UNDERSTANDING
PENELOPE FITZGERALD

Understanding Contemporary British Literature
Matthew J. Bruccoli, Series Editor

Volumes on

Understanding Kingsley Amis • Merritt Moseley
Understanding Martin Amis • James Diedrick
Understanding Julian Barnes • Merritt Moseley
Understanding Alan Bennett • Peter Wolfe
Understanding Anita Brookner • Cheryl Alexander Malcolm
Understanding Penelope Fitzgerald • Peter Wolfe
Understanding John Fowles • Thomas C. Foster
Understanding Graham Greene • R. H. Miller
Understanding Kazuo Ishiguro • Brian W. Shaffer
Understanding John le Carré • John L. Cobbs
Understanding Doris Lessing • Jean Pickering
Understanding Ian McEwan • David Malcolm
Understanding Iris Murdoch • Cheryl K. Bove
Understanding Tim Parks • Gillian Fenwick
Understanding Harold Pinter • Ronald Knowles
Understanding Anthony Powell • Nicholas Birns
Understanding Alan Sillitoe • Gillian Mary Hanson
Understanding Graham Swift • David Malcolm
Understanding Arnold Wesker • Robert Wilcher
Understanding Paul West • David W. Madden

UNDERSTANDING
PENELOPE
FITZGERALD

Peter Wolfe

University of South Carolina Press

© 2004 University of South Carolina

Published in Columbia, South Carolina, by the
University of South Carolina Press

Manufactured in the United States of America

08 07 06 05 04   5 4 3 2 1

              Library of Congress Cataloging-in-Publication Data

Wolfe, Peter, 1933–
  Understanding Penelope Fitzgerald / Peter Wolfe.
    p. cm. — (Understanding contemporary British literature)
    Includes bibliographical references (p.) and index.
    ISBN 1-57003-561-X (alk. paper)
  1. Fitzgerald, Penelope—Criticism and interpreration. 2. Women and
literature—England—History—20th century. I. Title. II. Series.
    PR6056.I86Z95 2004
    823'.914—dc22

                                                        2004016018

With love to
Heidie Maslo Wolfe
and
Vanessa Saracco Wolfe,
two nifty chicks from Chicago

Contents

Editor's Preface / ix
Acknowledgments / xi

Chapter 1
   The Benefits of Starting Late / 1
Chapter 2
   Hearts that Yearn / 35
Chapter 3
   Saying It Right / 48
Chapter 4
   The Great Museum Sideshow / 65
Chapter 5
   Oh, to Be in Suffolk / 93
Chapter 6
   On the Reach / 111
Chapter 7
   Keepers of the Discs / 137
Chapter 8
   Stagers / 160
Chapter 9
   Stumbling into Geopolitics / 184
Chapter 10
   Degrees of Exile / 212
Chapter 11
   Driving toward Modernity / 246

Chapter 12
  Kind of Blue / 271
Conclusion
  History Illuminated / 297

Notes / 303
Bibliography / 315
Index / 325

Editor's Preface

The volumes of *Understanding Contemporary British Literature* have been planned as guides or companions for students as well as good nonacademic readers. The editor and publisher perceive a need for these volumes because much of the influential contemporary literature makes special demands. Uninitiated readers encounter difficulty in approaching works that depart from the traditional forms and techniques of prose and poetry. Literature relies on conventions, but the conventions keep evolving; new writers form their own conventions—which in time may become familiar. Put simply, *UCBL* provides instruction in how to read certain contemporary writers—identifying and explicating their material, themes, use of language, point of view, structures, symbolism, and responses to experience.

The word *understanding* in the titles was deliberately chosen. Many willing readers lack an adequate understanding of how contemporary literature works; that is, what the author is attempting to express and the means by which it is conveyed. Although the criticism and analysis in the series have been aimed at a level of general accessibility, these introductory volumes are meant to be applied in conjunction with the works they cover. They do not provide a substitute for the works and authors they introduce, but rather prepare the reader for more profitable literary experiences.

M. J. B.

Acknowledgments

The author and publisher join hands in thanking those whose time and energy went into the preparation of this book: Roland Champagne, Geri Hoff, Rolf Mueller, and Lorna Williams, colleagues whose linguistic knowledge helped me make sense of some crucial passages in the Fitzgerald canon; Giuseppe Bolognese, for both translating parts of *Innocence* and sharing with me insights into the Italian background of Fitzgerald's 1986 novel; Linda Garvey, for locating important secondary sources; Thomas F. Staley, for helping me access the Penelope Fitzgerald Archive at the Harry Ransom Humanities Research Center at the University of Texas at Austin. The combined help of the following amounts to a major contribution: Ken Post, Rufus R. Jones, Elmer Crow, Moses Horwitz, Gary Sabourin, Bill Simmonds, Bob Holland, Hans Schmidt, and Max Schwabe.

CHAPTER 1

The Benefits of Starting Late

Penelope Knox Fitzgerald (1916–2000) has been intriguing readers for many reasons, the most basic of which is her family of origin. Both of her grandfathers were bishops (of Manchester and Lincoln, Penelope's birthplace). Further back, the bloodline includes a Bishop of Lahore, a chaplain to the East India Company, and a principal of a women's college in Toronto. This eminence carried forward, particularly on the male side. After spending some years writing parodies and theater reviews for *Punch* under the pseudonym "Evoe," Penelope's father, Edmund Valpy Knox, became the magazine's editor, a post traditionally honored by the unofficial title, "King of Fleet Street."

Edmund's brothers, all junior to him, also won distinction. His closest in age, Alfred Dillwyn (or "Dilly") worked as a cryptographer in both wars. A mathematician and translator of Greek texts, he helped break Enigma, the secret code the Nazis were using to signal each other during the Second World War. Wilfred, a don at Pembroke College, Oxford, served his country as a welfare worker in London. Though pro–birth control, this Socialist-Christian ascetic took vows of celibacy and poverty to fuel his attempt to reform the Church of England, which he believed was controlled by the rich. The youngest Knox brother, Ronald, converted to Roman Catholicism and later became a priest, a biblical translator and, more famously, a theorist and writer of detective fiction—a point of some relevance to his niece, whose first novel, *The Golden Child* (1977), was a mystery.

The years drained some glory from this distinguished legacy. In an angry act that may have been little more than symbolic, Ronald Knox was disinherited by his father for defecting to Rome. His defection might not have cost him much. As Harriet Harvey-Wood said in her *Guardian* obituary of Penelope, "Neither side of . . . her family was well off," as was indicated by the coldness of her parents' home, the only heated room of which was Edmund's study.[1] But just as chilly rooms would plague many of Penelope's characters, mostly in her last novels, *The Gate of Angels* (1990) and *The Blue Flower* (1995), a still sharper anxiety found in the novels stemmed from the domestic insecurity that dogged Penelope most of her life. At age seven she was taken from her home and sent to boarding school. At eighteen, when she was about to enter Somerville College, Oxford, where her mother had been an early female student, Christina died of cancer. A shaken, saddened Penelope nonetheless enrolled in Somerville, where she studied with J. R. R. Tolkien. She remained focused. Even though financial worries forced her to scramble for scholarships to finish her degree, she graduated in 1938 with honors.

The tenacity that helped steer her through Oxford would continue to help her. In 1944 she married Desmond Fitzgerald, a major in the Irish Guards. She had to summon all of her mettle to keep her marriage to Desmond afloat. Though trained as a barrister, he worked as a travel agent, and even that modest post was taken from him. An alcoholic, he drifted from job to job until he stopped working, leaving Penelope the burdens of raising their three kids and supporting the family. She held jobs at the Ministry of Food and the BBC, then clerked for a year at a bookshop that had been set up in an abandoned East Suffolk warehouse. Returning with the family to London in

1961, she taught at two schools for young actors—Westminster Tutors and the Itala Conti Stage School. Her students, though, may have been the least of her worries. The rat-infested houseboat the Fitzgeralds were living in at Battersea Reach sunk, taking with it Penelope's notes, photos, and letters, besides sending the shocked family into public housing.

Apart from telling an interviewer that Desmond "didn't have much luck in life," Penelope said little about her sad marriage.[2] But Desmond pervades her fiction in the likeness of the many misfits, losers, and have-nots that people it, those "born to be defeated" who may compel our admiration for their courage in the face of failure and loss.[3] Penelope Fitzgerald has a great gift for imagining herself in other people's shoes without patronizing them. This generosity of spirit also underlies her interest in alternative cultures—houseboaters, theater people, an English family living in Moscow.

The unfolding of this interest merits a careful look. Fitzgerald published her first book in 1975, a biography of Edward Burne-Jones, Victorian watercolorist and chief illustrator of William Morris's Kelmscott Press. (Burne-Jones, incidentally, also designed the stained glass windows for Manchester Cathedral, where Fitzgerald's paternal grandfather, Edmund Arbuthnott Knox, served as bishop.) Next came the well-received four-part biography of her father and his three brothers, *The Knox Brothers* (1977). This same year she published, at age sixty, her first novel, *The Golden Child* ("I have never been a young writer," she once quipped).[4] Although she often groaned that writing tormented her, she also knew that it was her calling. Any thoughts of retirement she might have indulged during her last years she quickly dispelled. As evidenced by the nine novels and one biography she wrote in her seventies and eighties, she kept to her desk. Rewards for her industry followed. This late starter's second novel, *The Bookshop* (1978), was short-listed for the Booker Prize, England's most prestigious literary award, as would be *The Beginning of Spring* (1988), *The Gate of Angels,* and *The Blue Flower* (1995). Her third novel, *Offshore* (1979), did win the Booker, and in 1998 *The Blue Flower* became the first novel written by a foreigner to win America's National Book Critics Circle Award, beating out works by native-born headliners like Philip Roth and Don DeLillo.

These honors were not flukes. Despite their artistic quality, her books were virtually unknown in the United States. Prompted no doubt by her having won Britain's Heywood Hall Prize in 1996 for a lifetime's achievement in literature, Mariner Books, a paperback division of the Houghton Mifflin Company, republished *The Blue Flower* the next year in a modest run of 13,000 copies. The book did well, eventually selling 100,000 copies and building a market for her other work. The market grew. By 1999, Mariner had made all of her novels available in the United States, and the next year Counterpoint reissued *The Knox Brothers*. Before her death, Fitzgerald had good reason to feel confident about her status. From the start of her writing career, reviewers had been friendly and encouraging. Then came the prizes, followed by claims for her greatness made by notables like Anita Brookner and A. S. Byatt.[5] Her prominence in the United States, thanks to the gamble taken by Mariner Books in 1997, lifted her reputation to heights so dazzling that critical acclaim rolled in from everywhere. "A great writer," pealed Philip Hensher in his *Spectator* review of her posthumously published book of short stories, *Means of Escape* (2000). In another review of the collection, from the *Times Literary*

Supplement, Hermione Lee called her "one of the finest English novelists of the last century"; writing for the *New York Times,* Richard Eder named her "one of the most remarkable British novelists of the last century"; finally, the first sentence of Harriet Harvey-Wood's obituary refers to her as "one of the most distinctive voices in contemporary British fiction."[6]

It is always hard to forecast the effect of time upon a writer's reputation. Compounding the problem is the flurry of interest, usually warm and friendly, in the years just following the writer's death. If justice is done, the neglect and even disdain that often sets in after this flurry wanes will bypass Fitzgerald. First, her art rests on a bedrock of knowledge as firm as it is wide. The graceful polished assurance of her 1989 *New York Times* review of a Canaletto exhibit shows her writing like a veteran art critic. "Most of us," the review begins, "see Italian landscapes for the first time over someone else's shoulder—the valley of the Arno, for example, behind Pollaivolo's martyred St. Sebastian, or the lake of Mantua through the back window in Mantegna's 'Death of the Virgin.'" These references flow smoothly from Fitzgerald's well-stocked mind—as do those to *The Aspern Papers* and *Death in Venice*—but they are not garnish. Never a passive reader, Fitzgerald quotes and rebuts the magisterial *Stones of Venice,* praising "the length and angle of the shadows" in a Canaletto that Ruskin dismissed as carelessly done.[7]

Fitzgerald's command of cultural history helps her fiction. What looks like a throwaway reference to a Wallace Stevens poem in *The Golden Child* in fact gives insight into the novel's deep structure.[8] Fitzgerald herself told A. S. Byatt that the meaning of *Human Voices* (1980) came from a poem by Heinrich

Heine.[9] Some of her literary references reflect her love of mischief, as in a passage in *The Bookshop* that displays her tendency to have fun with names. While wondering whether she should stock copies of Vladimir Nabokov's *Lolita* for her bookshop, Florence Green mentions that Graham Greene admired it.[10] The reference looks accidental. But another character in *The Bookshop* with little interest in reading either Nabokov or Greene is a local marshman named Raven, which is also the name of the main figure in Greene's *A Gun for Sale* (1936). Greene, a fellow Catholic, stayed on Fitzgerald's mind. A real estate agent who enters *Offshore* in chapter 5 is called Pinkie, the name of the demonic hero in Greene's *Brighton Rock* (1938), another novel, like *Offshore,* that develops near a body of water.[11]

But the allusions that add fun or intellectual fiber to a Penelope Fitzgerald novel need not be literary. As was seen in the civilized assurance permeating her piece on the Canaletto exhibit in New York, her knowledge ranges far. *The Rite of Spring* probes depths by treating archetypal Russian materials, as does *The Beginning of Spring,* in which Stravinsky's 1913 ballet is referenced. The philosophy being done in Cambridge in the early twentieth century plays an even bigger role in *The Gate of Angels.*[12] By banning metaphysics from philosophy, G. E. Moore and Bertrand Russell held that science should depend on direct observation alone. Scientists, they said, must begin with material data and, only after a long process of verification, embrace the safety provided by theories and laws. The Vienna School, led by Ernst Mach (who is mentioned in the novel, even though Moore and Russell are not [12]), tried to apply the principles of science to all human thought. Ludwig Wittgenstein, also a Cambridge philosopher in 1912, the time-setting of *The Gate of*

Angels, turned philosophy into linguistic puzzles. Ethics and metaphysics would be impossible if Wittgenstein (who is mentioned in *The Golden Child* [35]) was right. But the cutting-edge atomic research being done in 1912 by Cambridge's Ernest Rutherford would also have to be scrapped because atoms are unobservable.

Fitzgerald's homework, though, is more of an absorbed than an applied presence in her work. Her keen, highly informed mind lends her books a spontaneous unscripted quality. So thorough is her research that it recedes when she describes experience that eludes intellectual systems. She puts more art into her reading than she does reading into her art. She is a shrewd, sympathetic observer of the everyday passing scene whose novels keep faith with life's mess and muddle. They do still more. To make this absurdity credible, fiction must also impart a sense of dailiness and rootedness. Though short, Fitzgerald's novels are solid and well built. Blake Morrison hailed this gift in his November 1978 review of *The Bookshop* when he said that the book's author "has done her homework, and many of the details are carefully researched."[13] This praise applies to her other books, all of which convey an awareness of being alive at an exact historical moment. What keeps them fresh is her intimate knowledge of the world in which they unfold. As they move ahead, they refresh and renew themselves with references to customs and manners, clothing styles and eating habits. The Fitzgerald of *The Beginning of Spring,* for instance, knows what Russians in 1913 ate and drank on religious holidays. The book also supplies a pocket history of printing in Russia, noting changes in paper stock, typeface, and techniques of bookbinding. And when John Bayley praises Fitzgerald's "striking gift for recreating a time and place" in *The*

Gate of Angels, he might have been thinking of her recovery of the smells ("vinegar, gin, coal smoke, paraffin, sulphur, horse dung" [64]) pounding the hapless South London poor in 1912 as they rose to start their work day.[14] If a good novel brings a specific time and place to life, then *The Gate of Angels* ranks as a very good novel, indeed.

It has plenty of company in the Fitzgerald canon, thanks in part to the author's grasp of the particular milieu in which she is working. Few details escape her notice. Her 1982 novel, *At Freddie's*, which unfolds in a training school for young actors, includes the tiny aperçu that jewels worn by actors on stage should be soaped to prevent glare.[15] Comfortable with the humble and the easily overlooked, her sensibility warms to a common item like soap. When we are told in *The Gate of Angels* the brand of soap used in London hospitals one hundred years ago (157), we wonder how many other disposables she discarded before deciding upon Monkey Brand soap to shore up the social context of her book.

Sending her mind into many corners of society, she blends the researcher's zeal for background data, the journalist's sharp view of surfaces, and the social moralist's passion for justice. Informing all are her democratic principles. Content to be on equal terms with life at its simplest and plainest, she said in a 1988 book review that the ordinariness and not the preeminence of Mark Phillips's title character in *The Memoirs of Marco Parenti* "makes him all the more valuable as a witness of what he saw, heard, and did."[16] Witness is often borne quickly and early in her own work. Her first book, the 1975 biography of Edward Burne-Jones, both quotes and subscribes to William Morris's declaration of belief in art for the masses: "I do not want art for the few, any more than education for a few, or freedom for a few."[17]

Art remains a touchstone of character. The most sympathetic figure in *The Golden Child,* a man of common roots who has been knighted, leaves all his money "toward free admission to the exhibitions" (176) in the London museum where he keeps an office. A hands-on American journalist working in London during the Blitz says three times in *Human Voices* that, rather than interviewing notables, he wants to record the reactions of the "ordinary man."[18] The book's next chapter carries forward the idea of social parity. A forty-six-year-old BBC executive underscores his intent to bond romantically with a seventeen-year-old from Birmingham by celebrating with her at a restaurant called The Demos (139). Fitzgerald's next novel, *At Freddie's,* refers to the real-life Lilian Baylis having founded the world-famous Old Vic by turning a coffee house into "a Shakespearean theater for the people" (11).

This recollection comes from the book's eponym, Frieda Wentworth, or Freddie. A protégée of Baylis (1874–1937), Freddie keeps her mentor's bias as she tells the young charges at the acting school where she is headmistress to aim their words and gestures to the top rows of the balcony. Put more succinctly, "Freddie's heart was always with the cheaper seats" (56). Although it takes different forms, this spirit runs through Fitzgerald's works. *Innocence* (1986), which unfolds in 1955–56 Florence, describes the leveling effects of the Second World War: the abolition of titles for the nobility; the advent of cheap commercial air travel; and, above all, as in John Osborne's *Look Back in Anger* (1956), the effect of educational reform upon sexual bonding.

But the same mobility that fosters ties also threatens them. An ex-countess's husband returned alone to East Suffolk years before the present-tense action of *Innocence.* Her brother, in perhaps a bolder example of the folly of seeking trophy spouses in the post-Jamesian age, has a wife who left him and their two-year-old daughter to return to Chicago, where she stays during the daughter's Florentine wedding—an event that occurs without her knowledge. Elsewhere in *Innocence* an English debutante spends more time with her grandmother than with either of her separated parents. But if those who grew up in a time of war have failed at marriage, so have those who live in war's shadow. The first paragraph of *The Beginning of Spring* tells how Nellie Reid left her husband in Moscow in 1913—a year before the outbreak of the Kaiser's War and a time of political turmoil within Russia.

The traditional nuclear family faces risks at all times. Edward James is living apart from his family in *Offshore*. Daisy Saunders's father is long gone from the nest in *The Gate of Angels*, and then her mother's death orphans Daisy at age seventeen. Other orphans in the Fitzgerald canon include Annie Asra of *Human Voices* and the child actor Jonathan Kemp of *At Freddie's*. Modifying the Dickensian archetype of an innocent like Oliver Twist struggling to site himself in a fallen world, Fitzgerald's youngsters grow up quickly. Joan Acocella rightly calls them "outspoken, tough-minded, frighteningly precocious."[19] They outperform their elders in Fitzgerald's handy game of age reversal. Wisdom and skill belong to ten-year-old Salvatore Rossi in *Innocence* and the preadolescent James girls of *Offshore*, whose dazed parents, no example to them, fumble and grope.

Fitzgerald says in *Offshore*, "The crucial moment when children realize that their parents are younger than they are had long been passed by Martha" (20). Though Martha and her shrewd little sister, Tilda, are survival artists, neither is a genius. And perhaps they are better off, the two child geniuses in Fitzgerald's work dying early. Nine-year-old Jonathan Kemp of *At Freddie's* seems likely to become that rare stage genius who appears every fifty years or so and changes the very image of his country. Yet Jonathan's vocational drive routs his sense of self-preservation, duping him into taking a risk that kills him before his acting career has been properly launched. The vocal prodigy, Bernhard Hardenberg of *The Blue Flower,* who is called by a neighbor a "water-rat who'll never drown," does in fact drown, his death enacting Thomas Mann's belief that music has a purity and sublimity that, while refining the musician's awareness, also weakens the musician's hold on life.[20]

With a writer as careful and thorough as Fitzgerald, it scarcely needs saying that children appear in her books because she wants them there. Thus it makes sense for her to say, "Introducing children into a novel is helpful because they introduce a different scale of judgment."[21] As has been suggested, this standard can surpass that of their elders. But the childhood deaths in *At Freddie's* and *The Blue Flower* also show that, regardless of their wit, children need the protection of adults. Children in Fitzgerald walk in danger. Nor are they alone. A wise person in *The Bookshop* divides people into two categories—exterminators and exterminees (34), a split ratified by these lines of dialogue from *Offshore:*

> "It's not the kind who inherit the earth, it's the poor, the humble, and the meek."
> "What happens to the kind, then?"
> "They get kicked in the teeth." (67)

Further evidence of Fitzgerald's belief that "the nicest people" often suffer the most appears in "High Spirits," an online interview she did with Amazon Books. When asked by the Amazon interviewer about a statement made by a minor figure in *The Beginning of Spring* that life "makes its own corrections," she said she agreed with it.[22] We live in a self-correcting world whose rules come from within. And these rules favor twenty-six-year-old Fred Fairly. This Junior Fellow at Cambridge University tells some students, "There's no difference between scientific thought and ordinary thought" (*Gate*, 154). All thinking obeys the same laws. Moreover, thinking can be therapeutic. The classroom techniques Fred learned teaching Sunday school have sharpened his skills as a university lecturer. Also, he and his colleagues at the Cavendish Laboratories have all triumphed over the squalor of their workplace —icy, overcrowded rooms, patchwork equipment, outdated pipes and plumbing—to pride themselves in carrying on the tradition of "indisputable greatness" (153) the Cavendish has spent decades building. Their commitment to thought has proved redemptive. Contrary to B. F. Skinner's behaviorist creed, personal dedication to a higher purpose can override the constraints set by one's physical space.

But Fred's pride gutters. He and Sam Brooks, a BBC executive who virtually lives at Broadcasting House to avoid falling bombs during the Blitz, have both formed romantic attachments that clash with the jobs that mean so much to them. They must find other work. Perhaps their loss makes them tragic. They both have to survive the loss of something of value they not only wanted but even had. But should they be pitied? Very few of the other people in Fitzgerald's work enjoy happiness at all. In the same Amazon interview where she endorses the idea from *The Beginning of Spring* that life makes its own corrections, she posts a restriction: "If you wait long enough—if people have a chance to wait long enough—life does."[23] This restriction provides little help. Her moral beliefs have clashed with her creativity. The setbacks strewing her books show time either ignoring people or working against them. Her exterminator-exterminee division, with its built-in mockery of justice, still holds.

Those hurt most by it are the small and the old. W. S. Singlebury, who is axed from the clerical job he held for many years in "The Axe" (1995), says that losing his job will kill him.[24] Only after his departure does the office manager who fired him discover that Singlebury gave the firm excellent value. But having this knowledge prior to Singlebury's axing would not have changed the office manager's mind. The "discouraging trading figures" (*Means of Escape,* 65) reflected in the firm's books called for job cuts, and Singlebury's name headed a list of four the manager's boss deemed disposable. Unaware of his ex-clerk's efficiency, the boss also forgot that in a capitalist society, loss of job can lead to loss of freedom and, perhaps, of life. His ignorance of Singlebury's fine work suggests that he is closer than he knows to learning this lesson first hand. The whisper of the axe can be felt on *his* neck.

The aged title character of "Beehernz," published when Fitzgerald was eighty, is both the oldest and the most marginal figure she ever conjured. He is so cut off that his first name is withheld. He lives without books, electricity, and either a radio or a working piano to help him enjoy the music that has sustained him for decades. At age ninety-five, this world-class expert on the music of Gustav Mahler has been living reclusively "on an island off of an island" (*Means of Escape,* 50) near the Scottish coast. Whatever thoughts this hermit devotes to his career can only cause pain. Having spent decades conducting the works of Mahler, he is now parodying his man's life. And, despite Mahler's artistic triumphs, it was a sad life. Thrice excluded, Mahler was a rabbi's son who became a Catholic so he could direct the Vienna Court Opera. Then this Czech native lived as a Bohemian among Austrians, an Austrian among Germans, and a Jew throughout the world.

Florence Green learns Beehernz's lesson in *The Bookshop*. At age fifty-nine, she is almost old. Her widow's mite, her gender, and her shortness also push her to the edge of irrelevance in her raw East Anglian town. She is thus an easy target for abuse by others, like her solicitor and her dressmaker. The abuse spreads. Sensitive to the arbitrary but strong link between lack of size and lack of opportunity, Fitzgerald often shows Florence losing out in her dealings with others. We are told early about this grief, Fitzgerald saying of Florence in the book's second paragraph, "She had a kind heart, though that is not of much use when it comes to the matter of self-preservation" (7). This bleak lesson pervades the canon. Rejecting social orthodoxy and cultural consensus, Fitzgerald identifies with underdogs and outsiders, whose magnanimity has brought them more harm than good. The heart metaphor she uses to develop this sad irony can appear in her nonfictional prose. Her 1991 review of Alan Judd's biography of Ford Madox Ford proclaims, "Those who have 'heart' are perhaps better human beings, but they are liable to grotesque disasters."[25]

But disaster can snare anybody. A calculating, mind-driven life adds up to no life at all. The pains suffered by Fitzgerald's methodical exterminators equal in intensity those they inflict. But this justice is both bittersweet and cold. Everywhere in her writing, Fitzgerald insists that being fully human entails questioning social pressures, intellectual systems, and ready-made political creeds. Her introduction to the Penguin reprint of J. L.

Carr's novel *A Month in the Country* (1980) rehearses the dangers of embracing ideologies: "The death of the spirit is to lose confidence in one's independence and to do what we are expected to do." But then she decries any rewards the independent and the free-spirited might expect from bucking the majority; the self-reliant usually go unrewarded: "It's a mistake to expect anything specific from life. Life will not conform."[26]

This deprivation takes different forms in her fiction. Happiness is always fragile in Fitzgerald. Nellie Reid's sudden bolt ends Frank's serenity, and no sooner does Frank close with Lisa Ivanovna than he loses *her,* probably for good. Resourceful and efficient, seventeen-year-old Annie Asra of *Human Voices* has no romantic illusions about the middle-aged man she has fallen in love with. He is a selfish ingrate, and whatever sexual magnetism he offers is quickly waning:

> Vi wanted to be of help. . . .
> "He's old, Annie," she ventured at last.
> "He is," Annie replied calmly, "he's forty-six. I looked him up in the BBC Handbook, and it's my opinion that he's putting on weight. I daresay he wouldn't look like much in bed."
> "But what do you expect to come of it?"
> "Nothing." (98)

This last word causes regret. Unlike the empty-handed Jamesian heroine who had asked for everything, Annie seeks little but expects nothing. So dangerous to pursue and so difficult to gain, love rooted in self-knowledge should bring joy. Virtue should promote some good, too. From the genuinely good, only good should flow, not the misery of loss. In theory, Fitzgerald supports this optimism. Her epigraph to *The Blue Flower*—from the book's main character, Friedrich von Hardenberg (later more famously known as Novalis)—addresses our indwelling need for pattern and closure: "Novels arise out of the shortcomings of history." Novels ease stresses caused by the incoherence, strangeness, and discontinuity found in everyday life. Still mindful of this illogic, at the end of chapter 20 Fitzgerald has Friedrich, or Fritz, call nonsense "another language" (75).

These two statements mirror each other. Fitzgerald's search for a firm foundation for happiness has led her to the absurdists of mid-twentieth-century France. To the existentialist writers Albert Camus and Jean-Paul Sartre, absurdity dwells in the gap between the reasonableness of our expectations and an unreasonable, expectation-thwarting world. Fitzgerald has peered into this gap. And her response to it—no nihilistic shrug—also invokes mid-twentieth-century intellectual history. First, she rejects Dadaism's deadpan refusal to make sense, the poker-faced description of trifles found in the French nouveau roman, and the mathematical puzzles of Raymond Queneau. In a more positive vein, she follows the lead of absurdist playwright Eugène Ionesco by seeking meaning in prose that has not slackened and staled from overuse.

The search has taken her to metaphor. Metaphor evokes a world that finds its own corrections. As always in Fitzgerald, the affirmations bubbling up from these corrections can pass us by. Fritz von Hardenberg was expelled from a Moravian school at age ten for proclaiming his belief that body and soul are one. This organicism recurs in Fitzgerald, again in the shadow of pain and loss. A. S. Singlebury says in "The Axe" that "the mind is the blood" (*Means of Escape,* 70) a proposition repeated in *The Gate of Angels* as "thought is blood" (10, 14), and later disputed by a group of debaters. Attempting to refute the mind-body dualism, a debater claims that the body's tendency to flout reason when threatened proves that the body "has a mind of its own" (47). At this point, one of the debaters, Fred Fairly, invokes a Romantic tradition reaching from William Blake to D. H. Lawrence. Fred argues by analogy that, even though the process defies our understanding, the mind has a physical component, too.

Unfortunately, this organicism fails in practice. Speaking in her own voice, Fitzgerald says in *Human Voices*, "Truth ensures trust, but not victory or even happiness" (17). What is it worth? The truth is difficult and dangerous. Besides, there are too many truths to keep track of, even after noting the unfitness of language as a tool of communication. Florence Green's efforts to open a bookshop run afoul of a poltergeist that is based on one that "took the tiles off the walls" of the bookshop where Fitzgerald worked for a year.[27] If this destructive poltergeist squares with the Roman Catholicism Fitzgerald embraced in 1954, she never explained how. More benign is the ghost or ghosts inhabiting *The Gate of Angels*. Ghostly intervention in the novel, one might argue, both introduces Fred to Daisy Saunders in chapter 7 and brings them together at book's end. Fitzgerald had this reunion in mind when she called *The Gate of Angels* her only novel that ends happily.[28] But does it? Lovers squander chances to strengthen their bonds in *Offshore* and *Innocence*. Desertion and divorce throng the canon. What is more, the references in *The Gate of Angels* to both Maeterlinck's *Pelléas and Mélisande* (1892) and Verdi's *La Traviata* (1853), works that link Eros to torment and disaster, further darken the hopes of any union between Daisy and Fred—who, advisedly, do not appear together before us on the page at the end of *The Gate of Angels*.

The failure of this couple to click while in our view recalls many characters in Fitzgerald whose attempts to improve either themselves or their circumstances come to grief. But their grief may be denied the last word. Fitzgerald sees that, while the hopes and dreams of her people often defeat them, these same longings give them dignity. Though Florence Green's efforts to make a go of her bookshop deplete her financially and force her to leave town, Fitzgerald would have respected her less had she dodged the challenge. Where does this leave us? Can Fitzgerald both admire *and* punish Florence? Does her admiration of Florence drive her to crueler forms of punishment? An impression forms of a Kafkaesque world that scourges people for having innocently violated unwritten rules and guidelines. A world tainted by original sin also suggests itself, as it does in the works of Graham Greene. A belief in man's inborn depravity goes far in explaining why so many hopes in Fitzgerald run into walls.

But it also ignores the truth that her stifled female characters have a warmth, a sensuality, and a propensity for risk taking that their men lack. Unlike the quiet, uncomplaining women in the works of Barbara Pym, Fitzgerald's heroines kick against their low-key lives. They have to. Nearly every Fitzgerald novel includes a wastrel or ne'er-do-well whose ineffectuality, besides holding *him* back, cramps and constrains his intimates. The prototype of this ditherer, challenging Freud's insistence on the impact of early influences, is not Fitzgerald's busy, accomplished father or any of his three productive brothers, but her husband. The woman denied happiness and success, whether it be sixty-year-old Florence Green or Fritz von Hardenberg's fiancée Sophie von Kühn, dead from tuberculosis at fifteen, harks to both Christina Knox, who died when her daughter Penelope was eighteen, and the badly wed daughter herself. The daughter's reference in *The Knox Brothers* to Christina's "final illness," her being moved in vain to the seafront to help her recover (as would Sophie and Charlotte Mew's sister, Caroline), and Penelope's misery over being sent to a boarding school at age seven—all these woes point to the years of sickness on Christina's part that walled her off from her daughter and stopped her from knowing the daughter as a functioning adult.[29]

Too frail to inspire a fully developed character, Christina gives way to her lone daughter, whose wifely grief recurs symbolically in most of the fiction. And the cause of it? The glib, hard-drinking charmer, Boney Lewis—who wins the heart of a woman twenty-three years younger—reminds us of the imaginative use Fitzgerald continued to make of her husband, Desmond, whose own boozing both wrecked his career and degraded him in the home. Adult male delinquency always rivets Fitzgerald. Intriguingly, none of her delinquent men possess E. V. Knox's scariest trait—a hot temper (*Knox Brothers,* 207). On the contrary, as has been seen, the men Fitzgerald faults lack iron. And she finds them everywhere. It is as if she is trying to exorcize the pain caused by their prototype. William Trevor's father, for instance, was "too undemanding," she said in a 1994 review of Trevor's memoir, *Excursions in the Real World.*[30] Nearly twenty years before, in her biography of Edward Burne-Jones, she discusses the "failure in business . . . and inefficiency" (11) of the artist's father. To drive home the point, she puts her discussion on the first page following the book's front matter.

The archetypal figure reemerges in her biography of the poet Charlotte Mew—*Charlotte Mew and Her Friends* (1984)

—when she calls Mew's architect-father "a follower, not a leader," someone despised by his in-laws as "an uncouth interloper." And when she says that the passage of years cost Fred Mew his interest in life and that well before his death he "ceased to do very much at all," she could also be talking about her husband Desmond.[31] Edward Burne-Jones (1833–98) attracted Fitzgerald as a biographical subject because he fused in his personality elements of both Desmond and herself that she sought to understand better. In this vein, the passage from Jung she quotes in the first paragraph of the Burne-Jones biography shows her thinking about art as therapy: "If I had these images hidden in my emotions, they might have torn me to pieces" (11).

Burne-Jones and his biographer both needed therapy to lull the pain caused by death in the immediate family. Even though Fitzgerald kept silent about her mother's health problems in *The Knox Brothers,* she was "devastated" by them.[32] Her pain makes Burne-Jones's family of origin a skewed Victorian mirror image of her own. Burne-Jones's mother died a few days after his birth, following to the grave his infant sister, whom the artist never knew but thought about often. These losses worsened the pain of growing up poor and sickly in "the crude misery of Birmingham" (*Burne-Jones,* 19) with a father who failed at business (as would Annie Asra's Birmingham-based father in *Human Voices* [63]). He had good reason to feel deprived most of his life. "Fainting, weakness, and nightmares were part of Burne-Jones's tensely charged nature" (65), said Fitzgerald characteristically. Throughout her career, she always took to the stricken and bereaved, admiring their pluck in fighting hardship, a virtue she would have also admired in Desmond if and when she saw it in him.

She could not have seen it often. Thus her trademark sympathy for the hapless vanishes in her portrayals of ineffectual men. The portrayal of Edward James in *Offshore* or Giancarlo Ridolfi in *Innocence* delivers the force of her disappointment with her home life. Based on Desmond, these small-timers, though attractive, fall short of the shining example set by the Knox men of her father's generation. Some of her contempt for them is self-directed, Fitzgerald having had plenty of time to fret over being duped by Desmond. There were other lessons. Desmond's 1976 death showed her that drink could kill. The lesson stuck. In Charlotte Mew (1869–1928), she would choose a biographical subject who also died by drinking. But Lysol, "the cheapest poison available" (*Charlotte Mew*, 214), killed Mew, not whisky or gin, in a quick, agonizing death that symbolizes in inverted form the slow death that finally claimed Desmond. Aimless men would remain on Fitzgerald's mind. And her treatment of them shows that every coin she displays has two sides. The deistic optimism implied by the oft-quoted maxim in *The Beginning of Spring*, "Life makes its own corrections," has as *its* dark reverse side a realpolitik aimed at the weak and idle.[33]

Redress, appropriately, comes from within, and it takes the form of loss of focus or moral fatigue—not moral corruption. We are in the realm of Chekhov. The highborn Giancarlo Ridolfi of *Innocence* descends from people who never worked. And any salaried job this sixty-five-year-old took would soon defeat him, given the slackness bred into him by his family background. Maurice, the male prostitute in *Offshore*, dreams of going to Venice (43), but he will only get there if one of his johns takes him, an event as unlikely as Chekhov's three sisters making it to Moscow. Eddie James, the man who is about to drown together with Maurice at the end of *Offshore*, may have relished his days in the Engineer Corps just as Desmond Fitzgerald probably relished *his* service as a major with the Irish Guard. But, again following Desmond's sad example, Eddie is not "very successful in finding a job to suit him" (33). In fact, a legal action has been filed against him because he skewed the financial records for the launderette he manages. A change in both venue and occupation meant to boost his status in the workplace only weakens it. He has recently returned from fifteen months in Panama, where he went as a construction worker intending to bank most of his paycheck. The Panama job was a flop. Eddie has come back to London bitter and nearly broke, and his work performance was so bleak that the bad reference his boss gave him barred him from all but dead-end, low-paying jobs. Another bruised spirit belongs to the Irish Pierce Carroll, a teacher at the Temple Stage School in *At Freddie's*. During his job interview, Freddie, with her sharp eye for human weakness, spots him immediately as a victim. To enforce his low self-esteem and thus win his obedience, she tells him, "I'm doing you down" (22) while offering him the insultingly low salary she knows he will accept.

But spinelessness and low self-esteem can cost a man in Fitzgerald's works much more than a good paycheck. Milo North of *The Bookshop* is like a moral vacuum through which flows the interference of other people's aims and intents. He enters the novel thus: "Milo North was tall and went through life with singularly little effort" (22). This odd sentence logic soon becomes clear. Milo has not been cultivating the cool poise of the English public school man. He simply does whatever comes easiest. When Florence Green comes to his cottage—where she finds him "doing exactly nothing"—he says, "I'm glad you came. Nobody else ever makes me face the truth" (33).

Yet facing the truth defeats him; it calls for more resolve than he can muster. His submissiveness has made him everybody's flunky. But his policy of compliance soon costs him both his job and his live-in girlfriend. The blight spreads. Because she knows he will cave in to her, a local society matron uses him both to help her close Florence's bookshop and to run Florence out of town.

Her husband, General Bruno Gamart, who hosted the party in chapter 3 where Milo and Florence first talk in our presence, has also learned to submit to his wife, Violet. His deference could signal Fitzgerald's fullest statement on that supposedly heroic leader of men, the British Army officer. Both General Gamart and the retired Colonel Terence in "Our Lives Are Only Lent to Us" (2001) hark to ex-Major Desmond Fitzgerald. The retired Colonel is not only ineffective but also, as a cancer patient, damaged. And, since the cancer that has silenced him migrated to his throat, he will never bark out another order. The most this ex-daredevil of the trenches will do is to follow—a diagnosis put forth with cruel accuracy in his doctor's suggestion that he practice speaking by parroting the sounds made by his pet parrot. His counterpart, the general in *Bookshop,* is developed more amply. If Gamart's first name, Bruno, suggests that he is a dervish in combat, his kindness to Florence (as one of Violet's fellow victims?) bespeaks a gentle nature. He quotes poetry to her, reminisces with her about the war, and even visits the bookshop at the very time his wife is scheming to dismantle it. But he goes no further. Even the ex-combat ace disregards his conscience when following it means facing Violet's wrath.

Slavish devotion to society's rules, particularly the unwritten ones, always crushes the spirit in Fitzgerald. In *Offshore,* it nearly takes a life. After a houseboater breaks a rib, his rising politely to greet some well-wishers drives the jagged rib into his lung. The damage caused by such punctilio must be offset if Richard Blake is to survive. Thus the Port of London Authority Police breaks a rule by fetching some nurses to help him. This show of life making its own correction matters (*Beginning of Spring*, 15). It depicts the heart swamping both the law and the profit motive. But laws of physics can also be trumped. When Fitzgerald called *Gate of Angels* her only book that ends happily, she meant that the supernatural order intervened on behalf of three of the book's main characters.[34] Daisy Saunders's act of saving the life of the helpless blind Master of Cambridge's St. Angelus College delayed her long enough to set her in the path of Fred Fairly, the man who loves her. As has already been noted, the novel's recorded action ends either at, or shortly before, their meeting. Any marriage they contract would face hurdles. Besides offending his family by marrying beneath him socially, Fred will also lose his coveted Junior Fellowship, a post that can only be held by a bachelor. Similar worries face Fritz von Hardenberg in *Blue Flower,* another Fitzgerald hero who wants to marry down. As a German aristocrat, he is barred from any number of high-paying jobs that would help him support Sophie.

Fitzgerald understands the ripple effects, not only of marriage but also of other bonds. At issue are social arrangements and assumptions in place so long that they are taken for granted. Unless they are challenged, they will stay put. And their deep roots can withstand a lot of pressure. The defenders of the status quo, often acting from self-interest, even though they would deny it, will fight change; change threatens their security. But despite the force of their resistance, these self-styled conservatives often act from motives of cowardice as well as greed. Florence Green's lawyer acts cowardly when he refuses to help Florence fend off the attacks of Violet Gamart. Here and elsewhere, cowardice consists of yielding to pressure. When the community of houseboaters breaks up in *Offshore,* six-year-old Tilda James calls her former neighbors cowards (131). *Golden Child* shows cowardice parading as professional expertise and success. The director of the great museum that employs most of the book's characters uses an outmoded hierarchy to block innovations, particularly in personnel policy, that might jostle his power and prestige. The cravenness that figures in the late novel, *Beginning of Spring,* reflects Fitzgerald's progress from institutional satire to the dynamics of close personal ties. A man stands up the woman with whom he had made a lovers' pact to leave Moscow—but not without having first convulsed both the woman and her unsuspecting family.

Selwyn Crane's betrayal of Nellie Reid forces her distraught husband Frank to make some hasty decisions, some of which hurt him. Would that Selwyn acted more boldly or not at all. The guilt or cowardice that keeps him from eloping with his boss's wife invokes the archetypal Brechtian hero, who rebels imperfectly. Better for all had he resisted Nellie's plea to elope. Remember the compulsive conscientiousness that sent a spear of broken rib into Richard Blake's lung in *Offshore.* The shatter effect of caving in to protocol can pierce hearts as well as lungs. While Richard is lying speechless and immobilized in the hospital, his wife sells the houseboat he loves. Daisy Saunders cures a dying patient in *Gate of Angels,* but, because in doing so she also broke a hospital rule (taking the patient's story to a local newspaper), she gets fired. Fitzgerald knows the hazards of breaking rules to help others. Jeff Haggard, a BBC high-ranker, protects the morale of his countrymen by disconnecting the microphone into which a French Army general is urging the British people to surrender to Hitler. But Jeff's act of impetuosity also creates ten minutes of dead air on radios all over Great Britain. Did he do wrong? His dilemma is vintage Fitzgerald; her people must often decide within moments how to defend the bad against the worse, sometimes at great personal cost. The light punishment doled out to Jeff fails his own sense of justice. Writing in *World Literature Today,* Mary Kaiser says that, contrary to the beliefs of eyewitnesses, Jeff set off the unexploded parachute bomb that killed him.[35]

If Jeff blew himself up deliberately, his suicide follows a pattern familiar in Fitzgerald. Unifying the pattern are the men who shape it. The French General whose BBC speech is never heard by the British nation has had his face disfigured by a horse. Yet not only does he still love horses and horse races; he also marries a woman "addicted" to the turf. His own addiction runs deeper. Even though the horses he bets on "nearly always" lose, he keeps gambling at Ascot and Epsom with a "cheerful" face (*Human Voices,* 28). In chapter 11 of *Voices,* Fitzgerald patches in a short exchange between Jeff and an American war correspondent (who may be based on Edward R. Murrow) that might explain the General's attraction to what has been breaking him down:

> "Primarily I'm here to find out the reaction of the British people to attack from the air," Mac continued.
> "They don't like it."
> "Then how come they're all hurrying back to London?"
> (139)

Gripped by a force stronger than reason, these Londoners, like General Georges Pinard, may be enacting a goofy version of the myth of the eternal return. Perhaps fatalistic as well, they have chosen to die close to the things, places, and neighbors that their absence from London taught them to love.

They have immersed themselves in Joseph Conrad's destructive element. Artistic activity can speed the damage caused by this immersion. Listening to the music of Schubert, Debussy, and Liszt gives Annie Asra, who came to London from the relative safety of Birmingham, the sensation of drowning (*Human Voices,* 86). The drowning motif from the last line of T. S. Eliot's "The Love Song of J. Alfred Prufrock"—which includes the phrase "human voices"—sends out shock waves. In *Blue Flower,* Fritz von Hardenberg's singer-brother, Bernhard—who is called by a bookseller friend, "the little boy who likes the water" (169)—spends a great deal of time at the riverbank. At the end of chapter 4, when he runs across the deck of a barge after being feared lost, he says that he came to the waterfront because he "wanted to drown" (*Blue Flower,* 14). Water comes to define him. After hearing some hymns in chapter 44, he announces, "I'm going out to walk by the river in the darkness. That is the effect the music has on me" (178). Four chapters later, Bernhard says of himself "that he preferred to live by a river" (198). Live or die? Throughout his short life, music has been leading him to waters that could be reaching out to engulf him.

Perhaps he and the river both got their wish. The novel's afterword reports his drowning death at age eighteen (226). The link between art and death is even clearer in *At Freddie's.* At age nine, the brilliant child actor Jonathan Kemp is half Bernhard's age when he dies. He might also have twice the talent and dedication. He has been rehearsing the role of Prince Arthur in Shakespeare's *King John*. Arthur jumps to his death in the play's last act. A perfectionist, Jonathan believes that the fatal jump he is to perform as Arthur should honor the young prince's royal blood. Perhaps because a royal's death in antiquity often took the form of a fall from a high place, Jonathan decides to practice his jump from a height greater than any director or acting coach would have condoned. Furthermore, he practices the jump from a makeshift pile of rotting crates rather than a secure platform. Thus each of his practice leaps, though undertaken with the goal of achieving perfection, also improves his chances of injury or death. And die he will because of his dedication. Fidelity to a stage death will cause a real death.

This real death not only depicts the danger of blending art and life—it shows, too, that the total dedication good art requires menaces the artist; life does not make any corrections that help Jonathan Kemp. In fact, the role that is meant to launch his stage career ends his career along with his life. That Jonathan keeps jumping into a damp London night reflects his author's belief in life's difficulty and unfairness. No human attribute, perfection should be avoided rather than sought. But learning to live with uncertainty and ambivalence provides no key to survival, either. Unless God intervenes, the farsighted and the kindly meet grief in Fitzgerald. Already noted has been Daisy Saunders's dismissal from the hospital where she works for doing her nurse's job with more energy and imagination than the rules allowed. Georges Pinard of *Human Voices* has his promotion to the rank of General delayed because his lectures on the importance of airpower in combat anger his standpat chiefs (27). The Fitzgerald canon teems with characters whose truthsaying recoils on them. Their doom is expressed in a one-liner spoken by a cleric's wife in *The Beginning of Spring*. When told that being right is not always good, she answers, "It's good, but it's hardly ever safe" (66).

Emblematic of the wrongness of a world that punishes rectitude is dampness. Weather that is damp, dank, and clammy conveys the discontent that gnaws most of Fitzgerald's people most of the time. Every building but one—advisedly, the bank—in Hardborough, the physical setting of *Bookshop,* suffers from the damp blowing in from the North Sea. This same damp has permeated and thus corroded most of the houseboats in her next novel, *Offshore*. The pattern enforces itself. In *Gate of Angels,* violence flares out during a light rain. Three chapters later, though, it is noted that "the rain had stopped" (166) just before Daisy saves a man's life.

Had the rain continued—soaking the man through—it would have killed him. But if rain causes death, so do seas and rivers (especially tidal ones like the Thames). In *Bookshop,* the wife of Hardborough's senior resident drowns, and the last page of *Offshore* shows two men, certain drowning victims, clinging to a houseboat that a gale has hurled into the current (43, 141). Here is Penelope Fitzgerald at perhaps her grimmest. Full of salt water from the English Channel and, ultimately, from the great sea mother, the Atlantic, the Thames can kill. As in Flaubert's *Madame Bovary,* water imagery in Fitzgerald signals loss of control, even loss of life. The imagery occurs everywhere, reminding us of our kinship to the two victims careering into a squally Thames at the end of *Offshore;* like theirs, our bodies consist largely of water. This reminder resonates. The collective noise made by the crowds waiting to be admitted into a museum in *Golden Child* sounds "like the grinding of the sea at slack water" (7). The town of Hardborough, where *The Bookshop* unfolds, is called "an island between the sea and the river," an island, moreover, menaced by "the coldly encroaching North Sea" (12, 59). In *Human Voices,* Broadcasting House, home of the BBC on London's Great Portland Street, is compared to an ocean liner "lapped . . . round" by "damp sandbags" (10).

Fitzgerald's gift for compression helps her both sidestep predictability and play down the obvious. Motifs in her work can blend and serve multiple narrative purposes. In line with her familiar equation of music and death, a BBC employee in *Human Voices* says of a phonograph record she loved and lost, "I died the death when it fell into the river at Henley" (11). Death by drowning, the concluding trope of T. S. Eliot's "The Love Song of J. Alfred Prufrock," takes on a shocking reality in *Beginning of Spring,* where a newspaper describes "a pair of dead lovers, clutched together . . . frozen into the ice" (71).

In her oblique but deft way, Fitzgerald makes sure we remember this horror. Events in the book can be all but banished from the page to occur off camera in what looks like a chance reference. Nine pages from the end, apropos of nothing taking place between the characters, Frank Reid—who some weeks earlier read the article about the ice-locked lovers— mentions *Three Men on a Boat* (179). But Jerome K. Jerome's sportive novel, which has amused many thousands since its 1889 publication, has a dark side consistent with the calamity Frank read about in the *Gazeta-Kopeka*. A dog belonging to one of Jerome's vacationers will either drop or eat the dead rat hanging from his jaws in order to kill twelve swans. Continuing to thunder, the horror of these deaths culminates in the discovery of a corpse floating in the Thames.[36]

The cyclists seen in the first sentence of *Gate of Angels,* who look "like sailors in peril" (9), suggest that Jerome's vacationers judged well to row away from the corpse immediately. Floating bodies decompose. In Fitzgerald, the ugliness has an eerie, defamiliarizing effect. It bites into our civilized arrangements, copying nature's tendency to degrade the organized. This breakdown unnerves Fitzgerald's people, as when Frank Reid suddenly finds his status as a husband stripped of its usual guidelines. But it is here, when Frank occupies an in-between zone, that he most interests his author. Susannah Clapp says of Charlotte Mew, the subject of Fitzgerald's 1984 biography, "Her claim to be a writer of distinction rests on a small number of poems about people at the point of exhaustion."[37] A passage by Antonio Gramsci quoted by Jack Wakefield also notes the anxiety (Emile Durkheim's *anomie*) that sets in when established norms break down: "The old is dying and the new cannot be born; in this interregnum there rises a great diversity of morbid symptoms."[38]

Innocence (1986), in which Gramsci has a speaking part, displays many of these signs. First, political factions are squaring off in 1955 Italy, where the novel unfolds. Nobody can find their bearings. Because of changes that have occurred since the end of the war in 1945, the Italians we meet are bewildered by the direction they fear their country is heading. They are afraid that Italy is undergoing a collective neurosis nobody knows how to cure. Some are treating their bad nerves with antibiotics, whereas their elders prefer the old method of blistering. But Italy's problems go beyond the generational split. An ex-count lives in a small second-story flat in his once proud family's "decrepit" (15) palazzo while renting the choicer living spaces below. He also acquiesces—after some clever rewriting of his family's history turns his villa some miles away into a theme park.

A faster-changing environment is that of Moscow in *The Beginning of Spring*. The harshness of their city's winter makes all Muscovites yearn for spring. But spring's onset, following five months of ice and darkness, brings trials of it own. The book's 1913 time setting sharpens them. Under the Romanovs, the Russians lack freedom, fun, and civil rights. Yet the communists who are preparing their coup favor upheavals that, besides blindsiding business in general, endanger expatriate families like the Reids, proprietors of a Moscow printing firm since 1870. Furthermore, Frank Reid, the firm's Russian-born head, speaks Russian fluently and has a native's love of his homeland. This love clashes with his sense of self-preservation. When trouble with the police looms, he shrinks from the prospect of dismantling the firm and decamping to England. But how can a printery thrive in the reign of strict censorship that is ready to seize Russia? Margaret Walters pinpointed Frank's conflictiveness when she said of him in the *London Review of Books,* "Though he doesn't quite belong in Russia, he'll never be at home anywhere else."[39]

Compounding his woes of not belonging is the shock of his wife's leaving him without explanation. Fitzgerald depicts Frank's scrambled psyche—together with the "morbid symptoms" he has to fight off—with restraint, sympathy, and gentle humor. Writing for the *New York Times Magazine,* Arthur Lubow praised her as an original: "Fitzgerald has staked out a new kind of territory: the milieu of uncertainty."[40] He might have made his case with more force, uncertainty and ambiguity often being the milder worries fretting Fitzgerald's people. Compounding these and other cares, in any case, is the grief of being in-betweeners. Fitzgerald conveys this grief by capturing her characters in moments of transition. The artist hired to paint Sophie von Kühn in *The Blue Flower* (1995) wants to catch her likeness "just at the end of childhood and on the verge of a woman's joy and fulfillment" (117). His failure to do so shows that change or its expectation can cause as much anxiety as uncertainty does in Fitzgerald's other works.

The in-between zone many of her characters inhabit is, perforce, the frontier—a site occupied by fugitives and outlaws in the works of Graham Greene. Though most of Fitzgerald's people have something to hide, they face different problems. By showing people and things in flux, she charges her work with poetry. She will also drop the activated field they occupy into another, as in *The Beginning of Spring* when Frank Reid violates his wedding vows in the capitol of a disintegrating quasi-police state. This narrative strategy is original, as Lubow says. Technique makes it so. By placing an in-betweener like Frank in an unstable field of force, Fitzgerald can investigate both alternative life styles and the shifting relationship between a person and his/her government. The counterpoint of social norms and guidelines makes personal choice both important and dangerous. Fitzgerald introduces this fugue-like tension into *Innocence* when she refers to the seedy town apartment occupied by the Ridolfis as Limbo. Nor is it an accident that the Ridolfi with the most at stake in the novel is a seventeen-year-old Italian-American who was schooled in England.

The Fitzgerald novel with the most to say about unclassifiables like Chiara Ridolfi is the Booker-winning *Offshore*. Because the slapping, sucking, grinding action of water causes faster and deeper changes than air, *Offshore* also shows life in a state of hyper-flux. Nearly all the book's characters are riversiders, which makes them "creatures of neither land nor water" (10). Peter Kemp views them as misfits: "Amphibious in their life style, these 'tideline creatures' have not found a permanent niche in life, don't fit in anywhere."[41] Kemp is right. The tideliners of whom he speaks, moreover, regret their unfitness for life on dry land. To their sorrow, they live in the middle of a great city in which they are outsiders; passersby on the street find them unsavory and edge away from them. Then their houseboats, at the mercy of the bucketing Thames, protect them less than do the flats and office blocks of their urban foils. But they are not to be pitied. They have taken to their houseboats voluntarily. Always at risk should a hull be rammed by a drifting log or a pump handle rust out, they live more dramatically than these foils. They also understand better than most dry-landers the importance of bonding. Besides sharing food and drink, they help each other during emergencies. And the same dry-landers who scorn them are both deaf to the voices of the river and blind to the values of the treasure washed ashore by the muddy tides they barely glimpse from their windows. Like many other fine effects studding her early work, the clarity and balance infusing Fitzgerald's portrayal of the tideliners in *Offshore* justify her calling herself in a 1979 interview "the great hope of all late starters."[42]

CHAPTER 2

Hearts that Yearn

A believer in synergy, Fitzgerald favors participation and sharing. Speaking in her own voice in *At Freddie's* (1982), she defines good theater as a transaction between playwright, actor, and audience. An active audience can alchemize actors by transmitting energy to the stage. This magic sparkles and shines. But it also breaks hearts, vanishing forever at final curtain. No regrets, though; transience enhances its value, impelling again those touched by it on both sides of the curtain. They are forever joined by the evanescence of the beauty they have both witnessed and helped generate. Their emotional arousal typifies Fitzgerald's characters, nearly all of whom prize being over having. Nor need they be playgoers to be moved emotionally. A shared experience available to all is sexual love. Anybody can fall in love, not only those whose aesthetic sensibilities take them to the theater. But this anti-elitism carries a harsh recoil action in Fitzgerald, where love's promise usually differs from its actuality. Rather than enriching her people, it upsets them. While discussing the lesbian poet Charlotte Mew, Fitzgerald mentions the "nervous lover's perversion which backs away from what it most wants" (*Charlotte Mew*, 86). The beloved exerts such power in *Offshore* that she is both driven away *and* embraced. Similarly in *Innocence,* she emerges as an object of dread, something to run *from* as well as *toward.*

By resisting emotional clichés when writing about the clash of sex, Fitzgerald also avoids writing victim literature. Her loving couples, all straight, share several features that hurt their chances for happiness. The first is that of a big age difference. At thirty, Salvatore Rossi of *Innocence* is twelve years older than Chiara Ridolfi, a difference magnified by his also having qualified as a medical doctor. Chiara might have looked more closely at this disparity before her wedding day. Her own family history contains helpful information. The age gap between her father (who was forty-seven when she was born) and her mother (whom neither she nor Giancarlo has seen for years) probably surpasses the one dividing her and Salvatore. Love ignores common sense again in *At Freddie's,* where twenty-year-old Hannah Graves throws over thirty-year-old colleague to spend time with forty-three-year-old drunk.

The men in Fitzgerald act even more unreasonably when smitten. Like Dante did with Beatrice, a chemical engineer in *Gate of Angels* falls in love with a waitress the first time he sees her. Later in the book, Fitzgerald says of Fred Fairly, "After seeing Daisy [Saunders] at close quarters for let us say half an hour . . . he knew that he must marry her" (103). His heart works more slowly than those of most of the other smitten males in Fitzgerald. Vladimir Grigoriev of *The Beginning of Spring* falls for Lisa Ivanovna after seeing her briefly in a library three times, a figure Lisa dismisses as too high. Fritz von Hardenberg needs only fifteen minutes with Sophie von Kühn to know that he has to marry *her.* His passion rules him. Any attempt on his part to discuss her in rational terms ends, fittingly, in contradiction (*Blue Flower,* 113). He has been seized by her youth, her innocence, and her charm—qualities that defy analysis, the faculty Fitzgerald's men employ more comfortably than any other. But the more pragmatic these men try to be about love, the more wildly they act. Falling in love costs two of them their jobs. Two others drop everything to buy property where they can live with their sweethearts. Fritz von Hardenberg's brother would steal Sophie from Fritz in a heartbeat if he thought he could win her love.

Love's madness includes violence. Frank Reid threatens to beat up a friend he thinks is trying to dissuade him from having sex with his inamorata. Fred Fairly does pound a man for compromising Daisy's honor. That the pounding comes from an academic in "a university city devoted to logic and reason" (*Gate*, 9) links Fitzgerald's belief in sexual love's raw, brute power to that of D. H. Lawrence. Fitzgerald's women deal with this rough potency more ably than her men because, more at ease with their feelings, they are also more sensible about them. They neither try to wish sex out of existence nor call it something else. When Nenna James is rescued from embarrassment by Richard Blake in *Offshore*, her gratitude declares itself physically: "Nenna admired him and would have liked to throw her arms around him" (20). The erotic encounter Nenna will later have with Richard starts here, though neither of them knows it, just as Hannah Graves of *At Freddie's* needs to be reminded that she has already mentioned in conversation several times the name of her future lover. Either people in Fitzgerald enact their attraction for each other sexually, or sex gives them a natural outlet for an impulse that has seized them without their knowledge. This impulse overcomes everything, crushing barriers of age and breeding. The unlikely allure emanating from her much older boss, Sam Brooks, inflames Annie Asra: "She almost felt like asking him to put his glasses back. Otherwise, she wouldn't be able to go on much longer without touching him" (*Human Voices*, 139).

The 1993 title story of *Means of Escape* shows some of the effects of this sexual heat. The story's main character, an escaped prisoner, uses sex to flee Tasmania, then Van Diemen's

Land. His female companion, whose borrowed clothes he wears to foil detection, eagerly helps him escape the island—perhaps *too* eagerly. The story describes an action the exact reverse of the classic Jamesian drama, in which a bold deed is contemplated but never performed. The woman who calls herself Mrs. Watson spots the fugitive on a balcony near her window late at night. Recalling the events of the night in a letter written months later, the man, whose name, Savage, bespeaks the wild intensity of sex, writes about hearing on the dark balcony "a Woman's Voice suggesting a natural Proceeding between us." He adds: "When we had done our business" (*Means of Escape*, 20) the woman not only helped disguise him but also joined him on the Portsmouth-bound ship. All this develops logically from the "natural Proceeding" he detects in her tone of voice. Sex plays as much of a part in taking them from Hobart to Portsmouth as did that other act of recklessness—his prison escape.

Sex might also take Savage from one form of bondage to another. He and Mrs. Watson speak but briefly at her balcony window in a darkness that partly hides them from each other. But this same darkness also speeds the risks that sex always entails in Fitzgerald. These risks are daunting. Savage enters the story as "a rancid stench." His physical appearance also reminds Alice Godley, the rector's daughter he has shocked, of "a man about to be hanged" (5). In a foreshadowing of the scene on Mrs. Watson's balcony, Savage walks into the story hooded. Love is blind. But, as in Lawrence, this physical disconnect kindles other, darker sources of perception. Soon after leaving him, Alice puts Savage's reeking hood over her own head and asks her rector father about being replaced as the church's organist "if by any chance I had to go away" (11). Love's self-imposed blindness explodes into life in an atmosphere of filth and crime. A double-whammy plot twist ends the story. In the church aisle where Alice and Savage first speak, Savage agrees to come to Alice's window that night. But the darkness in which he sets out for her window foils him. The housemaid, herself an emancipated convict, inadvertently takes Alice's man.

This development could be one of life's corrections. The escaped convict Savage probably has a more promising future with a fellow ex-convict nearer his age than with a sheltered minister's daughter. Could Mrs. Watson have helped rather than hurt the young woman for whom she has always felt "intense affection" (21)? Is her silent parting gift to Alice that of life? As is suggested by the acrid lemons that symbolize sex in *Innocence,* Fitzgerald's people find sex unruly and bitter. The Irish song referred to in a passage in *The Beginning of Spring*— "I Met Her in the Garden where the Praties [i.e., potatoes] Grow" (113)—includes the line, "I'd rather be in jail, my boys, / Than be in love again."[1] We never know if Savage will regret trading his Port Arthur cell for the charms of Mrs. Watson. But the question occurs to us, as Fitzgerald intends. Revealingly, she devotes most of the story's second paragraph to a church organ. When Savage identifies himself as a poisoner, Alice retorts, "I should not have thought you were old enough to be married" (*Means of Escape,* 5). Could she be prophesying? Though sex is Savage's means of escape, it may also prove itself a vexation whose only cure is poison, a murder device, as Agatha Christie has reminded us, favored by women. Fitzgerald implies that troubles await Mrs. Watson and Savage by sending him in drag with her on a 12,000-mile voyage aboard a ship named *Constancy.*

When Savage addresses Alice as "ma'am," he is told, "You may call me Miss Alice" (7). After greeting Mrs. Watson that same night, he hears her say, "You may call me Mrs. Watson, tho' it is not my Name" (20). Fitzgerald's decision to keep that name dark, besides tightening her love-blindness analogy, also implies a belief that love thrives on mystery. Holding back can serve lovers well. The last line of the T. S. Eliot poem that supplies the title of *Human Voices* suggests that the frail must curb the rush of life they permit themselves. Analogously, the source of Annie Asra's surname in *Human Voices* identifies a tribe of slaves who die when they fall in love.

Savage's stay in Port Arthur sometimes makes him feel like a slave. But as *Constancy* puts out to sea, that brute, heaving, emblem of insecurity in Fitzgerald, Mrs. Watson's eyes are as open as his. They have to be; like him, she has put her life in the safekeeping of a stranger. Perhaps she will fare better than he. Her real name and the nature of the crime that sent her to Tasmania remain as dark as her motives. Then, Fitzgerald's women also expect less from sex than her men do. Boney Lewis's "heartwarming slights and evasions" (*At Freddie's*, 144), for instance, teach Hannah Graves that sexual bonding works better in a climate of deceit than in one of sincerity. Three years her junior, Annie Asra protects herself with Midlander pessimism because, she believes, one's hopes always misfire anyway. Perhaps she is right. Pierce Carroll of *Freddie's* and Frank Reid of *Beginning of Spring* will only have sex once with their sweethearts, and death takes Sophie von Kühn *before* she sleeps with Fritz von Hardenberg. Despite their low expectations, it is the women who usually instigate sex in Fitzgerald. Just as the tone of Mrs. Watson's voice beckons Savage to her bed, Hannah Graves asks Pierce Carroll to spend the night with her after several subtler overtures on her part go unheeded. Nellie Cooper undresses for Frank Reid without any encouragement from him. Her disrobing act is planned together with its aftermath. She has already thrown to the floor some objects that were strewn on her "white bed" (*Beginning of Spring,* 31) after maneuvering him into her room. Nellie remains headstrong even after marrying Frank. If Selwyn Crane can be believed, she—and not he—proposed the elopement he would renege on. She must have also incited the sexual activity that warranted an elopement. Selwyn's failing this tryst leaves her undaunted. Alone, she boards the train she had planned to take with him. Fitzgerald's women adapt better to the wild demands of sex because they are better grounded psychologically than her men. She subscribes to Fritz von Hardenberg's belief that "Women have a better grasp on the whole business of life" because "they particularize" whereas "we [men] generalize" (*Blue Flower,* 100). Though only seventeen, Annie Asra of *Human Voices* has learned to assess matters, especially feelings, on their own merits. Sam Brooks downgrades Annie's declaration of love with the words, "In a few years' time, you'll meet someone your own age" (139). Annie's reply—that his ideas about love come from books—cuts to the core of Fitzgerald's feminism. Sam *has* used a literary stereotype to dodge moral and emotional complexity. Only when he takes off his (reading?) glasses ("in capitulation" [139]) does he begin to catch Annie's drift.

Sex hones women's sensibilities. Nenna James of *Offshore* can sympathize with a sexual rogue even as she is rejecting him. When a stranger asks to spend the night with her, she notes that he smells of loneliness. Rather than condemning him, she feels "saddened by the number of times the man must have asked this question" (97). Daisy Saunders of *Gate of Angels* extends even more charity to a would-be seducer. Thomas Kelly, the married older journalist whose paper printed the article that got Daisy fired, exploits her weakness by booking a hotel for the two of them. Though Daisy never sleeps with him, she believes that two souls as pathetic as she and Kelly deserve each other. But when an enraged Fred Fairly punches Kelly for smirching her honor, he is scolded rather than praised. A lesser woman—or an ingenue in a melodrama—would have welcomed the violence he perpetrated on her behalf. Daisy recommends mercy to the same would-be violator who has sworn vengeance on her for bilking him sexually:

> Kelly's older than you, quite a bit [she tells Fred]. You must have noticed that if you got close to him. He has to pretend to be young in his line of business. His job's nothing to be proud of, but then he didn't have your advantages. You think of that the next time you come across a poor sod like Kelly. (159)

It is no wonder that Fred falls in love with Daisy. Despite being broke, hurt, and confused, she judges the histrionics instigated by Kelly with greater charity than all the others touched by them, even though these others are all older and more educated than she.

Daisy's defense of the cad who may have killed her chances for both employment and marriage reveals the same fusion of wide-ranging knowledge and deep thinking, of originality and clearness, we have come to expect from Fitzgerald. Her fiction describes the crabwise movement we make toward each other in our quests for intimacy. She has both studied the backlash of intimacy and described it. Resentment can simmer between longstanding friends, neighbors, and business partners. Lovers will deliberately hurt each other. They are often goaded by frustration. Most of her people either want to improve their lives or try to hold onto the lives they have made. Their efforts, though often frustrating, earn them a goofy nobility. As is conveyed by the gulping, slapping tides that threaten the houseboaters in *Offshore,* they are willing to risk danger to protect what they value.

They also sense that real happiness is a delusion. The prominence of accountants in the Fitzgerald canon tallies the cost of seeking it. Accountants play parts in *Bookshop, Freddie's, Beginning of Spring,* and *Blue Flower.* By putting the action in a hard glare, the Italian sun in *Innocence,* a book that features a big money deal, also invokes retribution; payment must be made even though no benefits may follow. This grim sermon takes a different form in *Offshore;* unless a houseboat's metalwork, timbers, and ropes are kept shipshape, the houseboat will sink. The changes starting to convulse Russia as revolution nears in *The Beginning of Spring* give accountants and accountancy a special prominence. A major scene in the novel begins in the countinghouse of a merchant (66). To deal more effectively with his firm's newfound international trading partners, Frank Reid later hires a costing accountant for the first time in the firm's history.

Accountants can report bad news. The one that Florence Green hires to balance her books in *The Bookshop* works with terrifying, sometimes unwelcome, efficiency. But not every accountant's client flusters as easily at the sight of a skewed balance sheet as Florence does. Freddie's accountant, "embittered" (*Freddie's,* 16) by his client's disdain for record keeping, might explode were he familiar with her everyday economies, some of which not only defy common sense but also safety codes, like using faulty, out-of-date wiring and plumbing.

Fitzgerald takes accountability more seriously than Freddie does. Yet she does not expect much from Freddie or her counterparts. Even though she records blunders and failings on their parts that could bankrupt them, she withholds judgment.

She would rather forgive. In her review of William Trevor's *Excursions in the Real World,* entitled "To Remember Is to Forgive," she praises Trevor's "exceptional powers of forgiveness."[2] Her characters can also manifest these powers. Short of blaming himself for Nellie's defection, Frank Reid of *Spring* refuses to judge his wife for bolting the home and keeps sending her money while expecting nothing in return. Elsewhere in the Fitzgerald canon, strangers offer help without hope of recompense. *Offshore* contains two such acts of kindness. Before the river police break a rule to help a wounded Richard Blake, an unnamed cabby drives a freezing, shoeless Nenna James home without charge at three o'clock on a wet, cold morning. Some important truths bypass the accountant's ledger book. Hardship, for instance, can close ranks rather than stir motives of greed and treachery. In the wartime setting of *Human Voices,* Fitzgerald's Londoners rise above the problems caused by food rationing and the housing shortage to help the needy, even when the needy are ungrateful.

Like the guilty, the ungrateful also have rights and needs. Writing in 1998 about human frailty, Fitzgerald said: "I have remained true to my deepest convictions. . . . I mean to the courage of those who are born to be defeated, the weakness of the strong, and the tragedy of misunderstandings and missed opportunities, which I have done my best to treat as comedy, for otherwise how can we manage to bear it?"[3] Her characters sometimes hew to this wisdom. Twelve-year-old Sophie von

Kühn laughs when asked for a lock of her hair. She cannot satisfy the request. As is implied by the cap she is wearing, she has no hair to give. But her laughter denotes insight as well as a sense of humor. Perhaps it joins her to those wise children who see further and deeper than their elders. Sophie is bald because the tuberculosis that will eventually kill her has taken her hair. But she has found a way to cope. Helped perhaps by a native German grasp of *Galgenhumor,* or gallows' humor, she knows that mockery tames adversity. Instead of mourning the loss of her locks, she laughs.

This polarity voices Fitzgerald's belief that stories are not smooth and that the surfaces of things can assume complex shapes that defy reconstruction. Humor celebrates the world's incongruity, but it also gets to the bottom of things. A sunny, redemptive moment like the one created by Sophie's laughter serves Fitzgerald's narrative purposes. Delving into the mysteries of perception, it defines character through a flow of unrecorded thoughts. Like subtext in Chekhov, it also charts the vagaries and the capriciousness of the private self. Life, though sometimes savored, is mostly an ordeal in Fitzgerald. But, as Sophie's laughter shows, it need not crush us. As in any other good novel, the ending of a Penelope Fitzgerald supplies no tidy mood, no easy justice, no purity of motives. Nor do clear resolutions crown her plots. But this lack of closure echoes experience. Fitzgerald rejects the clever tricks of postmodernism (e.g., endings that either collapse or rebut the logic preceding them, quotations in the text from obscure sources, an interest in form over character). Her aversion to neat endings buttressed by conventional images of happiness helps her depict the unruly, mysterious directions our lives sometimes take. At the same time, her portrayals of this waywardness respect the importance of narrative flow in prose narrative. The pull of storytelling keeps her writing from becoming precious or static.

Fitzgerald's 1997 review of Muriel Spark's *Reality and Dreams* includes the phrase, "the vast unseen presences on which our lives are dependent or contingent."[4] These same presences also dictate Fitzgerald's avoidance of proper endings. Like Spark, her fellow Roman Catholic convert, Fitzgerald believes that time provides its own endings to which we must submit. The mystery of unity decrees that fictional endings defy logic. The poltergeist in *Bookshop* and the ghost or ghosts in *Gate of Angels* voice Fitzgerald's belief in reason's inadequacy to explain God's role in our lives. The unreason of "the courageous drunkard" (*Human Voices,* 32), Winston Churchill, stopped the Nazi invasion many Britons were bracing for in 1940. Though a respecter of reason, Fitzgerald counterpoints the images of Florence, "the city of the mind,"[5] and Cambridge, "the intellectual city,"[6] with the antics of scientists who live in these centers of learning. Savants in the canon need to avoid smugness. All three doctors who try to cure Sophie von Kühn's tuberculosis in *The Blue Flower* fail her, and she dies at Weissenfels, near the University of Jena, whose faculty included the philosopher Johann Gottlieb Fichte (1762–1814) and the dramatist-poet Friedrich Schiller (1759–1805).

But neither Sophie's death at fifteen nor the surgical blunders she submitted to without anesthetic shatter Fitzgerald's faith in life's intrinsic worth. She seeks to be on a level with earthly things, even though everything earthly does not answer to reason. Why should it? This question has import to Fitzgerald. However faintly, moral theology always flickers over the everyday behavior of her people. Not only is she at peace with incongruity; she even revels in it. She called Antonia White's first novel, *Frost in May* (1933), "the most brilliant, and at the same time, the murkiest, of all convent school novels."[7] Her reviews keep providing insights into her beliefs. She said of Muriel Spark's *Reality and Dreams,* "It's not for us to distinguish between the tragic and the ridiculous."[8] She knows that tragedy can have a buffoonish look and that life can dispense laughs and knocks in rapid order. She is also comfortable with this incongruity. Her 1989 review of the Canaletto exhibit at New York's Metropolitan Museum of Art rivets upon the painter's interest in humble life, (i.e., "men urinating in quiet corners or stretched out in the sun"). Nor does her failure to make sense of everything that goes on in a painting block her fun. A picture of Venice's Piazza San Marco, for instance, shows "women . . . with baskets of black clothes, who may or may not be selling something."[9] She is just as modest and tentative in her search for meaning. Her faith in the value of the everyday can mock our quest for symbolism in her sharper descriptions. Sufficient unto themselves, many of the data she describes stand for nothing other than themselves.

At 226 pages, *Blue Flower* is Fitzgerald's longest novel. Do not let this figure mislead you. Her novels pack more meat and sinew than many longer ones. Rarely running to more than 180 pages, they consist of brief, pointed scenes that approach their subjects obliquely. The homework that bolsters them, their honesty about the differences made by money and social class, and their appreciation of the cost of sustaining relationships, particularly sexual ones, lend her treatment of big, interconnected themes like love, war, and the family a heft we would have never thought such slim, quietly told novels could support.

CHAPTER 3

Saying It Right

Fitzgerald has an easy, lucid, buoyant style. She writes gracefully and economically, and she has both a sharp eye and a nuanced feel for the intricacies of language. Basically, she avoids the lush and the grandiloquent in favor of a rhetoric that is trim, accurate, and uncluttered. Her sentences blend glide and snap, lightness and sting. Cleverness, after all, is a kind of insight, a truth that puts a quip like "Helping other people is a drug so dangerous that there's no cure short of total abstention" (*Human Voices*, 109) in some unchartered gap between the facile and the profound. Fitzgerald is not known as a stylistic innovator. But she does not copy the past, either. Viewing elegance as a function of economy, she mastered civilized writing—prose that is carefully weighed, paced, and pitched. These graces enrich her treatment of details. In both the selection and placement of details in Simon Ley's *The Death of Napoleon* (1992) she sees a skill she spent a writing career developing: "The details are so precise that the conspiracy [to restore Napoleon to power] goes forward under its own momentum."[1]

Narrative momentum in *her* work reflects this skill and originality. Even though her command is flawless, her manner is so unassuming that her mastery is easy to miss. Dialogue in the Fitzgerald novels moves the action along while also compelling us with the mellowness of its cadence and flow. It sounds like real, breathing human speech. The enormous research foregrounding her plots conveys the same ease. For instance, her knowledge that no hundred-ruble notes were printed in Russia in 1866 (61) and that only 1,500 cars or so were moving along Moscow's streets in 1913 (53) brighten the plot of Fitzgerald's 1998 novel. Jonathan Raban, another expert at capturing minutiae that seize the essence of a foreign place, has noticed that the hard work that goes into her novels erases any telltale signs of the lamp. In a *New Republic* review called "The Fact Artist," Raban cites her "abundant cosmopolitanism knowledge of the world." Then he adds, "Fitzgerald is the least academic of writers. . . . [Her] work is alive with the play of ideas, as if they were the stuff of ordinary civilized conversation."[2] Raban is referring to her ability to mask her urbanity. The words she writes are like everyday talk, but they disclose things we have never heard before. Besides being clear and succinct, her sentences are so relaxed that we marvel at their ability to cover such great distances. Like Chekhov, she can describe a noisy age quietly. Shades of gray are her palette. She has a way with the small, quiet image, for example, that sums up an irrepressible ache. Richard Eder praised this assured unintrusiveness in *Gate of Angels:* "The story of Fred and Daisy in a time of revolution is told largely in particular details and with a deceptive matter-of-factness."[3] Voice and vocabulary in her work do what she asks of them. Like Raban and Eder, Edward Wheeler has found in her unhurried, technically seamless prose a striking accuracy: "Fitzgerald is an uncanny, if understated stylist. Her style is so distinctive that the novels give pleasure by making us ask how she achieves her effects."[4] Balanced and varied in the sounds it makes, her prose also has the austere richness found in the later works of Saul

Bellow. Avoiding flash, it describes things so freshly and vividly that we often find ourselves rereading certain passages—not because they are clever (which they are)—but because they are true.

Few writers have created so much out of so little. Her astonishing ability to explore complex states of mind without smudging the clarity and harmony of her prose stems from a verbal economy that reflects her attitude toward both the reader and the very act of reading: "I always feel the reader is very insulted by being told too much," she once said.[5] She applied this epistemology with increasing rigor as her career advanced. According to her editor at HarperCollins, her work tightened with the years, relying increasingly on indirection and surmise in its flight from the epical and the earnest. Her latest books, said Stuart Proffitt, recall the "late period" of Beethoven, "where everything is getting pared down but the content is more concentrated."[6]

Proffitt is right. Though quiet, Fitzgerald's narrative voice demands our strict attention. Enormities come suddenly but without being voiced a jot louder than anything else. Atrocity arrives in the same tone and at the same pace as the whole deceptive buildup. This control reminds us that the best novelists have a finely tuned sense of restraint. They know when to pull back in order to stop a moving scene from curdling into melodrama. They also have the knack of choosing details that do the work of pages of brooding analysis. An accomplished novelist herself, Penelope Lively found in Fitzgerald's nuanced, condensed *Human Voices* proof of the idea that the more a writer leaves out, the more she is able to highlight what remains. Fitzgerald, says Lively, is "a deft hand with the descriptive phrase that nails a place or situation in a way that painstaking description would have failed to do."⁷

A fine example of the ease with which language, tone, and character join in Fitzgerald's work comes near the start of chapter 4 of *Offshore*. Fitzgerald is speaking of two houseboaters who see "at flood tide . . . the river as a powerful god, bearded with the white foam of detergents, calling home the twenty-seven lost rivers of London, sighing as the night declined" (45). Details included to impart epical grandeur to the Thames run afoul of the "white foam of detergents," which is tucked away, with Fitzgerald's usual cunning, in a phrase midsentence, where it is most likely to be skipped over. While a part of the Thames legend, Fitzgerald's strident detail nonetheless mars the sentence's lyricism. The ugly white patch smudging the majestic river also denies today's Londoners the heroic stature of those earlier riverfolk whose efforts built the legend. Like the God of Michelangelo or William Blake, Fitzgerald's river god has a great white beard. But it is a cartoon beard disgorged by the sinks and washing machines of London's postwar inhabitants. However much detergent these Londoners use and however hard they scrub, they will not remove the blot they have put on the Thames's long, proud history.

Fitzgerald's characters often worry about pursuing what they want, and they tend not to get it—or at least not in the way they expect. Mining the recesses of their personalities, her language captures the shifts of inner emotional weather in their lives. The language moves between plainspokenness and baroque wit with a fluency that registers tenderness, warmth, and humor. The channeling of this fluency into her finely burnished plots has invited comparisons with Jane Austen. A. S. Byatt, for instance, calls Fitzgerald "Austen's nearest heir for precision and invention."[8] She judges well. Gracefully and slyly comic, both writers use understatement and irony to skewer pomp with one well-aimed jab of the stiletto. The "precision and invention" Byatt admires in both writers refer to the wit, acerbic bite, and moral complexity marking their social and psychological insights. Like Austen, Fitzgerald has a sharp eye for vanity and pretense. Her inventiveness also recalls E. M. Forster's singling out Austen, in *Aspects of the Novel* (1927), as England's sole novelist of import who could portray characters in the round. Drawing upon concentrated reserves that rival those of Austen, Fitzgerald captures her people off guard, when they are most themselves. The news of his wife's absence from Pisa, for example, rouses warring feelings in Salvatore Rossi in chapter 41 of *Innocence:* "[Chiara] arrived a day later than Salvatore, who was furious to find out that she was still away, and immensely glad to have the extra time to dispose of" (134). In contrast to the humor characters of commedia dell'arte, whose behavior always refers to their ruling passions, Fitzgerald's people reel between conflicting values and needs. A communist bent on abolishing class distinctions secretly admires Salvatore for marrying above his social station.

Fitzgerald treats such absurdities with the same tough-minded affection that is also seen in her practice of referring to characters in narration by their first names. Here she parts company with Austen. Though she relies as much on atmosphere and language as her predecessor, Fitzgerald does not ground he compositional choices in narrative principles of harmony and order. Her preference for live action over summary takes her to the offbeat and the ridiculous. If *Human Voices* fuses "deadpan

English comedy and surreal farce," as Byatt claims, narrative selection kindles the fusion.⁹ It is the freedom and the vigor with which Fitzgerald both selects and handworks her materials that grab our attention. A woman in *Offshore* casually throws some cheese straws into a fireplace to warm herself. Things used for unintended purposes cohere rhythmically and destructively in Fitzgerald's next novel, *Human Voices*. Segueing from both a concert hall that is serving as a dormitory and a twist of wire that serves as a makeshift betrothal ring is an unexploded parachute bomb a BBC executive sets off because he allegedly mistook it for a taxi.

The executive's death is one of the book's surreal moments. It also typifies Fitzgerald. Britain's greatest popular artists—from Dickens to Chaplin to the Beatles—have a broad streak of sensationalism (which does not preclude subtlety or moral indignation). All the more shocking for springing from a context of gracious, understated writing, Fitzgerald's sorties into the raw and the urgent echo this clash. Her odd bursts of aggressive imagery also move the horrific into the realm of the everyday. A disquieting sense of menace punctures the ordinary when Florence Green of *Bookshop* is asked to hold the "large slippery dark tongue" (14) of an old horse so its owner can file its blunted teeth to help the horse chew the grass it feeds on. That the nag eats "like a maniac" (15) after its teeth are filed denotes the success of the filing operation. But it does not dispel our impression that the whole episode has an eroticism redolent of Thomas Hardy. Such jarring moments can occur at any time. Fitzgerald's flair for the macabre colors our reading of *Innocence,* as she intended. This intention is made clear by the events she includes in the book's first chapter. In the sixteenth century, the Ridolfis, who occupied the villa that still belongs to the family in 1955, were all midgets. To keep their daughter company, the owners supposedly brought a midget girl to the villa. But Gemma, the little ward, started to grow, and she soon stood higher than everyone else at the villa. To spare her the dismay of being different, the Ridolfis decided both to cut off her legs at the knee and to put out her eyes.

Whether these atrocities occurred remains unclear. Urgently clear, though, is the bear cub a rough-hewn Moscow businessman gives his thirteen-year-old son Mitya in *The Beginning of Spring*. Away from its habitat, the motherless cub is both terrified and terrifying. None of the children at Mitya's party know what to do with it any more than *it* knows what to expect. Objectifying a rhythmic compression reminiscent of Gerard Manley Hopkins, Fitzgerald's recovery of its essence, or whatness, clarifies their plight:

> The bear-cub at the Kuriatin's was disappointingly small, and its head looked rather large for its body and seemed to weigh it down. The skin was very loose, as though the cub had not quite grown into it. The dense fur, dark, golden and ginger, grew at all angles, except along the spine which was neatly parted, and on glovelike paws and hind feet. The protruding claws looked as if they were metal, and the bear itself was a dangerous toy. (57)

"Openly in need of protection for some time yet" (57), the cub is one of Fitzgerald's in-betweeners in that this oxymoronic "dangerous toy" can generate either havoc or fun. The fun disappears when the cub rises to Mitya's height after Mitya hits it with a billiard cue. When Mitya gives it vodka to impress his party guests, the havoc ensues. The children who watch it get drunk experience a gamut of emotions, both "laughing and [feeling] disgusted" (59). Guided by its keen nose, the drunken bear cub climbs on the dining room table, scattering crystal, plate, and silver as it guzzles from the vodka bottles standing at each place setting.

What happens next, a triumph of emotional and conceptual daring, both develops the dramatic potential of the bear cub episode and gives the episode the drive of metaphor. Hearing the commotion in the dining room, a servant runs in and throws a shovelful of red-hot coals on the cub, whose screams resemble those "of a human child." Already alight, it tries to protect its face with the same "front paws" Fitzgerald had earlier likened to "small hands" (58, 59). The cub has become one of her innocents whose destructiveness can hammer them. But more thematic goodness imbues the dining room scene. Mitya is another innocent and thus an alter ego of the cub—who is not only Mitya's father's gift to him but also stands as tall as Mitya does. Both act self-protectively—the bear to shield its face from fire and Mitya to *save* face with the party guests he wants to impress. The similarities continue, as the father's words—which he roars as he enters the smashed, reeking dining room—make everyone in sight a potential victim: "Why is that bear on fire? I'll put it out of its misery. I'll spatter its brains out. I'll spatter the lot of you" (59). Though as Russian as he is English, Frank Reid—who appears immediately on the scene—may soon find himself faced by a Russian juggernaut as strange to him as it is angry and hostile.

Key here is the absence of the female principle. Frank sent his kids to the Kuriatins because Nellie was not at home to watch them. But Mitya's mother is *also* away. These absences foreshadow another. "Dear, slovenly, mother Moscow" (35), the city where most of the action breaks, will soon surrender *her* young to the madness of the so-called workers' revolution.

In view of Russia's traditional association with the bear —depicted with brio in Yusef Karsh's studio photograph of Nikita Khrushchev—the bear cub incident in chapter 8 of *Spring* works brilliantly. It has the hyperreality of a nightmare. But for all its dash, the incident also shows Fitzgerald subverting connection and meaning while she both disarms and subverts subversion. Fidelity to concreteness impels her throughout. Her scenic genius here and elsewhere in *Spring* stems from both timing and an economy of means—as well as a rare attention to fact (i.e., the quiddity of the material world). This attentiveness won Philip Hensher's acclaim in 1998: "Fitzgerald is a writer rooted in the physical world, who, whether she is writing about a familiar or a strange world, always bases her abstract truths, her observations of character and morality on a concrete fact."[10]

Her grounding in the realm of facts has reaped some unexpected kudos for Fitzgerald, like being called by Raban "the funniest writer in English now alive."[11] Raban might be right. An accountant in *At Freddie's* who tries to show Freddie a tidied-up balance sheet is told, "'Put it away,' . . . in the tone she used to the [rather than a] local flasher" (50). In *Human Voices*, Fitzgerald jokes about a problem that escaped the architects and engineers in charge of converting the concert hall in Broadcasting House into a stopgap dormitory: "The sleepers were obscurely tormented by the need to be somewhere in five, ten, or twenty minutes. . . . Yet some slept on, and the walls, designed to give the best possible acoustics for classical music, worked just as well for snoring" (84). Not all of Fitzgerald's jokes are this dry. The concert hall inspires a different comedy in chapter

10, where it hosts the most vital performance ever given there—a woman "swaying like an animal fit to drop" (116) as she prepares to give birth. But the ensuing birth scene gives rise to laughter. With rare insight, Fitzgerald pairs Lisa Bernard with an innocent who, facing his first crisis, clings to the fast-fading hope that he has misread Lisa's symptoms: "'Shall I get you a cup of tea?' Willie asked in terror. He knew very well what was happening. Make me wrong, he prayed" (116).

His wild plea develops from Fitzgerald's narrative instinct. Rather than ending a big scene with a crescendo, she folds in a little drama to give fresh slants on the scene's meaning. Freddie wants to wrest control of an interview with a business tycoon accustomed to being in charge himself. The interview builds in tension as Freddie and Joey Blatt vie for the best conversational angles. Then she pierces his veneer of self-possession by telling him that he has an artist's hands (51). Self-composed enough to resist either looking at his hands or moving them, he nonetheless hears his voice jump a decibel. Blatt, who will appear together with Freddie during her last bow in the book, does have his poise shaken by her tribute, further proof of which comes in his later telling the accountant who introduced him to Freddie, "I've never thought of them as different from anyone else's" (54).

Details like these came slowly to Fitzgerald. For instance, she had to learn that making a noun from the adjective in the phrase, "the ambiguous situation" (*Burne-Jones*, 122) would have both saved a word and disposed of the empty vessel, "situation." Her first book needed more editing than it got. The construction, "her erratic behavior . . . begin to affect [rather than undermine or weaken] her health" (*Burne-Jones*, 124), hinges on a verb that names, without defining, a condition.

Wordiness can also bedevil the novice writer. The sentence, "Burne-Jones became interested in politics and in the perpetual delusion that *through political means we* [rather than *politics*] can *better the human condition* [rather than *help humanity*]" (162; emphasis added). *The Knox Brothers* is both wordy ("to conduct an attack on [rather than *attack*]") and soft on clichés (a married couple are "poor as church mice") (99, 103).

A recurring nuisance in her prose, also seen in *The Knox Brothers* (31), bleeds into *Golden Child* (20, 116) and even into *Bookshop* (49) and *Innocence* (136); it is the "in spite of the fact" verbal cluster. But stylistic flaws can appear anywhere. Greater care in proofreading would have both saved a word and disposed of a passive-verb construction in this passage from *Offshore:* "Her whole idea of the world's work *was* derived from what she observed there" (29; emphasis added). Verbiage also clogs sentence flow in *Human Voices:* "Only DPP [viz., The Director of Programmed Planning] was likely to *give an* answer *to* that" (76; emphasis added). Surprisingly, wordiness even obstructs *Beginning of Spring,* the "absolute favorite" in the canon of a writer whose voice is overwhelmingly candid, unhurried, and respectful of the reader's intelligence.[12] A party guest wears "skin *which had been* lined with canvas" (56; emphasis added). Similarly, one of Frank Reid's employees reacts thus to a business problem: "Apparently it did not interest him, or rather *there was* something else *which* interested him more" (89; emphasis added). These lapses should be noted. But they are only lapses. Deftly modulated and psychologically complex, Fitzgerald's prose delivers so many joys that it seems unfair and nearly pointless to bewail its defects. The joys take many forms. An admirer of the virtue of self-control (*Golden Child,* 146), Fitzgerald specializes in subtle, thought-provoking touches. A restless wife who will later sell the houseboat her hospitalized husband loves enters *Offshore* "cutting something into small pieces" (11). Chiara Ridolfi enters chapter 12 of *Innocence* in a run of thirteen straight monosyllables: "Small, thin, and still flat as a board, she wore a black dress" (160). The plaudits extended to Fitzgerald by Raban, Hensher, and others are earned. Witness the metaphor describing the worsening of a hospital patient's pain in *Offshore:* "Instead of having a pain he was now contained inside it" (127). The crossed front teeth of a rat seen from a middle distance (139) and the counterclockwise movement of jaws of a cow in *Gate of Angels* (137) also disclose in Fitzgerald observational powers as keen as the prose that registers them.

This synergy keeps astonishing us. Byatt asks, "How does she do it?"[13] Add to Fitzgerald's stylistic gifts that of the impersonator. Consisting of one long clumsy sentence, a municipal order sent to Florence Green in *Bookshop* (119–20) includes the flat Latinate words, the droning repetitions, and the gnarled syntax of legalese. A parody of Noël Coward in *At Freddie's* (61–62) not only alludes to Shakespeare's *Henry V* and *As You Like It* as well as B. G. De Sylva's 1926 song, "When Day Is Done"; it also brings Coward to life. In nine short lines, the lyric conveys, along with Coward's faux world weariness, his love of travel and the patriotism that inspired *Cavalcade* (a 1931 play he wrote, directed, and starred in). But the parody, a wonder of concision, serves up still more treats. The rhyme made by the words "speeches" and "breaches," recalling the line from Coward's "Mad Dogs and Englishmen," "The English detest a siesta," and the witty comeback in *Private Lives* (1930), "Don't quibble, Sybil," shows in Fitzgerald an alertness so keen and comprehensive it can only be marveled at.

A marvelous piece of mimicry comes in chapter 17 of *Gate*. As Nina King says in her superb review, the chapter consists of a ghost story told by a Dr. Matthews, "provost of the fictional St. James College, medievalist, [and] paleographer."[14] King adds that the story resembles in both style and subject matter those being written at the time by the real-life teller of ghostly tales, M. R. James (1862–1936), who was serving as provost of Cambridge's Kings College in 1912, when *Gate of Angels* takes place.[15] This congruence should be noted. Dr. Matthews's story does sound like vintage James. In her introduction to a 2000 collection of James's work, Fitzgerald may have been glancing over her shoulder when, speaking of the tale, "Martin's Close," she said that the language of Lord Justice Jeffrey "reproduced Jeffrey's style so exactly that it seems like ventriloquism."[16]

Undogmatic about the point of view from which the action of a novel is told, Fitzgerald will intrude either to generalize or to share a laugh with the reader. Sometimes, the intrusion takes the form of a pun. A man in *Golden Child* who finds cannabis seeds in a burial urn can be said to have discovered pot in a pot. The epigram from *The Bookshop*, "Morality is seldom a safe guide to human conduct" (100), is an authorial intrusion that works like a plot point, both setting a tone and providing an attitude that will prepare the reader for what follows. Another example of foreshadowing—the maxim, "Duty is what no-one else will do at the moment" (9)—appears on the first page of *Offshore* because of its relevance to the coming action. The job done by one of Fitzgerald's intrusions can depend on the intrusion's place in the action. After saying in the last chapter of *Offshore*, "A storm always seems a strange thing in a great city, where there are so many immoveables" (133), she cuts first to moveables like bicycles and then to seagulls and rats—both of whose behavior storms change—before turning to houseboaters who are just as moveable but more fragile than the craft protecting them.

Selection also governs the flow of the chapters in Fitzgerald's novels. The endings of these chapters often deny a Victorian preference for closure in favor of instigating new action. Rather than bringing a conversation to full development—or sometimes even to a logical pause—Fitzgerald will inject a strident note that refers to one of the issues brought up in the chapter. The stridency refocuses our attention, showing that the chapter had been moving in a different direction than we had thought. The metaphor ending chapter 26 of *Innocence,* for example, puts a man's fortunes in a shocking new light: "He disappeared into the lighted jaws of the bus company's câfé-ristorante" (205). Because diners serve food to their customers rather than make food *of* them, the metaphor's incongruity implies that the man is innocently walking into a cannibal's oven.

The recurrence of such aggressive tropes in Fitzgerald's fiction bespeaks an anarchic imagination. An image like that of the dark, slippery horse's tongue Florence Green has to grab with two hands in *Bookshop* evokes the challenges posed by simple physical existence. Stylistically, *Bookshop* is Fitzgerald's breakthrough book. Besides conveying the texture and mass of material objects, it also gives off emanations and auras, as in Florence's reaction to the bathroom of a house just ransacked by a poltergeist: "The bathroom, with its water supply half connected, had the alert air of having witnessed something" (17). The same chapter includes the remarkable Keatsian image of "tiny pinpricks [rising] through . . . golden mouthfuls" of champagne (21). Food inspires Fitzgerald's imagination as much as drink. The description of pasta in *Innocence*, "its sauce freckled and dappled golden from the oven" (22), reflects an insight into the qualities of objects that make the objects both vital and unique. Fitzgerald's later books introduce a new device to capture the presentness and authority of things. The things she selects are the same ones her characters deal with every day without probing their mystery. The following roster of cures for various maladies in *Gate* generates, through the carefully weighted images that comprise it, the molecular drive and sway of a power system that defines many interconnected lives:

> Down in the dispensary, the engine room of he hospital, ranged in alphabetical order, were the preparations of aceta (or vinegars), aquae (or waters), balsams, confections, conserves, decoctions, enemata, essences, glycerines, infusions. . . . In the wards the kidney sufferers, waiting to sweat into their thick flared night-shirts, were dosed with nitre, squill and broom. (81)

Having mastered language, Fitzgerald knows language's effectiveness as a mode of communication and expression. Always in flux, her multiform, absurd world will resist a construct as arbitrary and rational as the word. A fraught social encounter can sharpen into a wordless duel of wits in which victory is decided by silence and steadiness of gaze. Body language also has a nonverbal eloquence: "Vi had been able to tell from one look at her mother's back . . . that she had been hurt" (*Human Voices,* 161). Fitzgerald's sensitivity to the physical counterparts of feeling again bypasses the face in *At Freddie's:* "She saw the reflection of the back of his head and shoulders, where defeat shows absolutely" (148).

The acumen shown here chimes with Fitzgerald's treatment of face-to-face conversations. As in Samuel Beckett's *Waiting for Godot* (1952), her people often gag on their words while voicing their feelings and thoughts. "I don't love him any more," says Nenna James about her husband Eddie in *Offshore*. But when asked, "Is that true?" Nenna says "No" (105). Her confusion, which makes her look like an actor in a play (like *Godot*) who has not learned her part, delves to the quick of her psyche; she is too rattled to know her mind. This edge cuts differently in *Gate*. The following description of Daisy Saunders and Fred Fairly shows how the frantic and the overwrought will assault what they hold dear and defend what they oppose: "They looked at each other in despair, and now there seemed to be another law or regulation by which they were obliged to say to each other what they did not mean and to attack what they wished to defend." (159)

Words part company from human response in chapter 27 of *The Blue Flower*. Erasmus von Hardenberg snaps the thread of a heated conversation to stop it from lurching out of control. But where to go after fending off danger? The abrupt mood shift gives rise to an exchange of banalities that replaces the wrenching self-avowals Erasmus and Karoline Just had just started dredging up. They see the need to prolong the relief they have lucked into. Karoline knows that it is her turn to act. Food can help them. Though he is not hungry, a consenting Erasmus knows that keeping his mouth full will ensure his silence and thus quiet his and Karoline's nerves:

> Karoline collected herself enough to pull the bell. "I am going to ask them to bring some refreshments, which we don't want."

"Of course we do not," said Erasmus, who, however, when it arrived, ate large quantities of Zwieback, and drank some wine. (104)

Fitzgerald knows a thing or two about complex relationships and the blurry edges of sexuality, which is where Erasmus's talk with Karoline is sliding before she orders refreshments. Fitzgerald's observational powers and her grasp of the nuances of temperament alchemize this knowledge. Like two people in a Jane Austen novel, Karoline and Erasmus are funny in their distress. It is an Austenlike flair for sharp-edged, colorful characters that makes the distress vibrate.

Nor are these similarities to Austen accidental. Any fair, balanced assessment of Fitzgerald's art will invite comparisons with the best. The comparisons mount. Although the catalogues that enrich her later work lack the exuberance of Walt Whitman's, their freshness, sharpness, and carefully composed rhythms contain their own multitudes. Like found art, Fitzgerald's catalogues make the familiar new. They reflect, as well, a mind comfortable with the rough, the raw, and even the messy, as is borne out by a terrifying description of the deformed Antonio Gramsci, leaking fluids "from several parts of the body" (*Innocence*, 45) as he loses consciousness. But this toothless, reeking hunchback speaks with clarity, decency, and an unaffected wisdom when he can. Similar counterpoints of the courteous and the corrosive account for much of Fitzgerald's distinction. The genius with which she charts the counterpoint helps make her the world-class writer her reviewers have been lauding.

CHAPTER 4

The Great Museum Sideshow

The Golden Child has many of the traits of the traditional English detective story. Unfolding mostly in a confined setting, the novel provides a limited number of well-developed characters as murder suspects. Its plot is so well built that the naming of the culprit shows us that the clues dropped along the way might have helped us, had we been a bit sharper, to solve the crime ourselves. But Fitzgerald's idea of writing a detective novel to please her husband coexists with other narrative aims. *The Golden Child* is both a page-turner and a serious novel. A tension runs through her 1977 work that both rivals and helps it fulfill its goals as a whodunit. It is a mystery that also looks at complex social, political, and emotional questions.

A whodunit relies on believability to draw us into its plot. A satire, on the other hand, has to be absurd. Fitzgerald, whose humor often trades on the ridiculous, writes well enough to have it both ways. Her first novel opens in what might be "the most famous museum in the world" (66). Located in London and referred to as The Museum, this "place of dignity and order" (15) is facing several crises. The heads of departments like Woven Textiles and Unglazed Ceramics are scrambling for resources to beef up their holdings. A hierarchy, long in place, decides who can have keys and documents, access to office memos, and library privileges. This rigid protocol has created a collective can't-do mentality. The technical staff is denied reference tools that could speed their work. Management, besides competing for resources, frets about their juniors using dirty tricks to rise in the Museum's power structure.

And then there are the philosophical differences. A prissy, thin-blooded curator believes that Museums exist to amass and preserve art objects. Some of his colleagues, agreeing with him in principle, add that a museum should also store artifacts for the purposes of study and historical documentation. Here is the rub. Ignoring the general public, these attitudes forswear the idea that museums exist to teach and delight large audiences by displaying their collections. Most of the book's likable characters support this idea. Their ideological foes, who also favor the imperial ideals of maintaining order and keeping class distinctions clear, shudder to think that the privileges they have acquired may be scaled back. Imperialism works by crushing the disenfranchised. And once in place, its codes are hard to dislodge, even in 1977, decades after the British Empire had trimmed down to a Commonwealth.

Conveying Fitzgerald's disquiet over the sluggishness of bureaucratic change is the image of the maze. The Museum contains over half a mile of corridors. It is also exhibiting, as part of the Golden Treasure of the Garamantes, a ball of golden twine that evokes the labyrinth under the Palace of Knossos where the half-man, half-bull Minotaur lived. Early in chapter 2 of *Golden Child*, a foreign visitor speaks of "the clue of thread given by Ariadne to Theseus" (41), slayer of the Minotaur. Later in the chapter, the pattern formed by the displays leading to the Golden Treasure is called "an open maze" (55). The metaphor holds. In the last chapter, the Museum's outdated plumbing looks like "a maze of pipes" (158). The maze metaphor extends beyond the Museum. Both London and Moscow, where part of chapter 3 takes place, are cold, congested places full of frustrations and dead ends. Each city has publicly displayed an embalmed corpse that shivering people queue up for hours to see (viz., Lenin and the Golden Child), and at least one of them is a fake. Nor are London and Moscow the only cities that disappoint. A police inspector also finds Paris "a swindle" (156).

Fitzgerald knows the legacy of the city as maze. She recycles it again in *Offshore* together with its association with rats. In *Charlotte Mew and Her Friends,* she calls "the whole business of hurrying in desperation through a maze of mean streets" (61) a legacy of Victorian fiction. She is right. The legacy has carried forward from Bill Sikes's wild flight from the law in *Oliver Twist*. Ford Madox Ford describes life as a maze in *The Good Soldier* (1915); in Joyce's *A Portrait of the Artist as a Young Man* (1916), Stephen Dedalus feels trapped in Dublin's drizzling, mazelike streets; Patrick White's *The Tree of Man* (1955) develops, in part, on Sydney's dirty, noisy sidewalks, a concrete network that brings people to grief.

The grief caused by the modern city declares itself at the start of *Golden Child*. Quickly and economically, the novel begins on the first day of the exhibit of the Golden Child. Surrounded by his treasure is the mummified child, a boy king who died in the fifth century B.C. in his African desert kingdom of Garamantia. His corpse, wrapped in gold leaf, reposes in a coffin of salt next to a golden doll and a ball of golden twine, placed there to lead the king back to his burial site after visiting his friends on earth. A gaudy snatch in its own right, the exhibition featuring him has won the Museum some added prestige by coming there first after snubbing bids from rival fixtures in Paris and New York.

The crowds standing for hours in the Museum's forecourt under "a frozen January sky" (7) create a strong presence. Coach tours and student groups from all over the UK have descended upon the Museum to pay homage to culture. Though patient, the many queuers radiate tension. Because the novel opens on primary schools day, it describes, at its outset, six thousand hungry children "half unconscious with cold" (8) waiting for the museum to open. But these kids face still another worry. Leaflets scattered around the courtyard where they have been shivering warn them that the exhibition is under a curse and, further, "that those who look upon the Exhibition are doomed" (12). Showing how people close ranks during times of hardship, the children—and the tens of thousands queued up behind them to see the Treasure—build a mini-society of their own. A passage in chapter 5 describes the four-hour ordeal of waiting that unites the anonymous queuers, some of whom have brought "portable cooking-stoves . . . [and] short-wave transistor radios" (132) to help pass the time. Other diversions follow. One woman claims to have seen the Treasure every day since its opening, and she, along with anyone else who, like her, queued up for the Treasure the first three days of its showing, has the right to wear a special badge—showing a pair of sore feet against a golden background.

Such diversions breed surprises—but surprises that both conform to Fitzgerald's liberalism and show her rare ability to see the different sides of a situation. Her book's leading character, Waring Smith, forgoes the comfort of his Museum office to join "the six-time winding column of the queue" (131). Despite the awful cold, which rivals that of Moscow (155), he is accepted by his fellow queuers, most of whom, in a Tolstoyan fillip, rate their shared ordeal on the pavement higher than they do the prize of witnessing the Treasure. The Kremlin had it wrong, notes Waring: "The true international solidarity was not between workers, but between queuers" (132). Waring also notes that many of his fellow queuers are wearing clothes that look like those worn by British troops during the Blitz. That these clothes came from government surplus stores sharpens his impression that a war is being fought.

But against whom?

Sir John Allison, the Museum's forty-five-year-old director, an "awe-inspiring, gently smiling, wondrous blend of civil servant and scholar" (13), takes as little interest in matters of maintenance like plumbing and wiring as he does in the well-being of the queuers shivering outside his elegant office. Even more sniffingly contemptuous of the mundane is the effete curator of the Museum's Department of Funerary Art, Marcus Hawthorne-Mannering, or H-M. Besides trying to kill Waring Smith for allegedly filching his work, this fragile, "exceedingly thin . . . disquieting" (18) blue blood misses work so often because of ill health that others have to step in to do his job. It is surprising that he can function at all. His careful grooming is mentioned so often that he reminds us of a corpse. Known to his colleagues as "the May Queen" (28), this pale, mincing twit disregards the suffering of the queuers. When told that many of them spent the previous night riding on a train, he mutters, Pilate-like, "One's hands are clean" (29).

This frosty disdain sorts ill with the aristocratic image the May Queen affects. Though proud of his fine manners and high-toned connections, he is a ferocious careerist. The location of his family home—Poynton, Dorset (129), site of Henry James's 1897 novel, *The Spoils of Poynton* (the main action of which consists of a nasty feud over furniture)—betrays his elitism. Like

James's feuding high-borns, H-M is a fraud. The traditional English gentleman, with his sartorial finesse and wide general knowledge, shuns ambition. The homicidal fop H-M displays the unviability of this paradigm in our age of academic specialization.

Even more jealous of his turf if the Museum's director, Sir John Allison. This world-class expert in "French porcelain, silver, and furniture" (14) rates artifacts over people. The control these artifacts exert on his heart have made him a superb curator. But it has also twisted him. Like H-M, he would like to preserve the Museum's vast collection "in ideal conditions, unseen, unpolluted" (127) by the visiting public. The comparisons between the two mandarins mount. H-M says that he strangled Waring because Waring "went out of . . . [his] field" (127). He also confesses that he hated another character because he was not a "museum man" (55). Sir John later uses the same words to justify murdering this character, Sir William Simpkins (177). The aged Sir William had changed his mind about leaving his fortune to Sir John when he learned that the bequest had already been earmarked to bolster the holdings in Sir John's area of expertise. Fitzgerald's satire on the excesses of professionalism takes an ugly turn in Sir John's confession of his guilt: "I have broken the rules of my profession and attempted something for which I was never trained. About French porcelain and silver I know all that a man can know. But I don't know how to commit murder. I still do not know! I am out of my field!" (178)

The book's patricians are also its best haters. Sir John's belief that not only his victim's life but also his own lacks the value of one silver-gilt bowl designed by a master has reduced the act of murder in his mind to the level of a professional blunder. If this warped reasoning explains much of his conduct, the sense of self-preservation that feeds it reflects great shrewdness. In keeping with the smoothness that helped elevate him professionally, he silences the chiefs of two departments who come to his office to recount their budgetary woes. He finds a way to deflect blame when he discovers problems with the Golden Treasure. Then, after murdering Sir William, he takes the body to a place where its eventual discovery would, presumably, leave no trail back to him. Sir John it also was who scattered the yellow leaflets in the museum's courtyard headed by the words, "GOLD IS FILTH / FILTH IS BLOOD"(11).

Dispersed on the exhibition's first day, the leaflets warn the queuers that the treasure they have been waiting to see is cursed and, more portentously, that seeing the treasure will blight *them*. The leaflets' envoi—"GOLD IS DEATH" (12)—combines Freud's equation of money or gold with shit and the Manicheanism that feeds Sir John's snobbery. His notion of the ideal museum as a pristine, unpeopled space reflects his misanthropy. It posits a great danger, as well. The logical upshot of his sterile, airless paradigm, the closing of the museum to visitors, denies the vital exchange between artist and audience. Self-defeatingly, the director has created a means by which the clutter and filth he deplores can rush into the museum and swamp it. The phrase, "POO DUMP," from a cipher later used to solve the case, appears four times in the action (142, 148, 149, 151), first to remind us of Freud's famous equation and next to confirm Fitzgerald's faith in the synergy of "beautiful objects" and "the public who stood so much in need of them" (36).

This optimism comes to Fitzgerald from John Ruskin and William Morris. Museums, an invention of the nineteenth century, performed the fine service of moving works of art from the private collections of the rich to places of public access, often in high-density population areas, like London and Paris, where they could be enjoyed by more people. In keeping with this development, Fitzgerald traces most of her novel's affirmations to the collective efforts of flawed urban rank-and-filers. Human fallibility does not scare her. Would that all the novel's female characters agreed with her. As her name suggests, Miss Rank, the icily efficient personal aide to Sir John, shares her chief's belief in the claims of hierarchy. But the gentle, lilting cadence of her four-syllable first name, Veronica (125), invokes the girlish vulnerability (Veronica-vulnerable) to beauty that prompts her to put an illuminated book of gold foil in a place—her own desk drawer—that links the book to St. John's misdeeds and helps prove his guilt.

"He makes things" (163), Waring says of Sir John's opposite number, Len Coker. A skilled engineer, Len has a working-class dignity as far removed from political centrism as is the director's princely persona. But the inconsistencies dappling Len's character lend him a humanity that deflates Sir John's sleek image. A fierce left-winger, Len has studied conflict promotion (as opposed to conflict resolution). Yet he is very gentle and open-minded. He does drive a monumental spear through Waring's shoe after mistakenly thinking that Waring has been romancing his girlfriend, Dousha. St. Patrick, it is noted, once got so caught up in the sermon he was giving that he accidentally put his spear through a listener's foot (48). But St. Patrick is better known for having driven all the snakes from Ireland. The snake in *Golden Child* is Sir John. In the book's last chapter, Waring finds Len in the director's office—to provide him protection. The director had made Waring his private assistant in Miss Rank's absence in order to kill him, as he had already killed Sir William and *his* assistant.

Reversing the Toryism of classic mystery writers like Dorothy L. Sayers and Agatha Christie, Fitzgerald has the working-class artisan Len Coker nail the lordly, dignified Sir John. But she expresses her democratic bias in other ways, too. Several people—rather than a lone eccentric amateur sleuth like Sayers's Lord Peter Wimsey or Christie's Hercule Poirot—solve the case. And they join hands, not only to stop a murderer but also to honor Sir William, who angered Sir John by willing his money to a fund that would ensure free admission into the museum for all.

Though a team job, the sleuthing that nails Sir John comes mostly from Len. Fitzgerald shows her approval of his efforts by associating him with keys (72, 172), the symbolic potency of which culminates in his becoming a father by book's end. When first seen, Len is angry. Management has denied the museum's technical staff access to the Golden Treasure, a bad mistake in Len's opinion. Besides missing a chance to promote dialogue between the two branches, management has also ruled out any analysis of the exhibition's contents. The later firing of Len will have the same recoil action. Len loses his job because he is caught growing cannabis. But the cannabis seeds in question came from the exhibition, just as the stains on the royal garments turned out, under Len's analysis, not to be sacred wine but Pepsi-cola (146–47). Len has exposed the whole Treasure as a sham.

This revelation moves the book to its climax. While Waring is asking questions and looking for physical evidence, he comes under the eye of Sir John. Waring only realizes that he is at risk when he walks into the director's office and finds Len sitting there. Off the page since chapter 3 (71), the director first appears both to Waring and to us like one of James Joyce's flawed priests, "his back to the light" (169). Len's reply to his asking whom Waring has to fear creates a total shock: "You, cock" (170). The "uncouth" (170) Len's rudeness to his elegant host stuns Waring. More benefits follow from Fitzgerald's wise tactic of recounting the scene from Waring's point of view. The liberty Len takes with his language violates the dignity befitting the directorship of the Museum. Yet the tonelessness of Sir John's response to the epithet explains that Len has not misspoken. Sir John's leaden voice denotes a flatfooted dismay. His guilt—which, he knows, Len has inferred—strips him of any honor and prestige he might otherwise hide behind.

Len's demonstration of the evidence that proves Sir John's guilt brings another shock. Fitzgerald resists the doctrinaire satirist's urge to clobber her seemingly helpless villain. Len's recitation recalls Poirot's trademark practice of gathering all the witnesses and suspects in the library of the country house where the murder took place so they can hear him name the culprit. Unlike a Poirot or a Miss Jane Marple mystery, though, *Golden Child* ends in a flurry of physical action. A chase ensues, but, as in Graham Greene's *A Gun for Sale* (1936) and *The Confidential Agent* (1939), it reverses direction. Waring becomes the pursuer of the killer who had been pursuing *him*. In Sir John's mad rush, through rows and rows of earthenware pots and vases that he smashes, he is called "a great man . . . going mad greatly" (179). The paragraph in which he suicides also likens him to a bird, invoking his kinship with things of the spirit. Then Fitzgerald calls him "The Director" (182). This term honors Sir John. But it suggests, too, a separation on his part—not only from human values, rather from humanity itself. This touch suits Fitzgerald's purpose better than would a moral sermon. A murderer who believes his only crime consisted of acting outside his field of expertise *is* as cold-blooded as a bird. He has also blinded himself morally—as is implied by his looking at his accuser Len, his back to the light—through spectacles resembling "blank panes of glass" (170). Yet this "figure of authority and unrivaled scholarship" (170) holds one of the most highly esteemed jobs in the prestigious, cutthroat world of museum administration. Both his fine performance record in his two years as director and the popularity of his televised lecture series deny that his elevation was a fluke. Nor would he murder for personal gain.

Rather than probe the questions raised by his prominence, Fitzgerald's satire on the world of museum men folds in another, lighter, subplot. A visitor to the museum during the exhibition is Professor Heinrich Untermensch, the world's leading Garamantologist. But he is not just "the acknowledged expert in the Garamantian system of writing" (25); ancient Garamantian is also the language he speaks best, even though it died out centuries ago. The fun continues. He is the only living reader of ancient Garamantian, as well. To dissuade Sir John from killing him, he appeals as a fellow specialist: "Spare me! I alone can read Garmantian" (180), he shouts. Though deemed "the right plea" (180) by Fitzgerald, it fails to convince Sir John, who drops him from a high window. But Untermensch does not die. He returns to the museum after falling into a tank of water. Then, after stuffing the director's corpse into a ceremonial coffin, he intones, "May he rest in peace. . . . The life of scholarship is dangerous" (183).

Another distinguished scholar is the exhibition's sponsor, the eighty-five-year-old "ancient ruffian" (13) and archeologist, Sir William Simpkins. Self-taught, Sir William grew up poor in one of London's dockside slums. Now in "extreme but clear-headed old age" (10), this expert Garamantologist finds himself out of step with the museum's executive branch. But *has* his open-door attitude regarding access to the museum labeled him sentimental and rearguard? Through him, Fitzgerald creates a sense of historical depth that makes the question matter. He has saved letters sent him by his "long-dead wife" (111). Also, the work he did with the real-life archeologist Sir Flinders Petrie (1853–1942), besides looking ahead to Freddie Wentworth's apprenticeship under the Old Vic's founder Lilian Baylis in *At Freddie's,* lends the action a welcome resonance. First seen handling, with "almost transparent ancient fingers" (11), some old photos and a news clipping, he objectifies Fitzgerald's ability to portray oldness by joining it to data still older and crustier —rather than to the fresh, the dewy, and the new.

But he also enacts Fitzgerald's belief that, though age is inevitable, aging is not. His not being "a museum man," according to Sir John and H-M, does him credit. He sets no store by the dozen books he has written. To quell the dismay that greets the Golden Treasure's opening, he offers a pound, out of pocket, to every child who collects fifty of the nasty GOLD IS FILTH leaflets and puts them in a trash bin. Would that the Museum's directorate were this generous and free-spirited. He goes out of his way to share information that the directorate wants to hoard or bury. To him, the search for the truth is an active, inclusive process with political import. Democracies, he knows, depend on the free flow of information and ideas. In the Museum, this interchange could help rank-and-filers evaluate policy and, just as importantly, shine light in dark corners where special interests thrive.

Anticipating Fitzgerald's portrayal of Broadcasting House in *Human Voices,* Sir William says, "The function of the Press is to tell the truth—aye, even at the risk of all that a man holds dear" (32). He believes in sharing access as well as ideas. Rather than scold Waring Smith for peeking at some confidential files, he praises him, arguing that, once breached, secrets lose their power to harm. This argument has special import because each of the major figures in *Golden Child* knows the treasure to be a fake. Sir William's support of right of way also includes the easing of physical distress. The first thing said about him, before he shows his face in the book, by a personal aide, is that he would object to the crash barriers the Museum's security chief wants to install at each of the building's entrances for purposes of crowd control (7). The aide has spoken home. Several times in chapter 1, Sir William sympathizes with the bored, frustrated crowds packing into the icy Museum forecourt for as long as seven hours before stepping inside.

It is his love for Sir William that moves Waring to action when, in the last chapter, he hears the director call the dead old man a bastard and a Judas (175). This moment marks a climax because Waring has been, up to now, dithering and weak willed. John Mellors rightly calls him "an amiable, mostly baffled hero."[1] As an amateur detective, he calls to mind the passive, reluctant heroes of Eric Ambler who stumble upon clues rather than hunt them out. Fitzgerald takes pains to make this junior staffer at the museum ordinary rather than exceptional. Admitting that he is no gentleman, Waring sees himself as "not . . . terribly important" (44, 162). His background chimes with this modest self-assessment. "Young, normal . . . sincere, and worried," he grew up on Hayley Island, a Channel isle so small it rarely appears on maps or in atlases (26, 53). He then attended a mainland grammar school, as opposed to a top public like Eton or Rugby, before earning a university degree in Technical Arts.

As has been seen, his two-year tenure as a junior exhibition officer has stalled; he did so well on a cataloguing job first assigned to H-M, his boss, that the May Queen has hated him ever since.

He cannot afford to make enemies at the museum, what with his hefty monthly house note. This ache his wife cannot relieve because she took a low-paying typists job, where her university training went to waste, so that he could advance *his* career. Thus his moral indebtedness to Haggie swells into guilt when his new job as coordinator of security and public relations during the exhibition demands that he work overtime. His anxiety sharpens following Untermensch's announcement that the whole collection of Garamantian grave goods is a fake. If this secret ever becomes public knowledge, a scandal would erupt. Most critically, the museum would lose face as soon as the media starts bawling that the tens of thousands who paid fifty pence to see the Golden Child had been robbed.

A solution is proposed to relieve the Museum's distress. One of the world's leading Garamantologists teaches at Moscow State University. More importantly, the apolitical Professor Cyril Ivanovitch Semyonov can be questioned about the authenticity of the Golden Child with little or no risk that he will blab. The need to maintain secrecy and thus protect the Museum from scandal also dictates the mode of infiltrating the Golden Child into Moscow. To hide the importance of the operation, the courier will join a package tour to the USSR while kept ignorant of the treasure he is carrying. His proposed visit to Professor Semyonov will be strictly unofficial. Were he to know the value of his package, he might fluster and blow the operation. But the need to keep his paymasters' motives dark imposes still another bizarre condition, one that heightens the danger facing him. Though perhaps an object of great value, the treasure must not be declared at customs prior to being passed into the Soviet Union. Like the trouble-prone heroes of Greene, Ambler, and le Carré, whose miseries pile up as soon as they are beyond reach of help, the courier in *Golden Child*—namely Waring—is a small, luckless man entrusted with the biggest job of his life.

He is picked by his chiefs to do a dangerous job they will not help him with because of his ordinariness. His relative unimportance in the Museum's power structure supplies the good cover that will expedite the job. His chiefs—except for Sir William, who has been trying to further in him "an instinct for happiness" (27)—have sold him short. This instinct, while a shaky base for the guile of Museum politics, harks to the goodness and simplicity (but not simplemindedness) evoked by Sir William Simpkins's name. "Waring liked children" (75), says Fitzgerald in chapter 3, while he is seen talking to a child. She also shows him having dinner with a pregnant woman he will later visit in hospital after she delivers.

The literal birth he has come to celebrate nearly coincides with the symbolic one he is undergoing. Waring is one of Fitzgerald's innocents, and, like Henry Fielding's Joseph Andrews and Tom Jones, he has to learn to temper his goodness of heart with prudence before he can emerge as a responsible adult. This process transcends everything else in Fitzgerald's debut novel. Much of it takes a sexual form. Late in chapter 1, Waring penetrates the interior of the Golden Treasure, but to return, rather than take, something—the clay tablet upon which Sir William wrote his will. Later, at the ending of chapter 3—the book's halfway point—Waring ends up "in the holy of holies, the forbidden ground" (92) of the Kremlin, where he has been taken by the Soviet secret police. This penetration discloses to him the real Golden Treasure of Garamantia. The secret the Museum has been trying to hide was breached by the KGB weeks earlier. Both the Museum and the British government were duped by a third-world country lacking oil, an educational system, and a military arm (31). The bitter joke plays on. Professor Semyonov, whom Waring was sent to Moscow to see, does not exist. The plot of *Golden Child* has swerved into the realm of cold war politics, which were tense in 1977.

Waring's handling of the revelation that the Golden Treasure is sitting in Moscow rather than in London empowers him. His new strength surfaces quickly. Some questions asked him by the detectives who meet him at Gatwick Airport upon his return from Moscow reveal that the Defense Ministry knows less about the Golden Child than he does. Then, to protect his paymasters, he uses a neat dodge to avoid showing the Child to the detectives who ask to see it. The moral courage that helped him enact this dodge is felt immediately. On the book's next page (102), it is reported that Sir William and his assistant Jones both died while Waring was away. Though beyond reason, the coincidence of these deaths with Waring's absence from the Museum, where the deaths occurred, casts mediocre, confused Waring as a guardian spirit. Stripped of the protection conferred by his presence, two associates of the Museum who share both his outlook and his common roots get murdered.

But Fitzgerald, future broker in poltergeists (*Bookshop*) and ghosts (*Gate of Angels*), believes that certain forces in the world override natural law. Soon after returning to the Museum, Waring is greeted by both a promotion and a salary raise. In a profession where people fight dirty to keep their jobs, he has advanced without trying to. But his advancement is no mistake. When H-M asks him about his doings in Moscow, he finds the poise and self-presence to conjure up an indirect answer. The editorial comment Fitzgerald inserts here both endorses this equanimity and qualifies *Golden Child* as an initiation story: "Waring knew that he himself had hardened over the last few days. His puppyish desire to please and convince had gone, and had been replaced by a new perception . . . as to how the world was run" (126).

The book's next scene carries this new authenticity forward. Waring leaves H-M to go outside to mingle with the queuers. Lining up for four hours in the cold both gladdens and stimulates him. That Fitzgerald avoids naming any of his fellow queuers has import. Their government surplus store garb identifies them as the great sprawling middle class that makes the world go. His joining them in the cold prepares Waring for a still harder knock—getting shot by a fleeing Sir John in the book's closing pages. Violence seasons him. When a duty officer enters the area where the Director shot himself, Waring, asked about the Director's collapse, has the sangfroid to say ironically, "His heart has been affected by the accident, yes" (184). And right after this episode, he shocks himself by giving orders "for the first time in his life" (184)—to his supervisor, H-M, who is told to create a diversion to buy time while a replica of the replica Golden Child smashed by Sir John is made and then placed in public view.

But this coup does not crown Waring's self-definition. His canny author knows which of life's prizes are the most elusive. The plot structure of *Golden Child* makes this knowledge stick. Pressurizing and thus enriching the action are the domestic mishaps that befall Waring. At the same time his job is making new demands on him, he has innocently caused his wife to doubt his loyalty. Sir William's heavily pregnant secretary, Dousha Vartarian, focuses the confusion. Whenever Waring tells

Haggie that he will be coming home later than expected, he is asked whether he is going to see Dousha, whose existence she has mysteriously discovered. And he always is. But the good excuse he gives Haggie is always rejected. He takes Dousha to dinner at the request of Sir William, who recommends a night out to boost her spirits. Later, he will accompany Len to the hospital where she has just had her baby.

In a keen plot maneuver, Waring regains Haggie's favor through the intervention of Dousha, with whom he was suspected of cheating. Haggie's trip to the hospital where Dousha is lying in, during which Waring's innocence is established, reminds us, along with the deaths of Sir William and Jones, of Fitzgerald's ability to seat crucial action off the page. Besides tightening the plot, this maneuver also invites a closer look at Dousha. This daughter of a wrestler and a tumbler from Azerbaijan often arrives late to work and sleeps at her desk. Yet, even though as Sir William's secretary, she anchors a competitive, confrontational world, she holds her job. Why? In contrast to the Director's proficient, high-octane assistant, Veronica Rank, Dousha is "rarely seen either standing or walking" (49) and has a heavy floral charm that others warm to. This physical serenity has also tuned her to the natural function of birthing a baby. Blending her needs with her wants, Dousha follows her maternal instincts.

Though a feminist might balk at the development, Fitzgerald shows through Dousha (as Ibsen did through the character Thea Elvsted in *Hedda Gabler*) that Miss Rank's cleverness and her doggedness to excel thwart the quest for womanly self-being. In a novel that mentions Tolstoy (e.g., 86, 167), Dousha achieves the Tolstoyan ideal of gaining her goals by simply being herself. Fitzgerald admires her as much as Tolstoy would have. Dousha's drowsy, blossomy amplitude qualifies her for the role of dea ex machina. Besides giving birth in the book's present-tense action, she also rights Waring's shaky marriage. Waring calls her "soothing, undemanding, overweight, lovely, and brainless" (144). But he is not attacking her. As he will learn, her calmness and lulling softness give comfort. The peace Dousha exudes is even sexy. An alert, wide-awake Len Coker, who has the wit to prove the Director's guilt, falls for her. Fitzgerald would remain aware of her powers. In *The Beginning of Spring,* two and perhaps three men fall in love with a woman described as "quiet . . . slow-witted, nubile, docile . . . [who] hardly speaks at all in fact, sloping shoulders, half-shut eyes" (136).

A character who shares Dousha's common origins is Sir William's helper, Jones. This "solid, grizzled" (13) commoner has the working-class values that Sir William, himself a commoner, can trust. Like his boss, Jones angers the museum's establishment. His words of warning to the security chief regarding Sir William's disapproval of using crash barriers as crowd-control devices are the first he speaks in the book (7). He tells Waring that he is not a gentleman in the same conversation where he explains that Sir William's life is in danger. The warning that Len Coker later serves Waring, that Sir John is planning to kill *him* (170), thus fits a pattern. It is a pattern, moreover, which Fitzgerald will build on; Jones is called "old-fashioned" (107) for grieving over Sir William's death. He would be written off as a fossil if he said that the honor, courage, and comradeship he found in Sir William shores up everything worth working or fighting for in contemporary life.

Fitzgerald gives Jones the first name of Jones (155, 164) to show that he is so ordinary that he is strange—at least to the mandarins who run the Museum. The loyalty with which he serves Sir John angers these toffs because, to do his job properly, he has to bend or even break rules they have put in place. His ability to ignore their anger, though, finally defeats him. He has absorbed so much of his master's uprightness and integrity that he must die. Fittingly, it is the rank-and-filer Waring Smith and not stiff, pompous Sir John or the May Queen who says of Jones after his death, "He was a kind of fixture. The Museum feels strange without him" (164).

This tribute tallies with the book's democratic bias. At the start, both the Museum's hierarchy and its policy structure echo traditional English upperclass attitudes about social rank and property. These attitudes take a pounding—from Sir William's sympathy for the stalwart queuers, Len Coker's exposure of the folly of being denied, as a member of the Museum's technical staff, access to the exhibition, and Waring's trip to the USSR. By sending Waring to Moscow because they believe that his ordinariness will fool Soviet security, his chiefs define ordinariness too meanly. Vain and insecure, they ignore the truth that Waring's commonplaceness rests on an integrity that makes him a trusty servant. "To be ordinary, in these times," he is told, "is an occasion for bravo" (94). He is wrong to belittle his visit to the USSR as a series of blunders. His Soviet interlude gives him both the information and the moral fiber to improve his life.

Together with Sir John's guilt, Dousha's baby with Len Coker carries to completion a leveling outlook in a novel that also favors the spontaneous, the direct, and the foursquare over the formalities endorsed by conformism. *Golden Child* puts forth a healthy moral vision. Underlying it is the belief that the agitations and disturbances that vex us every day can help us if dealt with imaginatively. Waring feels clumsy and displaced during most of his stay in Moscow. Aggravating his malaise is the fierce January cold—until he learns that the cold tormenting his joints can also be a blessing. The same freeze that kills bacterial infection also defeated Napoleon (88). But such is the novel's economy that Moscow's chill provides still more fun. It is ironical enough that a collection of Saharan artifacts should be displayed "under a frozen January sky" (7) in London. That the packers, dispatchers, and insurers who inventoried the collection prior to its London showing were all taken in by its phoniness borders on the ludicrous. But the joke plays on. While the senior staffers at the Museum are whining about the deception, the real article is sitting in Moscow, whose winter is even more brutal than London's.

This irony provides but one of the many joys of reading *Golden Child*. Whereas most first novels can be trite, sententious, and dramatically awkward, Fitzgerald's fictional debut moves assuredly, displays an originality of image and symbol, and enjoys a wide range of allusion. It has its faults. The same cop is called both Sergeant Liddell (108) and Inspector Liddell (112). Fitzgerald also uses a barefaced contrivance to convey information to the reader. Thus Waring surreptitiously reads a top secret memo because Dousha, the secretary of the V. I. P. to whom the memo is sent, is sleeping at her desk when Waring enters her office. Nor is it ever explained how Sir John distributed, undetected, the yellow GOLD IS FILTH leaflets found in the museum's courtyard.

These faults notwithstanding, Susannah Clapp falls wide of the mark by calling the plot of *Golden Child* "over-inflated."[2] The book shapes itself to its sophisticated content without straining. Because art transcends national borders, the plot focuses on an exhibit of African artifacts in a London museum and segues to both Leningrad and Moscow. The first chapter foreshadows these doings. Fitzgerald has the skill to play out several different plot lines here, that she joins in the chapter's last sentence, "The police are in the building" (37). Another organizing principle she uses, perhaps to spoof Marxist dialectic, is binarism. Two murders occur in the book's fourth chapter; two windows are broken; two sets of keys disappear temporarily; two foreign experts visit the museum during the Treasure's installation; two employees of the museum go to Russia during the course of the action, one of whom, Waring, visits the nonexistent Professor Semyonov twice; Waring also spends time twice with Dousha outside the museum.

In line with its cosmopolitanism, *Golden Child* contains passages written in French, Russian, ancient Greek, and German. One German coinage, *Garamantischengeheimschriftendechiffrierkunst* (44, 114), which echoes the language's drift to word-bonding, means, roughly, the art of decoding secret Garamantian writing. It also invokes the author's Uncle Dilly (i.e., Alfred Dillwyn Knox [1884–1963]), a cryptographer and translator of Herodas, who is mentioned in *Golden Child* (137). Dilly certainly inspired the elaborate cipher, the decoding of which establishes the guilt of Sir John. Fitzgerald's treatment of Moscow, where Waring spends most of chapter 3, reflects the same care she extends to the cipher. Moscow's main feature, no surprise, is its numbing cold. But also bringing the town to life are the Russian words and phrases that stipple the text, the various public landmarks that come into view (St. Basil's Church is not one of them), and the worries foreigners face moving around Moscow. Not that Moscow is a joy for the locals; the drab, tatty clothes and the pinched gray faces of the

Muscovites Waring encounters convey the gloom the locals try to beat back by courting those two popular pastimes—the circus and, more often, vodka. But the gloom deepens. If Moscow inflicts upon Waring "the most unsuccessful Sunday he had ever spent," his clenched Russian counterparts find the "sluggish and secretive power" (85, 82) that rules them a constant strain.

But Waring's mission to Moscow succeeds—just as some of the questions that vex the others—like "What's become of Smith?" and "What's become of Semyonov?" (26, 91)—are put to rest. "The plot [of *Golden Child*] is as complicated and hard to unravel as the ball of golden twine that figures among the treasures," says John Mellors in *The Listener*.[3] He exaggerates. Fitzgerald guides the complex plot throughout. Notably solid is the murder case that pilots it. Multifaceted itself, it has three strands—the cipher that names the culprit, the alleged curse of the Golden Child, and the mechanics of detection. It is this third element that drives the other two. Fitzgerald's mastery of the basics of crime fiction sustains reader involvement. The search for means, motive, and opportunity—those staples of crime-busting—moves to the fore smoothly. The discovery of the Mafia connections of the museum's kitchen superintendent supplies the necessary red herring. Further reverberations come from the Museum's infrastructure. That two of the Museum's trustees were appointed by the Crown sharpens the threat facing both "the most famous museum in the world" (65, 66) and the British nation itself should the news leak that thousands of people have been paying fifty pence to see a fraud. The possibility that the Soviets, possessors of the real Golden Treasure, can go public with this damning news at any time provides the political shading found in Sir Arthur Conan Doyle's "His Last Bow,"

Christie's *Mysterious Affair at Styles* (1920), and P. D. James's *Shroud for a Nightingale* (1971).

Other conventions of classic literary detection come forward just as neatly. The enmity Sir William has roused in museum circles provides several suspects. A window broken from the outside supplies the classic device of the locked-room mystery, introduced in Poe's "Murders in the Rue Morgue" and later used in Conan Doyle's "Speckled Band," Edgar Wallace's *Four Just Men* (1905), and many works by John Dickson Carr. The curse fastened onto the Golden Treasure varies the hidden-treasure motif found in Chaucer's "Monk's Tale," Poe's "Gold-Bug," Dashiell Hammett's *Maltese Falcon* (1930), and John Steinbeck's *Pearl* (1947); in these works, the ownership and sometimes even the pursuit of treasure causes death. The solution of the crime in *Golden Child* also invokes literary posterity—in this case, Poe's "Gold-Bug," Robert Louis Stevenson's *Treasure Island,* and Conan Doyle's "Dancing Men." Some pictographs on a clay tablet put the blame for Sir William's murder on the Director. Then the appearance of the case-breaking message on a tablet that resembles hundreds of others in the collection of fakes reminds us that the secret in Alfred Hitchcock's film *The Lady Vanishes* (1939), for which several characters have risked their lives, comes from a scrap of a popular song. As is suggested by the tablet's association with both Len, who makes it and then deciphers the message on it, and Sir William, who inscribes the message, Fitzgerald has again plumped for the ordinary and the commonplace over the lordly. But the solution of the crime gives her more than just as excuse to reaffirm her liberalism. It also shows her layering linguistic scholarship into the art of misdirection. Her pictograph makes sense because it accounts for both the logic of intonation patterns and traditional modes of pluralizing singular nouns. Only after putting these features in place will she let Len translate the signs on the clay tablets into sounds and, next, show how the sounds make sense in English.

She continues to misdirect our attention. No heart attack killed Sir William. He was murdered, though not in the way first proposed. After he was lured into the director's private library, his smoking pipe set off the safety device that released the carbon dioxide that savaged his lungs. Sir John then took his body to another library and stood it upright between two moveable shelves. He wanted to give the impression that Sir William's heart gave out when the shelves slid together. But his ruse failed. The shelves that trapped Sir William's body could only slide together if pushed. Jones had to die because he was close to making this discovery. He had already connected Sir William's smoking pipe to the canister of the fatal carbon dioxide. But he reported this connection to the wrong man—Sir William's murderer. Like so many other homicide victims in the history of crime fiction, Jones died because he knew too much.

Waring's anxiety during the last-chapter demonstration of the evidence exerts a force that lifts *Golden Child* far above most whodunits. With added pressure coming from the coincidence of the murder case and the exhibition, Fitzgerald improves her book in still other ways. Her treatment of off-stage characters, for instance, promotes a welcome economy. Like those elders from early modern classics, Mrs. Moore of E. M. Forster's *A Passage to India* (1924) and Mrs. Ramsay of Virginia Woolf's *To the Lighthouse* (1927), Sir William acquires stature after his death, and Waring's wife, who, unlike Sir William, survives the novel, exerts force despite not being seen. Haggie's physical absence from the action helps the novel in other ways, too. Fictional detectives like Christie's Poirot, Hammett's Op and Sam Spade, Ross Macdonald's Lew Archer, and Walter Mosley's Easy Rawlins, routinely lack wives. The inroads made on Waring's marriage by his hectic work schedule lend *Golden Child* an impact that would be lost were Waring a bachelor. Moreover, the marriage stabilizes the action first by keeping Haggie alive in Waring's thoughts and next by including her as a telephone voice, a device used in some of Michael Connelly's Harry Bosch mysteries.

Such devices brighten the action. A new crisis erupts at the end—after Sir John's death. A facsimile Golden Tomb must be cobbled up quickly to appease the queuers who have been shivering outside for six hours. But first, the new father, Len, takes steps to bury the scrawny young African occupant of the tomb that broke into pieces when Sir John's corpse fell on it. Len then has about half an hour to knock off a copy—of a knock-off. The skill he displays improvising a tomb out of damp newspaper covered with gold leaf declares itself in the brief reaction of a visitor to the Golden Child that closes the book: "'Look, real gold!' said the man, turning. . . . 'It looks almost new,' he added. 'It might have been done yesterday'" (189).

The man's timing, of course, is off. The tomb he is speaking of was made minutes earlier, not yesterday. His error harks to some words the Director wrote in his private diary in chapter 3, his final act in our presence until he reappears many pages later in chapter 6 (71, 169): "The only emperor is the emperor of ice-cream." This line from "The Emperor of Ice-Cream" comes at the end of both stanzas of Wallace Stevens's two-stanza poem. The line preceding it in stanza one, "Let be be the finale of seem," with the first "be" serving as both a direct object and a noun subject, claims that appearances can stand in for reality. Just as flowers wrapped in last month's newspapers will charm the girls they are offered to, so can the cheap and the gaudy win our favor. It all depends upon packaging: "Let the lamp affix its beam," the poem says. A shoddy item that is packaged correctly and shown in suitable lighting will pass muster with us. This marketing strategy is deployed by the Museum, in chapter 3 and again at the end (65, 189), where orders are given to dim the lights above the Golden Child. Those who give the orders are reducing the chance that the Child will be spotted as a fraud.

Such a spotting is unlikely. Speaking of the tens of thousands who have seen the Child, H-M says, "They have come to be amazed, and they are amazed. What more can they ask?" (127). What more can anyone ask? Since both the centerpieces of the Golden Treasure on show at the museum have been fakes, the one in the Kremlin may be a fake, too. The very existence of the Golden Child, like that of Hammett's eponymous Maltese Falcon, has come under question. No soothing affirmations top off *Golden Child,* as in the traditional English whodunit. Why should they? By portraying a world hostile to reason, justice, and love (Professor Untermensch has not seen his wife since 1935), the novel challenges us to work out our own value systems. Perhaps we should look outside of public institutions. The Museum is a hierarchy used by those in charge to cement their power. Because of the struggle for status it provokes, it also blocks self-knowledge. Where to look for self-knowledge, though, is not revealed. Nor should it be. The tragicomedy of the Golden Treasure could make the governance of the Museum more democratic. Fitzgerald's silence on the matter of the Museum's future is meant to stimulate thought and discussion. If a great institution like the Museum cannot be trusted, then we must find self-being in ourselves. We need not stop here. This quest can be enhanced if shared. Both the team detection that names the culprit and Len's baby with Dousha posit a link between shared effort and affirm bonding as a source of health. Though never seen together, Haggie and Waring Smith of East Clapham also gain importance—as a couple—as the novel advances.

Along with the faith it expresses in love, *The Golden Child* has the coherent plot, credible sleuthing, and economy of language that give it a scope and a power rarely found in seasoned novelists, let alone in a newcomer.

CHAPTER 5

Oh, to Be in Suffolk

The Bookshop catches Fitzgerald coming into top form. It unfolds in a village near a North Sea inlet between Harwick and Clacton-on-Sea called the Naze (renamed "the Laze" by Fitzgerald). This part of East Anglia has a herring fishery and includes a spread of farmland where sugar beets are grown and livestock is raised. Would that the area promoted a similar elevation of the human spirit. Although Fitzgerald's 1978 novel nods in the direction of these activities, it does not celebrate the ways of the English countryside. It follows, instead, the socially acidic route blazed by the mid-1950s novels of Kinglsey Amis, John Wain, John Braine, and David Storey. These Angry Young Men often set their novels in the provinces, away from London, and, whether they were writing about a teacher, a budding jazz artist, a young businessman, or a rugby star, they pitted a young hopeful (Wain's 1958 novel is called *The Contenders*) against a corrupt establishment. *Bookshop* also counters the creativity of individual effort with a society hostile to it. But it adds a grim note to the clash. In *Bookshop*, the group is menaced, too.

Hardborough, the novel's dreary East Suffolk setting, has been losing out to nature at a fast rate in recent decades. The weather is always damp and sullen. Regardless of the season, sunlight usually fails to pierce the oppressive gray weight of the sky. Daily survival can also be a test in this "island between sea and river" (12). High winds and rough seas have weakened the local fishing trade. The soil, often wet from salt water that has crept in from the nearby estuary, barely yields. Industry has also declined; ever since the collapse of the bridge leading into town, Hardborough lacks train service, and there are no ferries. Anyone who wants to get there by car must take a ten-mile detour. The caving in of a sea wall has also made the harbor a caution for foot-travelers except at low tide. In fact, the wife of the town's leading resident died crossing the marsh. Her surviving townsfolk have little reason to feel safe. A faucet attached to one of the houses in a subdivision washed away by the sea's erosion gushes water "the color of blood" (94), as if the sea wants to gulp down more victims. Acting with animal wisdom, the herons have deserted the nesting spots built for them (31).

The heron's resemblance to the stork, symbol of both birth and longevity (56), suggests a continuing danger from the encroachments of the North Sea, with its "brutal salt smell" (93). There are other danger signs. Late in chapter 6, an edible weed that could be harvested and then sold as a delicacy in London for a high price comes into view. But the weed is ignored by the locals, and its name is missing from a botanical handbook of local flora. The old magic and the old wisdom have both all but abandoned Hardborough, making it easier for nature to swamp the place. Daily life in the nearby town of Flintmarket is probably just as harsh, as its name suggests. But at least it provides a trace of culture in the forms of a biweekly bridge game, a technical school, shops with a wider range of choice than can be found on Hardborough's High Street, and a bookmobile.

These amenities make Hardborough an outpost of an outpost. A spot of culture *has* been brightening the village in the form of a bookstore called Müller's. So stodgy is the town that enlightenment can only pierce its darkness with the help of a foreigner, a point Fitzgerald emphasizes by placing an umlaut over the first vowel of the name of her bookdealer—or ex-bookdealer; Müller's has closed its doors. Ready to fill the void caused by this shutdown, though, is a former employee, Florence Green. Florence brings light to her townsfolk. On the face of it, she is well suited for the job. Her first name evokes that of Italy's premier center of culture. Her last name suggests growth and renewal, powers she has both the clarity and sense of purpose to implement for the public good. Having supported herself since age sixteen, she is also well grounded. When the bank manager she goes to for a loan asks her if she plans to serve culture, she answers, "Culture is for amateurs. I can't run my shop at a loss. Shakespeare was a professional" (11). She has absorbed the no-nonsense practicality of Hardborough. While discussing the feasibility of stocking Vladimir Nabokov's abrasive new novel, *Lolita,* she calls herself a realist, a claim she lives up to. Even though she lacks the insight to spot a literary masterpiece, she knows whom to ask for a reliable opinion (69–70). She remains competent and capable. Methodically, she acquires an inventory, buying some of Müller's leftover stock while ordering new books from wholesale catalogs and salesmen. She shelves the books in ways experience has taught her will maximize sales. She buys accessories like postcards and bookmarks. Besides hiring both a shop assistant and an accountant, she also starts a lending library, and her skill as a window dresser runs so high that the crowds gaping at her shop window block the flow of foot traffic for the would-be passersby.

The spirit of renewal Florence serves includes self-renewal or, perhaps more accurately, an upgrade on the odds for a second chance. At fifty-nine, she often refers to herself as middle-aged (e.g., 10, 34, 65, 93). Just as often, she separates herself from the local elders, or has-beens, who spend their vast leisure time walking or knitting. This childless widow is giving herself a running pep talk to do a job that may prove her last chance to leave her mark. She has rejected such gendered roles as typist, volunteer nurse, and substitute teacher, irked by the inferiority they imply. Though neither sentimental nor nostalgic, she allows herself to be led by her love of books to open a bookshop. She orders 250 copies of *Lolita* as soon as she is convinced that it is a good book and, twice, she quotes the words printed on the endpapers of two Everyman reprints she owns: "*A good book is the precious life-blood of a master spirit, embalmed and treasured up on purpose to a life beyond life*" (39, 87).

She thinks it is a shared love of books that wins her a rare, much-envied invitation to a party given by the Gamarts, the town's leading family. The time is one of superlatives for her. She has already moved into the town's oldest building, the long-empty Old House, disregarding the presence there of the Rapper—a howling, screeching poltergeist that sweeps books off shelves, breaks dishes, and knocks her off her feet. Other knocks will soon remind Florence that, in the eyes of others, she is frayed, paltry, and negligible. Fitzgerald says of her, "She was in appearance small, wispy, and wiry, somewhat insignificant from the front view, and totally so from behind" (7–8). An unlucky handicap to Florence is her shortness, an attribute that either penalizes her in her dealings with others or aggravates the penalties she already faces as a manless woman (for the past eight years) with little cash.

No sooner does the Gamarts' invitation to the Stead lift her spirits than it deflates them. Even the dressmaker whose shop adjoins Old House bullies her. Once Florence decides to buy an ill-advised red dress for the Gamarts' party, she is stopped from changing her mind. Having dimmed the lights in her shop—a trick used in *Golden Child* to fool the public—Jessie Welford insists that the dress is garnet or rust, a merchandising ploy that only reveals itself to Florence after she enters the well-lit Stead. Florence's claim to another party guest that the dress *is* garnet or deep rust (24) stems from her hurt pride. She is peeved at herself for not standing up to Jessie. Her anger makes sense. The dress is not only the wrong color; it is also a poor fit. When, with a touch of self-irony, Florence says of it, "Perhaps if I try to stand against the wall most of the time," she is told that the dress will "come to" (19) her, as if the fabric has the wit to shape itself to her graceless form. Jessie clings to the sale. In a final affront, this dressmaker who claims, "I'm more used to dressing up and going out in the evening than you are," adds, "Nobody will mind you" (19). It does not matter how ill-clad Florence looks at the party; she will go unnoticed.

Her arrival at the Stead, "a house that had never been cold" (19), deepens Florence's gloom. Violet Gamart, the hostess, tries to talk Florence into vacating Old House, which "this natural patroness of all public activities in Hardborough" (24) wants to turn into an arts center. Uncowed by Mrs. Gamart, even on her own elegant turf, Florence refuses to change the subject she is challenged with any more than she yields to Mrs. Gamart. Old House had been untenanted for seven years until Florence bought it. Mrs. Gamart only covets it, despite the foot of water standing in its basement and the jackdaws and rats nesting in its corners, because Florence beat her to it. Equally selfish is her advice that Florence move her bookshop to the site of a former wet (or fresh) fish store. Built partly out of sand, the store's damp walls always reek of fish, as would any book bought there, even after having reached the home of its hapless buyer.

Florence's mettle is tested and proved sound. She is asked to a gala to have her new life filched from her by the gala's powerful hostess. She leaves the Stead immediately. This decisiveness typifies her. As Valentine Cunningham says, Florence is "a fighter."[1] Besides defying Mrs. Gamart, she stands up to the bank manager who tries to dissuade her from buying Old House (having learned that Mrs. Gamart wanted it?). Then she indicts her lawyer for "dithering" (37) when he proposes other sites for the bookshop. Here and elsewhere, the lines joining the personal to the political are blur, break, and cross. And all politics are local. Like *Golden Child* before it, *Bookshop* depicts the tentacularity of the English class game. Florence, who without much ado held the tongue of a hungry horse, has forgotten that people are either exterminators or exterminees (34). Intuitive and adaptable, she sees growth as process rather than goal-oriented. At fifty-nine, she is the same age as the century.

Also putting her in phase with reality are the two elders who champion her. Mr. Raven, the marshman, owns the horse whose blunted teeth he files to help it chew its food. He also oversees the local Sea Scout troop, some of whose members he sends to Old House to put up bookshelves. The reclusive Edmund Brundish resembles Raven in his age, his admiration of Florence's courage (12, 13, 83), and his continuity with nature. The town's senior resident, he looks like "a moving gorse-bush against the gorse, or earth against the hill" (12). Like that other widower, Sir William Simpkins of *Golden Child*, he has countered the frailties of age by keeping alert and clear witted. Thus he asks to join Florence's circulating library and invites her to tea to thank her for asking his opinion of *Lolita*. Her association with books has levered Florence into the two most prestigious homes in town. And marginal and undersized as she is, she impacts both places. Though their time together is brief and awkward, Brundish calls her his friend (114).

He uses this term while trying to persuade Violet Gamart, whose social overtures he has always spurned, to leave Florence alone. But the effort of walking to the Stead kills him. Other depredations follow, recalling the bleak aftermath of Clym Yeobright's mother's fatal walk across Egdon Heath in Thomas Hardy's *The Return of the Native*. Everything caves in on Florence after Brundish's death, as if his protective spirit has fled Hardborough. But, in an irony that Hardy would have relished —here in Fitzgerald's most Hardyesque novel—Mrs. Gamart gets her art center. Her will prevails. No matter that her proud new acquisition has entailed both the death of the town's most august presence and the ouster of its most vital force for cultural renewal. Speeding this bizarre development is Mrs. Gamart's lying insistence that Brundish had come to her home to congratulate her on the arts center idea.

Florence's ingenuity and enterprise have both recoiled on her. The neighbors who wished her well when she opened the bookshop now snub her. Set adrift by her lawyers once they learn she is not rich, she caves in quickly to the deception that both drives her from the shop and bilks her of any money from the shop's sale. Still worse, to clear her debt to the bank, she has to sell her remaining stock together with her car, a major source of freedom. She is trapped in a cycle of recurrence, a sign of defeat in Dante, Nietzsche, and Freud. This woman who lived in a flat before taking over Old House returns two years hence to another flat, but in London. The path between London and Hardborough is well worn. Every year, Raven escorts the Sea Scouts to London, arriving at Liverpool Street Station (60). But whereas he and his young charges return the same day to

Hardborough, Florence, who also arrives at Liverpool Street Station, does not see Hardborough again. Her thoughts, as she leaves us, though, have turned from herself. She is ashamed of her former townsfolk for not wanting a bookshop. Not that she is wholly self-detached; Mrs. Gamart's lie has made her feel betrayed by Edmund Brundish.

If Brundish is the book's oldest speaking character, the youngest is Christine Gipping, Florence's after-school helper in the shop. This ten-year-old probably heads the list of Fitzgerald's child characters who, says A. S. Byatt, are "intelligent and resourceful, aware of the deficiencies of their elders."[2] A middle child in a large mixed-race (31) working-class family, Christine has already learned a great deal about sex, a topic she discusses candidly. The same pictures of naked men and women in flagrante that shock Florence double up Christine "in laughter" (55). Her attitude toward sex stays hearty and frank. She says of a toad-faced man that she is surprised he has not given his sexual partner warts (88). When Florence tells her in chapter 5 that she expected Christine's elder sister to apply for the part-time job that Christine will take, Christine says that her sister is in the bracken with her boyfriend. But, she adds in a deft stroke of self-promotion, "You won't have to worry about anything like that with me. . . . Mine haven't come on yet" (53).

The prepubescent Christine becomes a reverse mirror image of an employer whose periods have stopped. Though unable to conceive, each of these females serves life. During a conversation that reveals their affinity, Fitzgerald notes that "the difference in age [between them] seemed less, as though they were no more than two stages of the same woman's life" (65). That woman is the recently widowed (1976) Fitzgerald, who published *Bookshop* at age sixty-one, both Florence's age during some of the work's present-tense action and a greater age than Fitzgerald's mother, Christina, reached in her lifetime. A third female has entered the equation. Under Christina's shadow, Florence and Christine reflect each other throughout. Just as the bank manager felt that the onset of age might have disqualified Florence from bookshop management, Florence resists hiring Christine at first because she does not "look old enough or strong enough" (53). But because as Christine, a model of embattled working-class dignity, says, "You can't tell from looking" (53), she is hired, which allows the traits she shares with Florence both to come forth and to build a strong bond. Each comforts the other in the shop, hands joined, while waiting out the onslaught of the poltergeist in chapter 6. Working together enriches both of them. A talent for organization she did not know she had helps Christine rearrange the shop's inventory. Warming to responsibility, she runs the lending library and locks up at closing time.

These skills matter because she has reached a crucial stage in her young life. As much as her job fulfills her, both she and Florence know that it must end soon. Christine will soon be taking her eleven-plus exams to qualify for grammar school. Because all her elder siblings have passed the exams, she has few worries. But those sibs did not have to contend with Violet Gamart. The acclaim Christine wins playing the role of Salome in a Nativity pageant angers Mrs. Gamart, who sees it as one more entrenchment for Florence at Old House. Like a patient pagan god, Mrs. Gamart has been biding her time. She knows that a failing grade on her eleven-pluses would not merely keep Christine from grammar school. It would also blight her whole future. Calling a technical degree "a death sentence," her mother claims it will kill her chances "of meeting and marrying a white-collar chap" (102). The mother's worst nightmare will take life, validating the sexual context in which she recounts it. The girl who played Salome will be symbolically beheaded. Mrs. Gamart has used her political clout to keep Christine out of grammar school.

But even she, with all her power and prescience, cannot foresee the brilliance of her coup. Christine does perforce go to a technical school, where she does not belong and from which she is soon expelled, smirching her prospects still more. Her disappearance from the novel after this sad news breaks implies that, as with her near-namesake Christina Knox, life made no corrections to help her. How could it have? Practicing a harsh economy of means, Mrs. Gamart has brought down both Christine and Florence with one blow. And even though she did not pick the moment to strike, she seized it as soon as she spotted it. The book's central event refers to the clash between the purity of human ideals and the stubborn complexity and ambiguity that defeats them. As in Joseph Conrad's *The Secret Agent* (1907), the key incident of which also takes place off the page, a child takes the hardest hit. Mrs. Gamart's smiling, gracious entry into the shop in chapter 7, construed by Florence as a peace offering, has created the chance to show her visitor how the shop's lending library works. But a Hardyesque stroke of fate materializes an unwelcome visitor who distracts Florence just long enough to set Mrs. Gamart in Christine's path. Accustomed to having her way, as is suggested by the chic Jaeger camel's hair coat she wears into the shop, Mrs. Gamart starts fingering the books Christine had carefully catalogued.

The next thing Florence learns is that, having seen Mrs. Gamart meddle with the books in the lending library, Christine rapped her knuckles. This ill-fated rebuke either revives or heightens the anger Mrs. Gamart directed to Florence when Florence flouted her indirect order to leave Old House. That the rapping incident occurs a chapter after the poltergeist's (i.e., the rapper's) bursting, screaming manifestation in the shop dovetails metaphysical with social power (Christine also enters the action a chapter after Mrs. Gamart). Neither Christine Gipping nor Christina Knox can repel such an axis of force. The effects of Mrs. Gamart's visit to the shop resound at all levels of local society. It also makes the characters part of a story larger than their own. October, the time of Mrs. Gamart's first and only visit to the shop (75), foreshadows, with its moody awareness of decline and loss, the grief that will squeeze Florence and Christine. The great popularity *Lolita* enjoys in Hardborough, following Mrs. Gamart's visit, puts forth a gleam of hope soon doused by winter's cold. Nor will the joy radiating from the Nativity play Christine stars in pierce the dark. Chill and gloom soon engulf all.

Speeding this engulfment is the mutually hurtful tie, instigated by Mrs. Gamart, joining Florence and Milo North. At first look, the tie promises well. Having worked in the mailroom at Müller's, Florence has aided communication, as does Milo at his job with the BBC. The motif appears elsewhere. By accompanying the Sea Scouts to London, Raven the marshman displays the communication skills to leapfrog two generations and fifty or sixty miles. Florence's other aging stalwart, Edmund Brundish, is so reclusive that his lone foray from home during the book's present-tense action kills him. Also labeling him an alien to communication is his "rusted-up" (51) mailbox. But this patriarch does exchange letters with Florence, whom he also entertains at his home. Then he surprises Mrs. Gamart with his accurate, up-to-date knowledge of local developments. His deep, earthy knowledge of the town over which he presides mystically exempts him from ordinary modes of communication.

Milo lacks this rootedness. Willow to Brundish's oak, he is so listless and craven that both his heart and willpower have shriveled. Christine is repelled by him, and Florence, normally kind and nonjudgmental, cannot resist calling him lazy and idle nearly every time they meet (e.g., 70, 94, 107). Logically enough, his apathy costs him his two vital connections to the world—his job and his live-in girlfriend, Kattie. Milo is an inverted symbol of the famous wrestler of antiquity whose name he bears and—expressing Fitzgerald's sharp narrative economy —also of that emblem of man's animal vitality, the rejuvenated horse of chapter 1. His sloth and lack of conviction (flaws that make him an inverted symbol of Christine, as well) stem from his fear of confrontation. Nothing deserves his effort. Rather than act on his beliefs, he does whatever is easiest. The course of action he chooses is always the one that costs him the least effort. To avoid awkwardness, he does not bring Kattie to the Gamarts's party in chapter 2. But in the process he also offends her. This probably happens often; the only time they are seen together, she has just been crying. She is better off ditching him. The red stockings she wears here (as opposed to blue) express a passion he cannot satisfy.

After Christine leaves the shop to study at the vocational school, Milo offers to work for Florence. But as soon as her back is turned, this tabby to Christine's terrier locks up in order to read in a comforting patch of sunlight. Then he deposes that the shop's dampness damaged his lungs so badly that it made him unfit to work. Most notably pathetic about him is that his lie cannot be called treasonous. Amoral, Milo simply signed the deposition to fend off trouble.

And the trouble he has been fending off would have come from Mrs. Gamart. It is suggestive that he talked to Florence before Mrs. Gamart did at the party in chapter 2. Mrs. Gamart may have already decided to use him as a cat's-paw to bring down Florence. He later tells Florence to expect to see Mrs. Gamart in the shop because she has "far too much self-respect" (62) to stay away. But she delays the visit she will not cower from. Having crushed Milo's spirit, she first sends him to the shop with a copy of *Lolita*. To prod Florence into stocking the book, Milo, again acting under orders, uses reverse psychology when he tells her that, according to Mrs. Gamart, nobody in "dear, sleepy little" (70) Hardborough would read it. The tactic fails. If Mrs. Gamart wanted to cause a scandal that would wreck Florence's business, she should have found a better go-between than Milo. With his usual ineptitude, he forgets to bring to the shop the second volume of Nabokov's two-volume novel. His telling Florence that *Lolita* will make her a lot of money (62, 70) shows him trying to recoup lost ground. But it also proves that Mrs. Gamart would have picked a better spokesman if she could. Milo does not know Florence any better than she knows *him*. Though in business to make money, she has always kept the policy of only stocking good fiction.

Like Sir John Allison in *Golden Child*, the evildoer in *Bookshop* is not a have-not but a nabob who wants to extend his/her domain. Also like that of Sir John (*Golden Child*, 169), her most important appearance in the book comes after a long physical absence and with her back to the light (72). Six months have passed since the night of her party, when she told Florence of her plans for Old House. Christine's recklessness revives her crusade. Yet even here she is passive. She never lured Christine into rapping her knuckles. As was seen in her manipulation of Milo, she works through others—the wet fish dealer who tries to bully Florence into buying his smelly shop, the solicitor who tries to keep her from Old House, and a slew of distant cousins and friends who pass laws to close the bookshop, to run a financially depleted Florence out of town, and to lower Christine's grade on her eleven-pluses.

These intrigues could have made up a good novel. Many novelists since Graham Greene have written about obsession. But only the sharpest, like Fitzgerald, can move away and look at it from a distance. Events in *Bookshop* accelerate through a series of misunderstandings, pitching innocence into a mire of loss and regret. Rather than conveying the experience of this poignant drama, though, Fitzgerald describes its effects. As is seen in her refusal to show Mrs. Gamart and Christine together in the lending library, selection gains her both trimness and compression. These virtues, as she wisely says, always promote greater reader involvement:

> I do leave out a lot and trust the reader really to be able to understand it.... [My books are] about twice the length ... when they're finished, but I cut it all out. It's just an insult to [readers to] explain everything.[3]

Yes, Violet Gamart is grasping, deceitful, and corrupt. And her eventual grab of Old House also shows how the heartless and the scheming prevail while the good go under. But another novel—one beyond the powers of the Penelope Fitzgerald of *Golden Child*—underlies this grim tale. Conscious of the vagaries caused by human ambiguity, Fitzgerald says, "I have remained true to my deepest convictions.... I mean to the ... weakness of the strong."[4] Mrs. Gamart has muscled her way to victory, but at the cost of deeper fulfillment (and without reckoning any plans the rapper might have for her). She would strike out again at Florence if given the chance. But fate spares her some unforeseen grief. Any power broker as skilled as she is must know that humility, suffering, and sacrifice can endure more than success. She has also stolen the initiative so often from her husband that he lacks the identity to help her build a marriage worth defining herself by. Childless, like the sorriest woman Fitzgerald ever wrote about, Charlotte Mew, she understands better than anyone the recoil action of her selfishness.

Her husband, the General, recites poetry. At sixty-four, he is afraid of dying. He quotes the following lines from the long-dead soldier-poet Charles Sorley: "It is easy to be dead. Say only this, they are dead" (21). Perhaps he envies Sorely's battlefield death at age twenty. The next chapter includes the detail that the life expectancy for Englishmen is 68.1 years (30). Even if this detail bypassed the General, its meaning has lodged in his heart. He tells Florence, a stranger, his age for the same reason he quotes Sorley to her (22). His mortality is gnawing him. Still worse, he feels blocked. As his solo visit to the bookshop in chapter 10 shows, he wants to help Florence. But, as he knows, he is too weak to cross his daunting wife.

His fine service record notwithstanding, he is as feckless as Milo North. This failing consigns him to a minor role in the action. Thematically, the roles of protagonist and antagonist in the book are played by Florence and Mrs. Gamart. That the women only appear on the page twice together supports this idea, even though they do not speak during their second meeting, at the bookshop, in chapter 7. Working through middlemen and behind the scenes, Mrs. Gamart depicts both the facelessness and the invisibility of power. The bipolar tension joining her to Florence is foreshadowed in the book's first paragraph, where Florence sees a heron flying with an eel in its gullet that keeps trying to flee before getting sucked partly back. The struggle will continue, Florence believes, because the creatures "had taken on too much" (7). Fitzgerald returns to this idea in chapter 2 of *The Beginning of Spring*, where a man recalls his father saying that "by the very nature of things we were never called upon to undertake more than we could bear" (20).

Never? Like the shrimp and the anemone in L. P. Hartley's like-named 1944 novel, the heron and he eel have blundered into a mutually destructive bond. If the eel flees the heron's bill, it will hit the ground and die. On the other hand, the effort of swallowing the eel will choke the heron to death. This sad little parable illuminates *Bookshop*. Florence will think about it at least two more times (34, 47). But it does not belong to her alone. Varying it, Fitzgerald materializes "an eel . . . swimming uncomfortably in a glass tank" (101) at Hardborough Primary School the same day Christine Gipping learns that she has been gypped of her rightful chance to study at the local grammar school. Mrs. Gamart has struck down both her and Florence in one deft stroke. This power play has also put them both in a glass tank, or fish bowl, in view of all who want to gloat.

But where does this leave Mrs. Gamart, whose totem, the heron, closely resembles its long-legged wader cousin, the stork? This childless woman's very association with the stork (and with the phoenix, whom the stork resembles) shows her at odds with herself, as befits someone whose only relationships are exploitative (the Gipping home swarms with kids). Nor does the book's deep structure forecast happiness for her. As has been seen, the rapper may be waiting to swoop. Also, the last paragraph of *Bookshop* shows both "the floods . . . and the fields . . . under shining water" (123). The same East Suffolk landscape that looks drowned in its own provincialism also puts forth an image of dazzling beauty (Fitzgerald uses the adjective, "shining," rather than the more disparaging "shiny"). Florence is both sad and glad to be leaving it.

By contrast, Mrs. Gamart evokes not only the heron of the book's first paragraph but also Tolstoy's description of Napoleon, in *War and Peace*, as a greedy monkey whose fist is closed around a nut in a narrow-necked bottle. She is too conflictive to respond to her surroundings in Florence's ambiguous but patently human way. Her anxiety sorts ill with Hardborough, an unsettling fusion of the ordinary and the ominous. Presided over by the heron-eel linkage, the townscape, at once soggy and gritty, includes Christine Gipping, who broke two teeth when a wintry gust blew a frozen vest off of a clothesline into her face. This oddity recalls that aggressive image, the first in Fitzgerald's fiction, in chapter 1, of Florence holding the tongue of Raven's horse. Survival in East Suffolk requires a sense of humor as well as toughness to withstand such a hard, fighting environment. In the last analysis, the Stead, the well-heated mansion where Mrs. Gamart lives, offers, as its name suggests, an alternate reality. But it cannot deflect life's cruelties; Florence, like her, is childless, and Raven's birdlike name chimes with her identity as the heron—suggesting that life along East Anglia's jagged coast has no favorites, including her.

Nor can the disfavored seek solace in the usual places. Poetry, a source of comfort and delight to many, invokes death throughout the book. The line of poetry General Gamart quotes at the Stead is not only about death; it also comes from a soldier who died at age twenty. In chapter 9, the General's fellow victim,

Milo North, reads some lines of verse that include the words, "flowers are dead" (109). He reads them to Christine, the younger counterpart of Florence, who heard the General quote Sorley in chapter 2. Finally, Florence met her husband Charley, whose first name is the same as that of the poet Sorley, when he was the poetry buyer at Müller's (8). But poetry is not the book's only starver of souls. Organized religion betrays its traditional function, too. None of the characters puts much stock in formal worship, and it is easy to see why. Coastal erosion has buried some local churches. The ones still standing lack public favor. According to Mrs. Gipping, neither the vicar nor the minister can rout the rapper at Old House. Perhaps these men are strangers to matters spiritual. Florence regrets that the canon of her church spends so much time raising money that he has none left to discuss metaphysics with her (68). The canon is not unique. Hardborough's clergy usually neglect their flocks. Although the vicar gives a slide lecture every third year on Picturesque Suffolk, he avoids discussing his parishioners' practical worries (26, 53).

Fitzgerald is too astute an artist to succumb to melodrama. Like the question of religion and religious leadership, the *Lolita* subplot is understated and unimposing. No passages from the novel are quoted, and, despite its aura of brimstone and taboo, it incites no tirades about obscenity or artistic freedom that could sidetrack us from the people. This discretion is typical. The sequence and flow of cause and effect in *Bookshop* convey a respect for narrative continuity. A fully realized work of fiction, *Bookshop* also confirms both Fitzgerald's hold on actuality and the cogency of her satire.

CHAPTER SIX

On the Reach

Offshore unfolds in London, as do Fitzgerald's next two novels, *Human Voices* and *At Freddie's*. A character in its immediate predecessor, *The Bookshop,* spoke of "the vastly different world . . . the 1960s may have in store for us" (9). Spanning two or three weeks in the fall of 1961, *Offshore* seems light years away from its frenetic decade of IRA bombs, cocaine parties, and the cults and charismas ignited by J. R. R. Tolkien and R. D. Laing. Also missing from the book are the paranoid tendencies and conspiracy theories of the cold war age.

Part of chapter 9 does take place on King's Road in Chelsea, the hub of Swinging London, where the town's first coffee bars stood and where teenagers bought buoyant, loose-fitting tie-dyed clothes in crowded shops that reeked of incense. This activity had to come from somewhere. Usually derided in the UK as a joyless decade of clipped accents and public service announcements, the 1950s brimmed with new ideas and new ways of experiencing the world. Rock 'n' roll was born in the 1950s, and when the 1956 movie *Rock around the Clock*—featuring Bill Haley and His Comets—came to Britain, jiving teenagers flocked to cinema halls. Yet Haley goes unmentioned in *Offshore,* as do the Beatles, whose songs "Please, Please Me" and "She Loves You" went into copyright in 1961 and 1962.[1] That two sisters of six and eleven discuss Elvis Presley and Cliff Richard matters less in the book than another big development of the 1950s—that source of instant gratification known as consumerism. Two pages from book's end, a cache of "record players, electric guitars, transistors, electric hair-curlers, [and] electric toasters" (139) springs into view to herald the strip-mall culture of the 1990s, which Fitzgerald survived and *in* which autonomy and abundance of choice both flourished.

Please note that most of the cast comprising *Offshore*—houseboaters living on the Battersea Reach—are too busy surviving to avail themselves of high-tech goods. *Offshore* (1979) is a pocket epic, packing into 141 pages the piecemeal dissolution of a way of life. By book's end, one houseboat has sunk, another has been drydocked, and two are up for sale. The last surviving barge—strikingly, the only one fitted with a gangplank to the shore—snaps its mooring ropes during a storm and hurls out to sea the two men clinging to it, likely fatalities. The wife of one of them, Nenna James, from Nova Scotia, departs the action shaken and distressed. Rescued by her sister, she has little besides her two daughters to show for her fifteen years in London. She is broke, and she has lost her library card, her watch, her photo collection, and her address book, "almost the whole sum of her identity" (129). Still worse, Thameside living seems to have denatured her. A youth says that she does not "look like a mother at all," and her husband, who has been living apart from her, blurts out that she is "not a woman" (109, 95). As shaken as she is by these words, she would probably collapse were she privy to the worst news of all—that her husband Eddie's efforts to reunite with her at the Reach killed him.

While displaying the same tightness and precision as Fitzgerald's first two novels, *Offshore* is more darkly expansive. Starting with the first chapter, it brings a hidden world to life, one with its own language, domestic economy, codes of conduct, and myths. Most of the houseboaters lead cluttered, haphazard lives.

Most lack the willpower to change, as well—even though they suspect that some character flaw or weakness has been keeping them wharfside in the midst of a throbbing, humming city they barely know. Ex-houseboater Penelope Fitzgerald knows their troubles. Yet, carrying forward the influence of Thomas Hardy seen in *The Bookshop,* she is more interested in circumstance or chance than in character in the realist sense. Most of *Offshore* hinges on the one-sided clash between life's elemental forces and man's helplessness. The river water has a "dead man's stench," and it always finds, "no matter what the obstacle, the shortest way home" (77, 79), heedless of the human cost. The Thames laughs at us and our plans. A barge slated to change hands six months hence, and thus net its owner a big profit, gets rammed amidships by a rogue log and sinks a week after the sales contract is drawn up. Fitzgerald's dark, subtle comic ingenuity sustains the menace. Though Nenna wrecks her marriage by buying a houseboat without Eddie's knowledge, she does flee the Reach. And, excluding the hapless pair careering out to sea at the end, Richard Blake, the houseboater who comes closest to death, owns the most expensive, best-maintained craft on the Reach.

His fellow tideliner, the male prostitute Maurice—effete and decadent like Marcus Hawthorne-Mannering (*Golden Child*) and Milo North (*The Bookshop*) before him—lacks Richard's competence and discipline. His wealth of heart knowledge, though helping him live more happily and deliberately than Richard, cannot shield him from the storm that whips him and his barge into the tide at book's end. Fitzgerald has put her familiar iconography in place to foreshadow his drowning death. "Maurice was *Maurice*" (132), it is said of him. Like his neighbors, he is known on the Reach by the name of his houseboat. He would have wished it otherwise, were he armed with a better sense of self-preservation. *Maurice* barely stays afloat because of its owner's fecklessness. With its insecure gangplank, it is barely connected to the land. And just like its owner-namesake, it is misplaced, having floated for years on a quiet Amsterdam canal, which, unlike the choppy Thames, is not tidal. *Maurice's* unfitness for the bucketing waves and running tides of the Thames comes across in its original name, *Dondeschiepolshuygen IV*, meaning, with prophetic accuracy, chased or driven out of the shipyard.

But even *had* Maurice installed the requisite fifteen feet of chain on his barge to hold an anchor that was not half corroded, he would still have met grief. Looking ahead to the drowned youth Bernhard in *The Blue Flower*, he is a fine musician (103) who, though attracted to the water, cannot swim. His good friend Nenna, a lover of boats (112) and a former student of music, exits London to prolong her life. But how good is her outlook? Despite her flexible attitude toward the truth (27), she acts most of the time as one driven to the edge. She is also as haphazard as Maurice, and she is heading for Halifax, Nova Scotia, a seaport with even rougher weather and stronger tides than London.

In any case, she will not miss the rigors of the dock, like being forbidden to bathe in the daylight because bathwater cannot be dumped on a rising tide. But recurring chores like scraping paint, scrubbing decks, plugging leaks, and replacing worn pumps could wear down souls sturdier than she. All these jobs must be done often because the flat-bottomed boats on the Reach lack keels, which could steady them when butted by tides most of them were not built to withstand in the first place. It is noted that, like the balmy canals of Amsterdam, the Seine at

Paris and the Danube at Vienna are not tidal (82, 108). Bobbing on the Embankment when they are not hunkered in mud, the boats and their owners, "creatures neither of firm land nor water" (10), occupy that dangerous in-between space that breeds exterminees. Living in the middle of a city whose social and economic movements exclude them, Fitzgerald's barge people often feel restless and unfit. Worsening their isolation in recent months has been the halting of mail delivery to the Reach, caused by a postman's falling twice into "the river's great load of rubbish" (14) while navigating *Maurice*'s shaky gangplank.

Richard Blake is the only tideliner we meet who lives on the Reach by choice. Moreover, his occupancy of *Lord Jim*, a converted minesweeper twice the size of any of the neighboring craft, has eased the toil of daily life on the Reach. He is also the only houseboater with a regular job. Woodie, the elderly owner of the "impeccable" (87) *Rochester*, is the lone barge dweller beside him who is well off. But this part-timer at the Reach is one of the "fair-weather people" (15) who move inland during the cold months. The others, except for Richard—all of them prey to the "great tideway" (10) on which their boats pitch and buck when they are not hunkered in mud—prefer life on shore. But they are all either running away, hiding, or being punished for having made a bad choice. In their plight, they also prove that rebellion or noncomformity is not always glamorous or carefree; the rigors of coping with the basics of daily survival have been wearing them down.

But they might stand even lower on the evolutionary ladder than a tribe of desert nomads. Fitzgerald likens them to amphibians (10) because the alternative lifestyle they have opted for rests on the quagmire that supports their craft at low tide, even as it wastes them. But these outcasts, though at risk, also know that, by leaving the Reach, they will be as clumsy and displaced as the amphibians who climbed from the primeval ooze eons earlier. Maurice is right when he says of himself and his cohorts, "It's right for us to live where we do, between land and water" (47). The tideliner, like the ironist, shrinks from hard decisions and thus makes no splash. He ends up with nothing. Some tourists who pass the Reach on pleasure boats are told that they are looking at an artist's colony. Wrong. The lone artist on the Reach cannot wait to sell his boat and move to shore. In fact, the book's first scene shows him discussing his plans to sell.

The discussion sets the moral tone of the book. Though Sam Willis, the sixty-five-year-old artist, has not been asking his neighbors to lie about the big leak his boat has sprung, he would nonetheless appreciate their not mentioning the problem to prospective buyers "unless direct enquiries are made" (9). He is asking his fellow tideliners to assume a borderline position between honesty and deceit. His request makes sense to them. As members of a subculture, they often join ranks. They do not want to cheat or defraud anybody. But still less do they incline to foil a cohort, a step that could hurt their own misfits' self-esteem. This self-questioning runs to waste. In line with the book's rueful humor, Sam Willis's *Dreadnought* becomes the only barge on the Reach both to find a buyer and to sink during the recorded action.

The sinking of *Dreadnought* robs Willis of the money he needs to move in with his sister. His setback is typical. But the domestic tie usually torn by houseboating is marriage, one character remarking inwardly, "Was there not, on the whole of Battersea Reach, a couple . . . living together in the ordinary way?" (68). The Woodies only cohabitate regularly when their barge is in dry dock. This arrangement salvages at least part of their marriage, which is more than can be said of their counterparts. Repelled by the Reach, Nenna's husband Eddie has moved to a remote part of town, and, during the course of the action, Richard Blake's wife abandons the dock to join her family in the shires. Thus both a husband and a wife have spurned houseboating, even if it meant walking out on a spouse. And, as is seen in Eddie's looming death aboard a foundering *Maurice,* the men in Fitzgerald who lose their women (e.g., Giancarlo Rossi of *Innocence* and Petros Zefri of "The Prescription" [1982]) suffer as much as do their foils in D. H. Lawrence.

Why, then, would anybody choose to live on a houseboat? When a lonely, stressed-out Nenna tells her sister "that it's quite an education . . . for the girls to be brought up . . . on the very shore of London's historic river" (26), she is speaking more truly than she knows. Her reassuring evasions have the ring of truth. Even though she never helped them, the girls have learned both to harvest and to market the treasure hidden in the Thames's refuse-clotted shores. Though only six years old, the younger child, Tilda, also faults a Turner painting she sees at the Tate because it violates the truth that "a seagull always alights on the highest point" (51) of a sailing ship. Her sister, the eleven-year-old Martha, has the maturity to keep a protective eye on both Tilda and their flappable mother—while having also cultivated the grace and poise to pour a young Austrian count a cup of coffee with a charm he would remember "to his dying day" (109).

The wharfside convention of calling the barge owners by the names of their craft shows that adults can profit from tidelining as much as children. By saying that they "felt the patches, strains, and gaps in their boats as if they were weak places in their own bodies" (13), Fitzgerald is noting their vulnerability to the quirks of the river. But she is also pointing out the vital link between the boats and their owners. As has been seen, a sequence of gangplanks joins all the boats, with only *Maurice* fastened to the shore; all the other boaters have to cross *Maurice* to go home. Nor does the boat's namesake-owner object. As comradely as he is ineffectual, he knows the importance of the fellowship joining the residents of the Reach. Thus at the end of chapter 3, he speaks indirectly of going to Venice. His indirection conveys a well-judged tact. Though permitted to talk about leaving the Reach, he cannot act as if he is better or luckier than his neighbors. The cohesiveness of the boat community must be affirmed even as it is being questioned, a truth reflected in Fitzgerald's opening the novel with a meeting attended by all the boat owners.

Nor will it be the only such meeting described. Displaying a tenderness and kindness found less often among shore people, the owners take up a collection for Willis after his boat sinks, do his laundry, and even feed and house him. Their efforts are as astute as they are noble. Artist Sam Willis is an intensified version of his neighbors, looking more deeply into things and making connections beyond their power. He has more imagination, too. Despite never having been to sea, he has enjoyed a long career as a successful marine painter. He has also learned how to surmount the hardships of the wharf. The same river that has sapped his health and smashed his houseboat gives him both the subject matter for his art and the leisure to develop his vision. Painting probably gave him the best life he is capable of. He and his friends on the Reach, though dropouts and discards, comprise a bedraggled elite, defying the codes of both land and sea. Though mostly scruffy and slapdash, they also share a stubborn pride as well as a fear of shore life. Sam's art keeps this pride aglow. Perhaps this same pride stokes the reluctance of Nenna's rich cosmopolitan sister Louise to visit the boats. She might fear their lure.

The docksider with whom Louise would have most in common, excluding her relatives, is Richard Blake. (Unlike Nenna, Louise married up.) In fact, she and Richard do speak on the telephone. Besides being the only boat owner we meet who lives on the Reach year around by choice, Richard is also unique among his counterparts in holding a full-time job. But he never does anything by half. Handy, capable, and conscientious, he keeps *Lord Jim* shipshape all the time. Though he may have bucked the norm for members of his social set by moving into a houseboat, he is a true conservative in temperament and style. His world is a tidy place where people queue, take their turns, and behave. He expects them to play by the rules. His modesty is striking. He prefers to leaven with self-denial the power forced upon him by his neighbors. Prodded by civic-mindedness, he hosts the meeting opens the book. If discipline and order do not come from him, he fears, they will not come to the Reach at all.

His sense of responsibility is too acute. Secretly, he fears that if he does not control circumstances, they will control him. This attitude solves some old problems but creates new ones. Maurice says of him, "He can't give up being half in the Navy" (47). Richard is looking for the moral authenticity and security he saw in the military. He also believes these values to be lurking somewhere on the edges of civilian life. But these edges are slippery, forcing him to devise his own code of conduct. It is as if this man who is asked if he is God (123) feels that God, by steering him safely through a torpedo raid during the war, now expects him to protect others.

But the clean athletic simplicity of naval routine keeps eluding him. Like the Joseph Conrad character after whom his boat is named, he has an ability in the abstract that runs afoul of his superfine moral sensibility. Richard suffers from the classically limited thinking of the overly dutiful. His ongoing failure to make his marriage work plagues him. A little imagination, though, might have told him that he has invited Laura into his fully formed life rather than built a life *with* her. First seen "cutting something up into small pieces" (11), Laura feels cut off from everything she values. Like Ibsen's Hedda Gabler and the woman at the dressing table in Eliot's *The Waste Land,* she is a bored society beauty whose boredom has grown destructive. Whereas a mountain of cares threatens to bury Nenna, Laura feels that she is drying up from enforced idleness. Richard has organized their life so well that he has left her nothing to do beside resent him.

Despite his solid, handsome ship and his moral fastidiousness, Richard is anxious. He does not need to be told by a business colleague, "You're living nowhere, you don't belong to land or water" (57). His marriage provides him no anchorage. When Laura announces that she is going "home" (59) to her family for at least two weeks, he tries to dissuade her by taking her to an expensive restaurant. The words ending chapter 5, "they went out" (61), mark the novel's halfway point. Fitzgerald does not say that the dinner failed to warm up the fast-cooling marriage. What she does instead, after giving the dinner a pivotal place in the book, is to omit any description of it. Unlike a business lunch earlier in the chapter, in which the restaurant, the food, and the conversation between the diners all stood forth in detail, the wished-for communion feast is passed over. Perhaps it falls so far short of its partakers' hopes that, in

Fitzgerald's view, it does not deserve our attention. These hopes may have also been unrealistic. (Laura, who is used to having all her whims and dislikes taken for gospel, had already violated a communion feast of sorts when she threw some cheese straws into a fire to stop Richard from sharing them with Nenna.) The next morning, Nenna's daughter Martha says that Richard looked strained and tired en route to the restaurant (64–65).

Richard's virtues are weighing him down. This paragon who stows everything on his boat in the proper place and who always locks the hatch of his boat but never forgets the key to it has seen everything he prizes come unglued. Nenna may well ask him why he has such low self-esteem (106). Like many other stoics, he is self-critical. Because he distrusts impulse, he is always raising his standards of personal conduct and, as a corrective, ceding others the charity he denies himself. He stays disoriented. The most important things that happen to him are both unforeseen and beyond his control—having sex with Nenna, being knocked out by a thief, and having *Lord Jim* sold by Laura while he is lying speechless and immobilized in a hospital. This innocent who oversaw a circle of barge people now relies upon others to survive; nor can he rejoice in the knowledge that all of his neighbors at the dock have left it.

This exodus has been ongoing. In John Ryle's words, "Behind the brass-bound portholes, holds are leaking and hearts are breaking."[2] One of those hearts belongs to Richard, even though he denies it as long as he can. In chapter 9, the duties he has grudgingly undertaken nearly kill him. A crook named Harry—a man who is violent, dangerous, and evil in the religious sense—has been stowing contraband in the hold of *Maurice*. In Harry, Fitzgerald describes moral evil without losing her lightness of touch. A great deal of artistry, it needs saying here, also went into Fitzgerald's portrayals of the two mudlarks, Martha and Tilda James. Victoria Glendenning speaks of the girls "avoiding school but acquiring specialized knowledge of the river."[3] Of the two, Tilda is the more remarkable. Rowdy and mischievous, she has fun pretending to be both Sam Willis's granddaughter and Richard Blake's daughter. Highly adaptable, she also helps serve dinner in a hospital, and she has no qualms about going to Canada. Having made the best of her London life, she is ready to start anew. She even loves the "villainous smell" (63) put out by burning driftwood. This ability to live fully in the present helps her fend off Harry, who gives signs of wanting to rape and kill her. Richard, on the other hand, despite his combat service and business success, comes close to dying at Harry's hand when, rather than minding his own business, he questions Harry about his presence on *Maurice*. Harry plays Gentleman Brown to Richard's Lord Jim. In fact, so effortlessly does he dispose of Richard with one well-aimed blow of his spanner (or wrench) that he is surprised. Nor does he give Richard a second thought after leaving him for dead.

Richard, the man who left nothing to chance, will owe his survival to strangers. He also yields to the muddle and mystery of emotion—though with Nenna, not Laura. Having sex with Nenna has a rightness to it that tempers its lawlessness. Feeling "neither Canadian nor English" (83) after many years in London, Nenna is Fitzgerald's classic in-betweener. Besides having a smudged national identity, this denizen of the Reach, a straddler of land and sea, has also been living apart from her husband. Richard's comment about her marriage, "I'm not too sure what the situation is" (14), needs to be developed to explain how the daily pressures that have been squeezing her also steer her toward Richard.

Explanations are surely called for if the book's most capable, reliable figure and its most casual one have sex while married to other people. The most likely answer comes from their both having been rejected hours before by their respective mates; Richard read Laura's note saying that she has gone to stay with her family, and Nenna felt spurned by the husband she had tried to reconcile with. Despite her haphazardness, Richard has always found Nenna attractive. Although pity may lead him to invite her to have a drink and some cheese straws with him and Laura after the *Dreadnought* meeting in chapter 1, he also notices the "very fine golden hair" (18) covering her forearms. (In her childhood, her family had a summer cabin on Bras D'Or Lake [17].) Ironically, this sexually provocative hair, a legacy from John Donne, Ibsen, T. S. Eliot, and Dylan Thomas, flusters Laura more than it does Richard. Unhappy offshore, the tipsy Laura has already noted the resemblance between her jersey and the one Nenna is wearing. But she uses it to point out her jersey's superiority to Nenna's, implying that both her boat and her husband surpass Nenna's, too. Annoyed that Richard has been looking at Nenna's arms, she strikes out at both of them.

Her peevishness does not exactly throw them together. The rut Nenna has with Richard is a consolation prize for both; they would rather be embracing their mates. To convey this lack of uplift, Fitzgerald summarizes the rut indirectly and briefly from the point of view of Richard, whose conservative morality blocks any expression of joy he might be feeling (106). *Offshore* is a book of small and few satisfactions, with chance trumping reason and logic. If chance materializes the wicked Harry on *Maurice*'s deck at the same time Richard is passing by, it also brings Richard together with Nenna at a moment when they are both stressed by their mates' resistence to offshore living.

Having upgraded the lighting and heating systems on his boat, Richard cannot understand why Laura has left him. His bafflement compounded by his loneliness, he invites Nenna for a ride in his dinghy. Her acceptance of his offer sparks a trademark Fitzgerald moment. Two people hovering somewhere between marriage and single life are cruising the Thames at four or five A.M., a time that "wavered uncertainly between night and morning" (102). Another expression of the uncertainty that dogs Nenna (her first words in the book are, "I wish I knew the exact time" [16]) comes when Richard turns off the dinghy's engine. Uncharacteristically, this slave to duty and self-control opts to drift.

His drifting rather than straining to do the right thing culminates when, feeling "at a loss" (106), he submits to Nenna's influence. Though neither of them realizes it, they have been moving in this direction. Richard admits to Nenna that he has been waiting for her to turn up on the wharf. He puzzles her again when, after giving her some boots to protect her feet, numb and bleeding from her long walk from Eddie's, he tells her that her feet are small. She interprets his words as a rebuke ("Richard liked things to be the right size" [100]). Actually, he finds her feet sexy, just as he was stirred by the hair on her arms in chapter 1. Fitzgerald has a rare gift for disclosing hidden resonances in what seem to be wildly disparate things. Enriching her mosaic is the truth that, during the predawn encounter of chapter 8, Nenna is wearing the same jersey she wore in chapter 1 (93, 126), whose rolled-up sleeves revealed the fine, glistening hair on her forearms.

Fitzgerald sustains the sexual aura of the predawn episode even as she spoofs it. Describing Richard's pressing of the button that starts his dinghy's outboard engine, she says, "Richard's

Johnson . . . came to life at once" (102). Nenna adds to the aura. Her gratitude to Richard after his quick thinking and tact douse Laura's anger in chapter 1 takes a sexual form: "Richard spoke with calm authority. Nenna admired him and would have liked to throw her arms around him" (20). A circuit has formed. Richard's competence is as erotic to her as her defenselessness is to him. When, earlier in the chapter, she complains that she cannot not fold a map, he offers to teach her. The erotic charge released by his offer is duly noted—but not by Nenna: "Laura's eyes seemed to move close together. She was concentrating intensely" (17). This commonplace moment in which very little happens takes on the wordless psychological tension of a scene in Henry James. Fitzgerald's shift in point of view both validates Laura's charged response to Nenna's jersey and the looming tirade that Richard defuses.

But the erotic associations of map-folding stay with Nenna. Just before she begs Eddie for a sign of his love, she tells him, "I want you every moment of the day and night and every time I try to fold a map" (94). In the same vein, her last words about Richard, which may also be the last words she speaks in the book, are, "He was going to show me how to fold a map properly" (131). Whether or not he follows through on his plan to see her on one of his business trips to Montreal, he will always live in her thoughts; every time she sees a map, she will think about him.

Has Fitzgerald also suggested that Richard will become more than a memory to Nenna? Nenna's being told by a stranger, "Your hair is quite pretty" (88), denotes the dynamism of sex in the novel. This dynamism persists. On the page just after she sleeps with Richard, Nenna is "struck by the difference in her older daughter since she had seen her last [viz., the previous day]. Her hair was out of its fair pony tail and curled gracefully, *with a life of its own*" (107; emphasis added). If Fitzgerald's symbolism is consistent, Martha has had sex with Heinrich, the sixteen-year-old Austrian count she took to the King's Road to see Swinging London; Heinrich says that being parted from women for months at a time drives him mad, to which Martha replies, "There's a great deal of sin in me" (118). But if, at age eleven, she has no worries about pregnancy, the same cannot be said about her mother. Perhaps the difference Nenna notes in Martha only hours after having had sex with Richard stems from a change in herself. Her other daughter, Tilda, will need only one look at her cat Stripey to say, "You've got kittens on you" (120). Such is Fitzgerald's sense of mischief that Nenna might have conceived at the same time as Stripey.

In her *New Statesman* review Judy Cooke calls *Offshore* "a tightrope of a novel, stretched between absurdity and pathos; the river flows beneath, a dominating presence, both threatening and sustaining."[4] What sustains *can* soon threaten. *Offshore* reflects modernism's sense of the provisional and the unknowable. Even the book is a schematic, artificial chart of the unknowable, like a Chekhov play. Its mightiest, most mysterious presence, though, as Cooke says, is the river. And the river's most imposing, insistent feature is its oft-mentioned tidal flow; the tides rule the people's routines and define their freedom. Also, the astronomical link between the tides, the moon, and, through the moon goddess Diana, the menstrual cycle, calls forth another link equally vital to the book—the many parallels, repetitions, and counter-rhythms in the lives of the people that mimic the flow of the immortal, rolling Thames.

Like voices in a fugue, the events depicted in *Offshore* dovetail into motifs and melodies that echo back and forth in patterns. Thus after coshing Richard, Harry walks toward the King's Road (124), where he might cross paths with Martha and Heinrich. But how does this coincidence stoke the idea that Nenna might have started a baby with Richard the night of the dinghy ride? Nenna stands at the center of much of the book's apparent randomness, which is to say that, beleaguered as she is, she could also be an organizing principle. Martha is her daughter, as is Tilda, the last person Harry speaks to before he smashes Richard. Then Nenna's husband, sister, and brother-in-law all read the news report of the sinking of *Dreadnought* (82, 91). Naught were the consequences Nenna dreaded when she slept with Richard. And Richard, though normally sensible and mindful of consequences, was "more at a loss" (106) than Nenna when they boarded *Lord Jim* at first dawn. The wildness of the moment ruled out birth control.

Their mutual surrender to the attraction they have been feeling for each other is not described any more than was the central event of *Bookshop,* Christine Gipping's attack on Violet Gamart. But neither is the epigraph to *Offshore* translated nor its source given: "Those whom the wind loads, and whom the rain blasts; and those who meet with such sharp tongues" (*The Inferno,* canto XI, 71).[5] So subtle and glancing has Fitzgerald's art become that she highlights the importance of an event by either omitting it or nodding to it in a foreign language. The discovery of her pregnancy after returning to Canada would shock Nenna as much as any bucketing wave would have shocked her houseboat, *Grace,* during her time there. Dante's "sharp tongues" suggest the gossip that will arise once her discovery becomes public knowledge. But the gossip would subside, and Nenna would have a new child to replace the childish Eddie. This two-part drama, while reflecting the ebb and flow of the tides that govern so many of the decision of the houseboaters, conveys both the persistence and the breakdown of the family, a major proposition in *Offshore*. An act of violence like the ripping of a log into the hull of *Dreadnought,* or Harry's coshing of Richard, can smash up the meandering, roundabout lives of the houseboaters. And so can sex. But sex also renews the family, a fixture that nurtures hopes just as its absence breaks hearts. Sex is always there—the more repressed or disallowed, the more likely to cause psychic damage. Eddie James moved from *Grace,* which Nenna bought in his absence, largely because its design disallowed him and Nenna the privacy they needed for a normal sex life. Sexual frustration fuels his rage. The continuity between healthy, fulfilling sex and the family also shows why the loss of his family coincides with his loss of life.

Now none of this proves that Richard and Nenna conceived a child together. But it does let us say, knowing what we do about Fitzgerald's fondness for hints and omissions, that were a child conceived the night of the dinghy ride, she would have written the last subchapter of chapter 8, during which Nenna and Richard board *Lord Jim,* in the same oblique, glancing way she did. She would have also avoided stating her belief as a Catholic that God inhabits the everyday world. Instead, she dramatizes another belief—that the job of the religious artist is not to create a new order of life, but, rather, to find someone hidden in our midst, perhaps like Nenna, who fell short of her musical hopes and also wrecked her family—and then to lift her from the sludge and make her shine, just as Nenna's daughters do the precious tiles they find in a drift of tires, boots, and broken crates that wash ashore. Metaphysics runs strong in *Offshore,* echoing Jung's belief that people have a spiritual aspect essential to their evolution. Once again, Nenna's boat is called *Grace,* and only God's unmerited favor has kept the sad old tub afloat. This idea has snagged the ex-convent schoolgirl Nenna's mind. When she takes the long trip to Eddie's lodging, she introduces herself to his landlady as "Grace" (87).

Others are drawn into the drama, as they should be, without moral exception. Just as Judas supports the Christian myth, so does Harry, the scurviest wretch in the Fitzgerald canon, engineer Richard's translation. Asked by Richard why he is on *Maurice,* he answers, "Who made you God here" (123)? His words are more apt than he knows. Though Richard did not create the Reach community, he, more than anyone, has, Vishnu-like, been holding it together. And his charity, generosity, and hard work earn him a beating, which his humility—another Christian virtue —nearly turns into a fatality; rising to greet a visitor, he sends a jag of broken rib into one of his lungs. Christian materials also pervade the long episode that culminates in Richard's having sex with Nenna. Resting on the foredeck of *Lord Jim* after her long trip home from Eddie's, Nenna notices that her feet are bleeding. "A hint of some religious association disturbed her" (99) is the book's next sentence. Turmoil for her often evokes religion. Like her sister, she married outside the faith. She lets her girls skip parochial school. She is about to violate the sacrament of marriage. But she does make a long, punishing night journey that will end, not with a birth, but, perhaps, a conception. The drama that began with her reaching out with love to Eddie culminates in Richard's cabin. The absurdity of it all reflects Fitzgerald's approval of God's alleged sense of humor. And, like God, she also prizes good-heartedness like Nenna's.

But she knows too that Nenna's efforts to redeem herself have been flagging. Nenna loses the squash rackets Eddie entrusted to her before his fifteen-month work trip. Her throwing a bank book at him in a pique shows her literally throwing away family assets, an act Eddie will repeat when he throws her purse, somewhat insultingly to her, at a rat (39, 139). Is she the rat he wants to smack? She and Eddie often sidetrack their love for each other by committing stupid, wasteful acts. While he was away, she depleted the family's savings to buy *Grace*. Then, to delay the angry outburst she is dreading, she gives him the address of the boatyard office as her own. Her purchase of *Grace* has dismayed her. She loves Eddie. But she will not leave *Grace*, as he asks, even though it is unsafe. Eddie thinks the barge means more to her than he does. He is wrong. She wants his respect and approval for having bought it. But she also knows that buying *Grace* was a mistake, if only because it broke up her family. Nenna cannot let her self-esteem drop any further. Though she writes to Eddie every day, she delays going to him because, if the visit proves a bust, she will have used up her last hope to revive her marriage.

Mollie Hardwick calls Eddie "a drifter who prefers to do his drifting on land."[6] The temptation to compare this underachiever to Desmond Fitzgerald is strong. Though trained as an engineer, Eddie, "not very successful in finding a job to suit him" (38), has mismanaged a launderette and done construction work in Panama. At present, he is clerking for a small firm in a low-rent district of London. This sad sack, Nenna knows, will never succeed in business. She loves him anyway. He had contracted to work for fifteen months in Panama because he planned to bank most of his earnings. This Nenna never thought he would do. Such prudence and self-sacrifice would clash with the character of the man she loved (38). She loves him for— rather than in spite of—his weakness. This mature love she takes with her to his bedsitter in chapter 8. But all explodes in a fit of repressed sexuality. An unbearable moment Fitzgerald captures with devastating grace is the brief time they spend alone together. Though both parties want to make up, they cannot stop fighting. Rejecting Nenna's pleas that he spend one night with her on the boat, Eddie insists that she sell *Grace* immediately. Nenna, who rarely recognizes a good opportunity, resists. She and Eddie lose grip, and it is soon clear that their overwrought feelings could land them anywhere except aboard *Grace*. Within seconds of telling her that he is glad to see her, he contradicts himself. They sink to the floor, anyway, to make love.

Then farce intrudes, reflecting Fitzgerald's belief that our most shining, lyrical moments can fizzle in a heartbeat. Eddie's landlady bursts into the room and Nenna, who had been clinging to Eddie and claiming that "she loved him and could never leave him" (93), is back on her feet, getting dressed. In another five or ten minutes, she is on the street, facing a five-and-a-half mile trek to the Reach; a trek it must be because, having bolted Eddie's room in a rage, she forgets her wallet, which contains both her money and her all-day bus ticket. But pride keeps her from going back upstairs, just as the landlady's entry into Eddie's room had chilled her sexual heat. She had told Eddie, "I want you . . . every time I try to fold a map" (94). The map reference stumps him. Ignorant of its association in her mind with male competence and mastery, he accuses her of raving. Normal guidelines blur in what ensues. Sexual frustration panicking them both, they contradict themselves, bark non sequiturs, and switch frames of reference so unpredictably that each thinks the other is jabbering nonsense. Flustered, they blurt out the ugliest insults that come to mind. They are soon drained. Eddie tells her, "You're not a woman" (95), and the next sentence finds her in the street below. Perhaps the fight with Eddie *has* denatured her while crushing her spirits. In the next chapter, she is told that, according to Heinrich, she "doesn't look like a mother" (109).

But perhaps Heinrich sees her as a siren—or an *expectant* mother. The life described in *Offshore* is so unruly and fractious that it defies analysis. Nenna is intense, edgy, and easily flustered. The only person she can relax with is Maurice. Everyone else either throws her off stride or backs her into a corner. It is Maurice who can best comfort her after the fiasco at Eddie's. This homosexual has learned what she is like without being distracted by sexual desire. What he has discovered is a kindred spirit. Careless and absentminded, he and she are also both borrowers. Yet both have loving hearts. It is said of her bond with him: "She confided in him above all the others" (45). The two of them have long, rambling conversations that go on for hours. These dialogues, about subjects like sex and jealousy, friendship and music (103), gush emotion. By contrast, the practical, goal-oriented Richard favors results and definitive answers; dialogue in which something is not clearly evaluated and resolved he scorns as a waste of time. Chance, though, turns up Richard—and not Maurice—on the wharf the night of the disaster with Eddie. But it is a lonely, confused Richard, one more shaken and vulnerable than Nenna has ever seen. His heartache has put him within her emotional reach. Besides, unlike the wayward oracular Maurice, he can give her sex, a prize that, after her long, grueling day, she values more than words.

His foil, "the incurably sympathetic" (12) Maurice, speaks well of everyone and helps anyone who asks. He can be trusted when he says that he loves everybody (138). In fact, he reveres all living things. When Eddie attacks a rat, he screams in protest, "It's one of God's creatures!" (139). He is beautiful, but because of his shirker's avoidance of work and moral slackness, he is also damned. His universal benevolence is thus corrupt. In his folly, he is reminiscent of Desmond Fitzgerald. But he also harks to the classical scholar and Bishop of Lahore, Thomas Valpy French (1825–91). Fitzgerald called her maternal grandfather "a saint, holy in the noblest sense of he world, and as exasperating as all saints." Her next sentence explains the Bishop's ability to exasperate: "A poor judge of character, he always believed the best of everyone . . . and was so generous that his friends dare not mention their wants, for fear of his ruining himself" (*Knox Brothers,* 12). While indirectly causing Richard's downfall, Maurice has already degraded himself by letting Harry use his barge as a drop for the goods he has been fencing. Someone whose survival skills are this weak brands himself an exterminee. The river death of a rich Dutch entrepreneur whose "glittering . . . impressive" (31) dinghy, like the bedraggled *Maurice,* came from Rotterdam, foreshadows *his* end. Despite Maurice's gift for fortune telling, he has forfeited a future of his own.

He dies soon after the book's savagely dark, mesmerizing final scene. The swirling undercurrents of the Thames pull *Maurice* from the shore. Eddie, who came dockside to rejoin Nenna, had boarded the boat. His encounter with Maurice on the deck of his juddering, lurching boat piles mayhem upon mayhem. Both of them drunk, Eddie and Maurice are also unaware of each other's identity. Connecting them is the skittish Nenna. Maurice, her best friend, she can talk to companionably for hours. Eddie she cannot be with for five minutes without both of them acting like maniacs. Yet as her husband and the father of her kids, he has a tie with her as formal and legally binding as the one joining her to Maurice is free and open ended. This disconnect, worsened by Nenna's absence from the pier, metastasizes.

The man who came to the Reach to reunite with her now departs with her best friend, a man whose existence he never heard of. It tallies with the absurdity of *Offshore* that these two Desmond Fitzgerald surrogates should die in drunken ignorance of their curious bond. The slightly worn phrase Fitzgerald puts in the book's last sentence, "the two of them clinging on for dear life" (141), conveys the urgency of their plight. At stake here is survival.

The sensual descriptive style of Fitzgerald's closely interlocked narrative makes the physical world where the plot unfolds much richer and livelier than the people in it. *Offshore* conveys an awareness of existence at a precise geographical spot. Rendering offshore life with intimacy, it includes specific details that set the Reach off from the rest of London. The place seems vivid and knowable, on the one hand, yet freakishly remote on the other. Betraying no sense of strain or self-indulgence, the images and rhythms used to stage it are beautifully chosen. Indeed, how better could the texture of Fitzgerald's shadow world be expressed? The effect is like that of music, which often uses color, movement, and imagery like that found in *Offshore*. (Maurice and Nenna, two of the book's leading figures, play music.) Fitzgerald's uncanny gift for describing the commonplace, the utilitarian, and the overlooked galvanizes the flow. She names the different parts of a barge and their functions; she is familiar with barge maintenance; she knows how the tools that keep barges afloat should be stored. Finally, she describes with accuracy the effects of the tides upon barges and their inhabitants.

Narrative tempo sustains this immersion in the world being conjured. Though the book may look fragmented, it creates a community before our eyes. The story of a whole subculture creeps through the pores of the individual stories. *Offshore* is crammed with a bustling, ludicrous humanity worthy of Dickens. There is also an element of folly in the people but rarely the suspicion that Fitzgerald is looking down on them. She would rather know them than judge them, and insight comes to her through her practice of disrupting guidelines and boundaries. Not only does Nenna introduce herself to someone as "Grace" (87); a "ball of oozing clay" (41) turns out to be a cat that flees rather than pursues rats. The darkness fuses river to sky in the middle distance, and the river plays tricks with sound. Sam Willis says of the leak that will sink his craft within minutes that "he was not sure whether it was inside or out" (76). In this scene, reliable supports—like a saucepan or a leg of the bunk he had slept in for fifteen years—strike out at him.

Such defamiliarization signals danger. At the end, Eddie sees a rat on *Maurice* that would not have been there had Maurice greased his mooring ropes, as he had been told to do. Again, when the rat runs away, its tail thumps "like a rope" (139), a discord that precedes by moments the snapping of the ungreased ropes that flings *Maurice* into the tide. Rope dominates a manifold drama of disintegration or deevolution in which things and people (innocents who do not know the ropes) run together and lose their defining marks. But it is the storied Thames that performs this drama of dissolution, a truth that explains why the book ends with the word, "tide" (141). Like the many repetitions, dovetailings, and correspondences in *Offshore,* the tidal flow evokes the limits of human opportunities, exerting the same relentless force as the sky in Forster's *A Passage to India.* Cheer and optimism did not win *Offshore* the 1979 Booker Award for Fiction. Gloom outpaces grins in the novel. But, rather than hold Fitzgerald hostage, it oversees a vision that is intellectually complex and artistically rewarding. History will decide if *Offshore* is a great book. Like the acclaim it has won, the close reading it rewards proclaims it, at the very least, the work of a master.

CHAPTER 7

Keepers of the Discs

Like *The Golden Child* and *Offshore* before it, *Human Voices* takes London as its setting. But Fitzgerald's 1980 novel also harks to the later *Innocence* and *The Beginning of Spring* in demanding from us an acquaintance of the political climate in which it unfolds. This climate is tense and dangerous. As is reported in the book's second chapter, France fell to Germany in June 1940 (26). She fell quickly because her people lacked the heart to fight, France having lost 1.4 million men in the First World War.[1] Her defeat she blamed partly on Great Britain, as an exiled French General tells some BBC staffers; the men and materiel from the UK that she needed to defend herself never arrived: "We French, do we trust you English? The answer is: not at all. . . . You led us unprepared into war with Germany and . . . having done so you have deserted us. . . . We are ruined, and we blame it on you" (31). A tendency to blame the Brits has a long history in France. Historian John Lukac calls France's aversion to Britain in 1940 a function of longstanding Anglophobia rather than a byproduct of military policy or political ideology:

> They [the French] were convinced not only that the British were hypocritical and selfish but that their system and their view of the world were old and probably useless, which was not the case with the new order of Mussolini or, alas, of Hitler either.[2]

This indictment of Britain as stale and obsolete also found voice at home, as is seen in Virginia Woolf's statement, "They [the Germans] seem youthful, fresh, inventive. We plod behind."³ If plodding meant a foot-dragging reluctance to challenge Hitler, Woolf was right. Many Britons acquiesced in Hitler's efforts to right wrongs dealt Germany by the 1919 Treaty of Versailles. There was also the rankling suspicion that fighting Germany would ultimately favor the Americans, the international Jewish business community, and the communists. This last issue bulked large. Frightened by the early success of the left-wing Spanish Republicans in their 1936–39 war against General Francisco Franco, Britain prized Germany as a bulwark against the USSR and the spread of Soviet communism. There was also the fear that the British Prime Minister, Winston Churchill (1874–1965), was both too conservative and too old to stop the ruthless, fanatical Hitler, a man fifteen years his junior; fresh in the collective British memory was Neville Chamberlain's notorious appeasement flight to Munich in 1938, undertaken at age sixty-nine.

Human Voices describes the immediate effects of Britain's declaration of war against Germany in September 1939. Foremost among them was the Battle of Britain. In August 1940, Nazi warplanes began bombing RAF airbases. The following month saw the start of nightly air raids of London. Besides wanting to crush British morale, the Luftwaffe hoped to destroy airpower that could thwart a Channel invasion by German ground troops. These attacks have shaken the London of *Human Voices*. Barricaded by sandbags, the BBC calls fire alarm drills at all hours. Statues have been removed from places where they stood for decades. While the trains still run, the platforms of the London Underground have been turned into dormitories to house the many thousands who spend nights there. A bomb smashes the Hammersmith house of an unlucky family we have come to know and like.

An event that is omitted from *Human Voices* but that adds to the book's clenched mood is the evacuation of the British Expeditionary Force from Dunkirk in northern France in late May of 1940. Fighting off attacks by German aircraft, the British navy managed to repatriate 330,000 troops from Dunkirk. This operation, which coincided with the present-tense action of *Human Voices*, could not be hailed as a victory; the BEF surrendered strategic territory to the enemy. On the other hand, the evacuation need not be scorned as an act of cowardice. The troops it repatriated gave Britain the manpower to stop a Nazi invasion. This ambiguity focuses *Human Voices*, a book whose wartime setting sharpens the uncertainties and oddities that always color human affairs in Fitzgerald. This absurdity comes forth at the British Broadcasting Company. During a speech on the BBC aimed at the British nation, the French General Georges Pinard refers to "the courageous drunkard whom you have made your Prime Minister" (32). The reference is accurate. Writing in 1994, David C. Cannadine described the wartime Churchill as "widely distrusted as a man of unstable temperament, unsound judgment, and rhetorical (and also alcoholic) excess."[4] But Churchill overcame his flaws to win the hearts of his people. Wisely ignoring reason and logic, he united the British by addressing their patriotism and pride. The United States could dally as long as it liked. Churchill promised to fight to the end to protect British freedom and democracy, even if he and the British armed forces had to do it alone.

Certain aspects of *Human Voices* carry over from *Offshore*, like the motif of pregnancy. As in Joyce's *Ulysses* (1922), birth occurs in the presence of its opposite number, death. Thus the first words spoken in *Human Voices* come from an expectant mother who will deliver before book's end. We may not be through with pregnancy. In chapter 8, a character (here, a man) takes a long night journey by foot through London that ends in sex (98), as did Nenna James's trek in *Offshore*. On the next page, a youth intones, "Love is of the body and the spirit" (99), sounding like Maurice, another innocent whose lofty ethics have gone untested by experience. A collection to buy flowers for the family of a recently dead associate at the BBC recalls the one undertaken in *Offshore* for Sam Willis after the sinking of *Dreadnought*. Then, just as the boat owners in *Offshore* went by the names of their boats, so do the people in *Human Voices* refer to each other by the acronyms that designate their jobs at Broadcasting House. RPD, for instance, is Sam Brooks, the BBC's Director of Recorded Programming, and Jeff Haggard, the Director of Program Planning, goes by DDP.

Along with a dozen or so other BBC workers we meet, these two men serve an ideal set forth by lovable Sir William Simpkins in *The Golden Child*: "The function of the Press is to tell the truth—aye, even at the risk of all a man holds dear" (32). Susan Salter Reynolds's review of the 1999 paperback reprint of *Human Voices* in the *Los Angeles Times Book Review* applies this credo to radio broadcasting. Reynolds calls the BBC of *Human Voices* "the lifeline between London and the troops in wartime, the dispenser of uncensored truth to the public."[5] The truth reached listeners not only without sugarcoating but also, whenever possible, fresh. To insure accuracy, the BBC would transmit live whenever possible. Its aim was consistency. If it lied about the losses inflicted on Britain and her allies, it would be disbelieved when it hailed the victories.

Fitzgerald calls this commitment to the truth "the strangest project of the war, or of any war" (17). By equating the truth with Shakespeare's Caliban, who always spoke truly (141), in contrast to the beautiful liar Ariel in *The Tempest,* Fitzgerald is reminding us of the dangers that accompany honesty's supreme importance. Though graceful and charming, Ariel wanted most of all to stop working for Prospero. The amoral Caliban wanted to *kill* Prospero. But he did not have to. Everything came right without violence. After Prospero freed Ariel, he left the island where he had found him and Caliban. Caliban—the ugly truth—stayed behind. He owned the island, to begin with, and it reverted to him (141). The many casualties inflicted by the war make him a metaphor for the evil side of humanity that must be served lest the race die. Our devils cannot be killed if our angels are to survive.

This fact has resisted the corrections of time. Always dangerous and difficult, the truth can crush "the noble, absurd, ungrateful, and incorruptible truth-tellers" (108) charged with dispensing it. It can also vex those who hear it. Churchill called the BBC "the enemy within" because of the dogged accuracy with which it reported military and civilian losses. And he was citing only one area of activity where the truth is threatened by the wish to safeguard virtue and morale. Other areas, just as crucial, refer to the rank-and-file. Though committed to the traditional values of loyalty, respect, and devotion, the wartime BBC was run by flawed individuals. Alfred Corn judges well to claim for it "a collective personality, selflessly patriotic and pixilated in equal parts."[6] In order to do its work, its members had to suppress their rivalries, grievances, and dread of falling bombs. This collective act of suppression calls for the self-detachment of a religious mystic. Most often, we are amazed—not that the BBC functions well, but that it functions at all. But function it does, staffed, as Gillian Reynolds notes, by people whose foibles and fears have intensified through lack of sleep.[7]

More is the pity because these staffers need to be alert and attentive. How alert and attentive, we can imagine. The intractable, relentless waters pushing through *Offshore* stream across *Human Voices* in the running metaphor Fitzgerald uses to describe the BBC's offices on Portland Place as a sea liner (10, 11). "Built like a ship" (59), Broadcasting House, or BH, must maneuver stormy seas. Different arms of government are jostling each other for air time and space allocations. At a time when its resources must be maximized, BH also faces staffing problems. Violet Simms, a Junior Temporary Assistant of eighteen who has worked at BH for six months is esteemed by some of her colleagues as a senior employee. The awe they feel for her makes sense. Much of the work at BH falls to JTAs of Vi's age. Like the museum in *Golden Child,* BH is "a cross between a civil service, a powerful moral force, and an amateur theatrical company that wasn't too sure where next week's money was coming from" (35). Uncertainty always looms. Guidelines blur, and the makeshift often trumps precedent. Staffers also try to avoid the dangers of falling bombs by sleeping in one of the many bunks set up in the concert hall. Cubicles and dressing rooms are allocated by rank but, like everything else at BH, give way to the pressures of time, need, and availability. Then all BBC staffers must take classes in first aid, sometimes working together, regardless of rank, on the same splinting and bandaging drills.

Fitzgerald both mocks and admires such efforts. Processing the five thousand phonograph records used weekly by the BBC are the Junior Temporary Assistants, who also manage to complete the job despite the distractions caused—by their chiefs. Yet these harried chiefs, some of whom have stuffed their office cabinets with fresh clothes against the prospect of working around the clock, face more pressure than the JTAs. They control both the content and the flow of information on the airwaves. But the war presses upon all. Many Londoners have decamped to escape the nightly bomb attacks, and those who remain have trouble functioning. Recording discs get lost en route from shelves to turntables; those kept in the studios sometimes melt from the heat of the teacups placed on them, or they freeze in a winter transit to a storage depot (destruction in both cases described in watery terms). Downtime rules: "The corridors were full of talks producers without speakers, speakers without scripts" (11). This disconnect owes nothing to laziness. Rather than work, staffers huddle in the canteen or in stairwells because they want company if a bomb hits.

Yet the BBC soldiers on. Free of both the War Office and the Ministry of Information, it makes its own policies and sets its own agendas. It takes this freedom seriously. Staffers at all levels sacrifice their welfare to keep transmitting (i.e., "scattering voices into the darkness of Europe . . . for the sake of a few that made their mark" [77]). How few does not matter. Their truthspeaking empowers all BBC staffers with a pride that offsets the bitterness and resentment that the daily plod of dealing with constraints has inflicted on them. Yet serving an institution forbidden to lie also stymies them. The pride they take in doing a job both useful and honorable can be felt by these insiders, but not expressed. They need not fret. An ex–BBC staffer herself, Penelope Fitzgerald voices their collective pride alongside their woes. Like most good historical fiction, *Voices* fills the gaps in the record in order to show the acts of heroism and folly that typified BH during the war but were never written down. The book's setting extends the narrative possibilities of commonplace materials. With danger always threatening, Fitzgerald's counterpoint of professional and private tensions resolves itself in a craziness that, when played through, makes beautiful sense.

But the whole differs stubbornly from the sum of its parts. One man whose job at BH lets him indulge the full range of his self-indulgent personality is forty-six-year-old Sam Brooks. Called RPD, this head of the Department of Recorded Programs at the BBC oversees thousands of pounds sterling worth of equipment. He has earned this trust. This brilliant technician's ability to regulate radio frequencies has produced a clarity of sound new to BH. "While the war lasted, if the BBC wished to record itself, it needed Sam" (108), says Fitzgerald, explaining his prominence at BH. But Sam will not bask in his colleagues' esteem. He has of late been working so hard to improve the sound reception of miked windshields that, in his words, the job has come to mean more to him "than happiness or health or sanity" (45).

It should not. Toiling too long and too hard, while making him a star employee, has loosened his hold on life. For diversion, he spends time lounging with his office staff, nearly all of them young women. He likes to tell the members of his Seraglio, as his office is called throughout BH (7), his problems —particularly now that his wife has decamped. During one of his recitations, he even put his head on a sympathetic listener's shoulder and nodded off. To make her feel special, he will tell a listener that she reminds him of a figure in a well-known painting. He has fed this story to so many JTAs, though, that it has become an institutional joke. But it matters not. Sam stirs women's protective instincts. Though patronizing, he affects women as someone who needs looking after. The coddling he both bids for and gets bites him. He needs to grow up. He claims that he was born to be deserted by those he loves (136). But he always does the deserting. His relationships with his charges are thus much more fleeting and superficial than they are intimate. He will not let them develop. Using his rank and his age to shield himself, he engineers them to glow brightly but briefly within a tight frame.

This regimen changes with the entry into BH of Annie Asra in chapter 5 of the novel. Though but seventeen years old, Annie helps Sam apply to himself the BBC's preference of truth over consolation. Her entry thus speeds and sharpens the action. A "little square curly-headed creature, not a complainer" (63), this only child has come to London from Birmingham to work after the death of her piano tuner–father left her orphaned. She could use a lucky break. The syntax Fitzgerald uses to summarize the day she arrives in London joins her to loss and privation: "That was on the 8th of July, the day they announced the tea-rationing, two ounces per person per week" (67–68). Annie, though, shrugs off setback. She later gives part of her tea ration to someone worse off than she. An older woman says in chapter 9, "A woman's possessions are part of herself. If she loses her things, her personality undergoes a change" (105). Not Annie; chattel counts little with her. She brought few personal goods to London to begin with because she rated her chances to find work in the capital low.

Annie has always managed on very little. "Less is more, sometimes" (139), she says in the last chapter, alluding to the coping power the deprived must develop to get by. Disregarding comfort, she slept on two chairs in the hallway outside her father's death room, and she checks her bags at Paddington Station before taking the Tube to her interview at BH—where she is expected. Thinking ahead, she has made an appointment before her arrival, preparatory to which she got letters of recommendation from both her vicar and head teacher (69). This competence comes naturally to her. Assured, unflappable, and "a serious tranquil believer in life" (65), she knows what is important and what deserves her efforts. Her belief in life recalls that of Tilda James of *Offshore*. It also includes a frankness about sex reminiscent of Christine Gipping's in *Bookshop*. Accepting the truth that her attraction to Sam Brooks is sexual, she discusses his physical attributes with a friend. Nor does the weight that has recently padded his middle-aged frame jade her desire—even though, she claims, "he wouldn't look [like] much in bed," she finds herself aching to touch him the next time she is alone with him (98, 139).

Composed and self-assured, she will not waste energy. Years earlier, when a schoolmate tied her pigtails to the back of her chair, she remained seated, silent and tearless because she would not give the schoolmate the satisfaction of hearing her cry for help. Her attunement to reality is so keen that at times it looks like the product of second sight. Without ever having been there before, she turns up for her job interview at Broadcasting House, with its shiplike look, wearing nautical garb consisting of a "white blouse and navy blue skirt" (68). This congruence foreshadows her job performance. "Annie . . . gives the novel its heart. . . . Annie sees life steadily and is unafraid," said P. H. Newby in *The Listener*.[8] He is right. She works with quiet efficiency. Confident without being smug, she always calls her superiors by name. She also fits in well at the Simmons's house—in contrast to their previous boarder—by doing little domestic chores, like shelling peas, with a cheer that even the Simmons kids cannot match.

But her biggest splash comes at BH. And it shines with the legacy of her father. Like a piano tuner, she does not build from scratch but, rather, repairs something that has fallen out of tune or become misaligned. But her job is tougher than her dad's. In Sam Brooks, she is working for a person, not on a piano—a workaholic, moreover, who is out of tune with himself. Fitzgerald makes it clear that a struggle awaits Annie. Her last name comes from a poem by Heinrich Heine (1797–1856), whom the young Austrian Heinrich quoted in *Offshore* [119]). The poem, "Der Asra," tells of a tribe of slaves who die when they fall in love. But this portent carries an added weight. In addition to its use in Heine, the name Asra is an anagram of the name Sara; Annie faces the uphill fight of babying a lover nearly thirty years her senior. The perfect pitch she developed accompanying her father on his rounds hurts her chances for happiness while, ironically, heightening her appreciation of the prize she seeks. Again, German literature forecasts her defeat. In Thomas Mann, art, and especially music, provides the most sublime ecstasy we can know. But Mann also links music to lust, disease, and decay. The concertgoing of young Hanno Buddenbrook in *Buddenbrooks* (1901) becomes an education in death. In *Doctor Faustus* (1948), the syphilitic eponym, a great composer, carries death inside him.

This legacy from Mann matters because Annie's connection with Sam leaps forward in the presence of music. They are first alone while music is playing. Annie, who likens hearing the work of Schubert, Debussy, and Liszt to the sensation of drowning (80), enters Sam's office in chapter 7 because he wants her to hear a new recording with him. Their brief time together displays Fitzgerald's ability to show changes taking place in characters so quickly that the characters do not know they are happening. The scene also shows how a routine social encounter can seethe with tension. Sam is learning something here about himself, and his emerging self-knowledge is painful. Within minutes, he looks at Annie "impatiently," speaks to her "with dangerous calm," and even shouts (81). By contrast, she remains quiet and self-composed. Wearing her learning lightly, she even repeats the claim she made during her job interview that she is not "particularly musical" (81). Her modesty gives her pronouncement that the singer she and Sam have been listening to is "a twelfth of a note flat" (81) the force of a jackhammer. These words jar Sam. As much of an inventor as Annie's father was a refurbisher, he uses the success of one of his inventions to rationalize his taking his staff of JTAs to an elegant French restaurant; even during times of want, anything and everything are available to those with the right contacts and the right money. So badly does Sam want to impress Annie that he orders a cab to take her and the other JTAs to Prunier's for lobster. The sexuality unconsciously prodding him comes forth in his attention to her hair. In chapter 9, he twists "the outlying curls of hair made ragged" (111) by a friend's clumsy attempts to cut it. Then he claims to be "very good at cutting hair" (111) himself to improve his chances of touching her hair again.

This attraction seizes others during the visit to Prunier's in chapter 8. Maximizing her resources, Annie wears a white dress to dinner—a tactic, however unconscious, that prompts the headwaiter to seat her next to Sam. If Fitzgerald's people fall in love without knowing it, those around them intuit the circuit they have sparked and encourage it. The circuit continues to vibrate. Impulsively, Sam gives Annie "the best" (96) gift he can imagine—a ring made of a twist of wire from a champagne cork and crowned with one of the currants from a dessert tort. With her usual poise, Annie leaves the hand to which Sam fitted the makeshift betrothal ring on the table, in view of the other dinner guests. But immediately this calm gives way to the sensation of upheaval. She realizes that she loves an older married workaholic "who said the same things to all the girls" (97). Because Sam "squandered young people and discarded them" (103), she faces the prospect of becoming one in a series of flirtations. Sam's self-pity is so strong that it has blinded him to her merits. He wants to be soothed, often by several women at the same time. As his dismal record as a husband shows, he could turn away from the more mentally anchored Annie on a whim.

As her urge to touch him shows, Annie wants to give Sam more than comfort. The convulsing of BH by a German bomb sends her straight to his office. The threat of death has propelled her to the side of her beloved. As in Greene's *The End of the Affair* (1951), danger speeds the flow of emotions in *Voices*, specifically hers. Entering his office, she sees him reading a children's book. He claims that he has been wanting to see her—but not for any reason she would welcome. He is sad because some supplies he had requisitioned have been denied him. Even before she met him, during her job interview at BH, his secretary had told her that his name was Seymour Brooks, adding, "You're not likely to have much direct contact with" him (69).

Annie need not see more of Sam than she does in chapter 7, when they listen to recorded music together, to read his character clearly. She knows that he is selfish. But *can* she steer him into a bond more vital than the sentimental episodes he has been enjoying with the other JTAs? When she says that self-knowledge is useful, he replies, "It's painful" (138). Yet he does take off his reading glasses in "capitulation" (139). And if she embraces him before waiting for him to make the first physical overture, he does invite her straightaway to celebrate their new bond over dinner. Removing his glasses has directed his attention to his heart.

Sam also shows a welcome maturity by resigning from the BBC on the spot. Happiness is only possible when its limits are recognized and accepted. Like Britain's King Edward VIII, who is mentioned earlier in the book (18), Sam chooses love over duty; his bonding with Annie would set a bad example for his junior colleagues at BH were he to keep working there. Forget for the moment that any marriage he embarked on with Annie could be as troubled as that of the Duke of Windsor and Mrs. Wallis Simpson. Though much older than Annie, Sam lacks her steadiness. But he values steadiness. His quitting a job that means everything to him, besides counting in his favor, shows him following her good example. It also gives their union a strong, promising start.

Unlike him, his more accomplished and charismatic colleague, Jeff Haggard, grumbles about retiring but keeps to his office. The Director of Programmed Planning at BH, cerebral, compulsive Jeff is facing a midlife crisis. Jonathan Raban calls him "the cleverest, most ironically detached character in the book."[9] Is Raban off target? Jeff is Sam's mirror image writ large. Though both men served in the First World War, Jeff saw combat duty. And whereas Sam hides inside his Seraglio, Jeff does all his own office work. His heroics here and elsewhere have given him the best-known face in the BBC—and also, because his three divorces have won him plenty of time to do so, he has cultivated a persona. This persona, or mask, reflects the stoical indifference of the English public school man. In his case, the indifference borders on disdain. Jeff prefers a low profile. Unless cornered, he will not admit that he speaks fluent French and Turkish (and perhaps Russian). People who have known him for years are ignorant of his battlefield heroics. Continuing to play down his achievements, he expedites problems quietly and rebuffs the attempts of others to give him credit. His self-effacement, though, tallies a high cost. He never goes home—either by train or by the taxi requisitioned every night to take him there.

Many of his coworkers find him puzzling. Allegedly cold and dry, he enters the novel wearing a "pale, ruined-looking face" (14) and ordering a double whisky. Jeff has been feigning cynicism to hide the truth that he cares about people, especially Sam, whom he tries to keep at bay while often having to rescue him from trouble. These interventions are revealing; Jeff will more likely break a rule for others than for himself. And he acts quickly and alone. His most notable intervention occurs in chapter 2. France has just fallen, and the elderly French General Georges Pinard has come to BH to address the British nation. His words die in the studio. Sensing that he is coming apart (in fact, he will die within the hour), Jeff unplugs his microphone. But the ten minutes of silence Jeff creates on the national airways count little alongside his sparing his countrymen the distress of hearing that Great Britain should surrender to Hitler when his troops invade in two or three weeks' time. Jeff's decisiveness has earned the BBC a bargain.

Perhaps the first warning sign Jeff picks up came from Pinard's telling the program engineer in charge of the broadcast, "I have something to say from the heart" (30). Jeff distrusts the heart—mostly because he has been struggling with his own. His internal struggles have failed him. A junior colleague accuses him of not meaning half of what he says (106). The accusation is nearly gratuitous. Jeff chafes at having distanced himself from others. Like Sam, he sees himself as overworked. But no Annie Asra will charm him into relaxing and having some fun. His self-destructive habits of mind persist. An American newsman tells him, "You don't recognize a giver" (51). The comment can be extended. Jeff, a compulsive giver, is being told indirectly that he lacks self-knowledge. So low is his self-esteem that he feels unworthy of other people's generosity.

What he craves instead is control, lest the unpredictable flood in and disrupt his routine. Thus, like Richard Blake of *Offshore,* he prefers to help others covertly. But this help can recoil on him. He sees to a greater degree than Richard that helping others both encroaches upon their freedom and curbs their coping power. Few of us will struggle for a prize if we can get it without effort. But, in the process, we lose a chance to grow. Jeff knows that his generosity has been a cheat to his friends and colleagues. In chapter 9 he notes inwardly, "Helping other people is a drug so dangerous that there's no cure short of total abstention" (109). But he cannot act on his insight. Just as Nenna James and Maurice of *Offshore* borrow, Jeff gives. His suicide is an act of punishment, self-inflicted for refusing to rejoice with Sam after Sam tells him that he has found someone to love. He also knows that Annie's capable presence in Sam's life preempts his own. He fears being shamed as well as cast off. Annie has the classical repose and serenity that he can only fake. He has been outperformed—by a child, no less. What is left is for him to die after physically leaving Broadcasting House for the lone time in the book. Unprotected by his workplace and the structure it imposes, he loses his life.

Several minor figures flesh out the action, both peopling the seven floors of corridors, offices, and studios at BH and providing useful slants on the main characters. An "expert in human behavior" (22), the young JTA Della aspires to the world of style and celebrity glitz. This opportunist who never goes out in public "without looking her best" (38) rates having fun as high as she does the chance to better herself. Thus she deserts her friends in Kensington Gardens to go dancing at a time when they could have used her help. But singing, not dancing, is her passion. At about the same time Annie comes to London, Della leaves the BBC for Manchester, where she apparently launches a promising career as a singer. At least, she is heard singing "Look for the Silver Lining" on Manchester Radio. An eye on the main chance she has always had. She resents sharing an orange that luck brings her way, and she applies for a job transfer after learning that the staffers in her unit have been forbidden to accept gifts from the public.

It is said of her, after her departure from BH, that she never got along well with her boss, Sam Brooks, because they were too similar. This judgment makes sense. Both Della and Sam use people only to discard them—Sam because he likes the safety net provided by frequent change and Della out of an urge to shine. Sam's emerging prominence in *Voices* shoulders Della aside. The novel no longer needs her. In fact, her ongoing presence would weaken its narrative economy. Thus she is swept aside with the same callousness she routinely displays while discarding others. A good thing it is, too—Annie has enough selfishness to deal with in Sam.

If the self-centered Della is a foil to Sam, then Fitzgerald uses the JTA Willie Sharpe to warn us that charity like Jeff's can also be a dangerous form of egotism. So young that he pays only two pence for coffee at BH's canteen, Willie is a relentless improver of both himself and the world. This self-starter believes in preparing himself for everything. He will not light the darkened hallways of BH with a flashlight because learning to see in the dark will make him more effective in night combat. Combat he does accept—but as a step toward achieving the goal of world harmony, a paradise where action blends with thought and where one's private impulses serve the commonweal. Willie has even factored eating into the politics of his ideal world state. People will only eat every other day "to ensure world plenty," with food servers and servees alternating roles "in strict rotation" (94) so that today's waitstaff will have tomorrow's meals brought to them.

That this regimen denies freedom of movement and choice has bypassed Willie. He has other blind spots. When told that he must have a school certificate in mathematics to pilot a plane in the RAF, he says that Hitler needed no school cert "to command the Nazi hordes" (13). He also cites Hitler as an example when he talks about concentrating his will and needing a strong-willed people to implement the new humanity he envisions. Perhaps he has unconsciously modeled himself on Hitler because, like Hitler (and also Napoleon, Stalin, and Al Capone), he is small (91). His statement about the cooking of lobsters, "They plunge them head first into boiling water. . . . That instantly destroys life" (93), could have come from Hitler as well as from Maurice of *Offshore*. But, as is seen in the differences between Fitzgerald's treatment of Richard Blake and Jeff Haggard, politics count much more in *Voices* than in *Offshore*.

Gentle and kindly like Maurice, Willie Sharpe is nonetheless associated with sharp or pointed objects, symbols of the ruthless male ego that has primed him to take charge. He uses a knife to slice an orange and a pair of scissors to cut Annie's hair; in chapter 4, he prods Jeff Haggard with a pencil (57). Strikingly, coincidence links him most often (in chapters 1, 4, and 10) to the combat veteran Jeff; in chapter 4, when they are partners in a first aid exercise, Willie lectures Jeff on the happy, thriving world he sees shaping itself while London lies in a rubble of glass shards and twisted metal. Could he be right? Divided by decades of experience as well as by official rank, Willie and Jeff nonetheless have a natural affinity that keeps joining them. Both are destructive innocents whose behavior tallies with their alleged beliefs. Both gravitate to violence. Willie not only uses sharp or pointed objects; the words "sharp," "sharpened," and "sharpening" also occur four times within three paragraphs, both in a musical context and in the presence of a piano tuner who will soon die (64–65). Jeff later sets off a parachute bomb that kills him. If he and Willie are not proto-fascists, they nonetheless endorse values that kill.

Another character who adds to the book's restive wartime mood is Lise Bernard. First seen as "pretty, but shapeless, crumpled, and depressed" (8), Lise is drifting at a time when she needs to set down roots. Her life is strife-ridden enough to justify Willie's saying that she cries a lot (13). Half French, she conceived a child with a French soldier who has since cast her off. Her accidental reunion with Frédé in Kensington Gardens, coming at a time when 200,000 French troops have joined General Charles de Gaulle in London, lacks definition and closure. No sooner do Frédé and Lise begin talking than their discussion lurches into nonsense. Impressions blur, as if seen from a distance or through a moving crowd. To start with, Lise is much bigger than the "disheveled khaki creature" (40) who keeps pushing her away from him. But he is not the only one she dismays. Like her physical clumsiness, the French words she yells at Frédé vex the English girls who came to the gardens with her;

they feel, to their alarm, that this shrieking eyesore is revealing her true self to them for the first time.

The Gardens incident conveys both the dark humor and the grim absurdity of living through a war. A fight starts while Frédé is repelling Lise. Frédé's face gets bloodied by an unidentified assailant, and the bread rolls a volunteer made for the homesick French soldiers streak the air like missiles and then get tromped into the earth. These bread rolls represent the loss of guidelines that always means trouble in Fitzgerald. Though a refuge to many foreigners from Nazi-occupied lands, the London of *Voices* also brings foreigners to grief: Frédé gets beaten up; a "swollen . . . ugly" (41) Lise has nowhere to go after her parents reject her; General Pinard and the eccentric old academic, Dr. Josef Vogel, both die.

Tempering this grief are the unbidden acts of kindness warming the action. After Lise's fiasco with Frédé, Della goes dancing. But her colleague Vi Simmons takes Lise home with her, paying her bus fare, and lets her share her bedroom. But Lise, acting "without explanation" (61), soon bolts both the Simmons home and her job at the BBC. Then Vi, breaking a rule for Lise, gives her her own ticket to sleep in the BBC's concert hall, which is now serving as a makeshift dormitory. It is here that Lise gives birth. Luckily for her, Jeff Haggard is nearby. Acting with his routine competence, Jeff orders an ambulance to take Lise and her baby to the hospital. Although not the book's most likable figure, Lise is the neediest. Sam's secretary, Mrs. Milne, who is threatened by younger women, often disparages both her and Annie. But her assistant, a minor character called Mrs. Staples, "in the grip of a force stronger than reason" (124), steps out of the shadows to invite Lise and her baby to share her flat. As is also suggested by her loyalty to an ancient law, Mrs.

Staples's name signals a Tolstoyan faith in the decent and the foursquare. The war keeps stirring responses traceable to deep sources. Having learned about Mrs. Staples's generosity, Annie gives a sulky, ungrateful Lise a pair of baby socks and some of her precious weekly tea ration. Lise's unpleasantness has been negated, two strangers having reached out to her both to protect and preserve two lives at risk.

Speaking of *Human Voices* in 1981 Penelope Lively said, "There is not a great deal of plot. . . . It [the book] is not so much a narrative as a series of sparkling episodes."[10] Her observation needs to be qualified. *Voices* does much more than amass a variety of stalled fragments. As in *Offshore,* the patient buildup of glittering details it comprises form a unified portrait. *Human Voices* is, above all, a story of private lives. Again, with *Offshore,* Fitzgerald needs to be praised for having recreated a world that might otherwise be lost. Undaunted by the truth that war heightens the ambiguity and confusion of the human personality, *Voices* knows exactly where it is going and how to take the reader there. Its title appears once, advisedly at the end of chapter 6, its midway point, where Fitzgerald calls the BBC's "scattering [of] human voices into the darkness of Europe" (77) a labor of both love and faith.

She also mentions T. S. Eliot (131), author of "The Love Song of J. Alfred Prufrock," the last line of which supplies the title her 1980 novel. She had this famous line of verse—"Till human voices wake us and we drown"—in mind when she has Annie observe that hearing classical music gives her the sensation of drowning. But the novel's action also takes Fitzgerald's mind elsewhere. The closing chapters urge a rethinking of W. B. Yeats's (and Willie Sharpe's? Yeats was often called Willie by his friends) claim that the "terrible beauty" of violence can create fresh new life. Unfolding mostly during the worst moments of the Blitz, the book depicts sidewalks shuddering, walls buckling, and a terrace collapsing. As BBC staffers slog through air thick with smoke, they hear water gushing from pipes burst by a fallen bomb. But having sent two men out in a storm to drown in the last scene of *Offshore,* Fitzgerald does not want Jeff to die by water. The narrative logic of *Voices* satisfies her wishes. The book's deep structure decrees that Jeff, whose blocked desires have already brought him near bursting point, should blow himself up.

Whether he deliberately sets off the parachute bomb that kills him instantly remains unclear. But his death cannot be shrugged off. Though absurd, it rings hideously true. A casual reference to Elizabeth Gaskell's novel *Cranford* evokes Lively's assessment of *Voices* as "a series of sparkling episodes." Like Fitzgerald's novel, *Cranford* (1853) substitutes details taken from ordinary life for formal plotting to describe a closed society. The people in both novels also act alike. Though the Cranford women compete with each other, they forget their quarrels to come together during a crisis. By refusing to celebrate with Sam and Annie, Jeff spurns the solidarity the moment demands. This self-punisher has no place in a ridiculous world where men of forty-six couple with teenagers who know more about life than they do.

Fitzgerald's style conveys this freakishness admirably. It is fluent without wordiness and poetic without being showy. Her meticulous practical attention to craftsmanship and detailing always to the fore, she deserves acclaim for both her undemonstrative casual rightness and the seeming nonchalance of her best effects. A good deal of hard work stokes her ability both to transmit information and to build mood in a tight space. The marvel in this, it merits repeating, is her ability to make it look easy. The following passage shows her using the imagery of smell to evoke an extended collective nightmare: "Recordings . . . were apt to be misplaced. They looked alike, all 78s, aluminum discs coated on one side with acetate whose pungent rankness was the true smell of the BBC's war" (11). With the same drypoint accuracy, she captures the counterpoint of sounds greeting the survivors of a night bombing raid as they face a new day: "After the first week of September [1940] London became every morning a somewhat stranger place. The early morning sound was always of glass being scraped off the pavement. The brush hissed and scraped, the glass chattered, tinkled, and fell" (104).

That this lovely auditory cascade is sourced in the madhouse of war calls to mind the book's critique of strong-arm politics. Like most of Fitzgerald's other effects, the invocation is subtle. But it still invites a look at, if not a reassessment of, postwar British politics. Only the best novels keep jogging our minds after we put them down. Deeply satisfying, *Human Voices* delivers what we have come to expect from its author: a well-crafted plot with sensitive emotional understanding, prose graced by shining moments, intimacy and immediacy, and engaging people who are trying to sort out their lives in the teeth of disaster.

CHAPTER 8

Stagers

Fitzgerald's first novel to be published in the United States, *At Freddie's* appeared here in 1985 without much fanfare, as is reflected in the twelve-year wait before another one of her books came out on our shores.[1] As she did in her earlier London-based novels, Fitzgerald builds *Freddie's* around a fixed point, a tactic noted by Penelope Lively in her review of the 1982 novel: "*At Freddie's,* like *Human Voices* and *Offshore* . . . offers . . . a string of elegantly contrived episodes involving a group of people caught up in an institution."[2] That seedy, august institution is the Temple Stage School, a landmark and monument placed "in the middle of Covent Garden, which in itself is in the exact middle of the heart of London" (23). The actors, singers, and dancers performing in venues like the Theatre Royal and the Opera House troop to work through the fruit, flower, and veggie stands of Covent Garden. In the eyes of many, the Garden, its "rotting debris" (23) and all, had become part of London's theatrical tradition, as the opening scene of Bernard Shaw's *Pygmalion* (1914) shows.

The Temple School helped shape this tradition. Staffed in part by a dialect coach and a fencing instructor, it has been training youngsters in Shakespearean drama for forty years. It also sends them to theaters producing plays with juvenile roles like *Peter Pan* and *The Nutcracker*. A lucky break can help the school and its eager pupils at any time. At the time *Freddie's* opens, the fall of 1963, a local theater has been staging a musical version of Dickens's *Dombey and Son,* which includes a children's chorus. And midway into the book, a local company begins mounting a production of Shakespeare's *King John,* which has in its cast a juvenile role. To fill this role and others like it, theatrical producers routinely go to the Temple School. But do these roles surface often enough to keep the school afloat? Its formidable headmistress, Frieda Wentworth, or Freddie, has been ignoring a growing demand for child actors in movies and television. She is not trying to sink the school. She is just neglectful. Early in the first chapter, Fitzgerald calls it "not far from destitution, with crippled furniture, undraped windows, and floors bare to the point of indecency" (9). More is at stake, though, than decency. Besides being shabby, dirty, and rundown, Freddie's school menaces its pupils, staff, and faculty. A floor is about to cave in, the ceiling leaks, and both boiler and the incinerator could go at any time, along with the building's plumbing and electricity. But these threats, though frightening, are being laughed off. Like the people in *Bookshop, Offshore,* and *Gate of Angels,* Freddie and her companions have been transcending the constraints of a squalid physical environment to enact mighty deeds.

Overseeing this ongoing, many-sided process is that "very old stager" of seventy-three winters (11), Freddie.[3] By turns selfish, calculating, and charming, the imperious Freddie knows how to survive. Were she a man, she would be called a "macher," someone who gets things done. As a woman, she has learned that ruthlessness is often a necessary survival skill for those of her gender. But Fitzgerald's careful portrait of her also includes the grating effect of this ruthlessness upon others. Freddie is not the only extravagant, larger-than-life woman Fitzgerald wrote about. She ended her short 1990 essay about the Victorian land reformer Octavia Hill (1838–1912) by saying, "Evidently, to achieve so much, Hill had to be an impressive but also infuriating woman."[4] In *Charlotte Mew and Her Friends,* Fitzgerald says of a woman whose gift for both friendship and efficiency ran afoul of her eccentric, demanding nature, "It is easy to criticize such people, difficult to do without them" (107). It is with reason that the Temple School is known chiefly as Freddie's. She runs the place, rarely budges from it, and controls everything that goes on there. Without the governance of this extraordinary, irritating woman, the school would have folded long ago. And having no Temple School to run, Freddie might have folded her own wings. She and the school are mutually supportive. When she hears that the architects of the National Theatre on the South Bank want to endow a junior acting academy "with particular attention to training in Shakespeare," she falls to the floor and says, "I imagine I am about to die" (107, 108). Death spares her. Priestess as well as proprietress, she occupies an office that suggests a "church vestry" (9). Any meaningful discussion of her must flout natural law. Called "a solid piece of darkness" (9), she glides amid the somber appointments of her dark office. She and the office she navigates so flawlessly have even come to resemble each other, as if the decades of her occupancy there have smoothed the differences between them.

She continues to defy everyday standards of judgment. Compared to "a sea creature on dry land" (18) and disfigured by a stroke that has immobilized one side of her face, she fuses the ugly and the sublime, the ragged and the elegant; a fine cashmere shawl covers the spare, thin mattress she sleeps on. Besides harboring a treasure trove of anecdotes about the stage, she knows everything about the plays being produced locally, the actors and production staff, and the theaters where the plays are being rehearsed or performed—their history as well as their physical resources. She has a drawer full of complimentary tickets to current plays. This largesse has come to her as a matter of course. Because of the clout she has gained as the doyenne of a fabled theatrical institution, she can also coax the most reluctant house manager into sending her rugs and upholstery not in use. Her mastery of the art of coaxing, cajoling, and bullying is legendary. In fact, someone who comes to her with a grievance but winds up giving her goods or money is said to have been "Freddied" (9). The verb "to Freddie" (24) has become synonymous in theatrical circles with striking a shrewd deal or perhaps even cheating; Freddie acts as if she is doing you a favor by fleecing you.

While the product of an overweening ego, this cunning and chicanery serves a selfless cause. In chapter 3, Freddie explains the need to keep up the school at whatever moral cost when she says, "without a great theater you never have a great nation" (35). She is always acting on the school's behalf. For instance, in chapter 13, to fend off a teacher's request for extra pay for teaching an overload, she thwarts the request before it is made. This guile comes into play often. Spotting the chance to shore up the school when it seems to be foundering, she solicits letters from influential friends and patrons with the same aplomb she marshals to pry a roll of leftover wallpaper from a stage manager. The efforts of this sacred monster usually succeed. Her forty years at the helm of the school have gained her the support of the British nation. Having kept Shakespeare alive in the nation's collective psyche for so long, she has elevated herself and the school to the status of a permanent fixture or even a national treasure. "Remaining the same requires an exceptional sense of balance" (47), it is said of Freddie and Freddie's. Both have withstood the changes caused by time, chance, and shifts in theatrical tastes to rouse in the public mind links not only with Shakespeare but also with London and Christmas. The school's very existence comforts and reassures friends of the theater all over the UK. And now that Freddie and Freddie's are both in decline, they are amassing more of their anxious compatriots' devotion than ever; rampant change prompts a craving for stability.

But this devotion needs constant tending. Freddie knows she cannot dissolve into the grandeur of her role. Vishnulike, she often preserves her earthly store through passiveness. She can, for instance, ignore bill collectors, bailiffs, and tax authorities because she owns no personal property. Although her careless bookkeeping riles both her accountant and her solicitor-brother, she can tell them, along with her fuming creditors, that all the items that help her survive belong to the school and thus, as the source of her livelihood, cannot be attached to pay delinquent bills.

Her sharp instinct for survival has also taught her the uses of activity. Thanks to her eye for human weakness, she knows how to get the upper hand quickly—over a student, the casting director of a theater, or an employee. Anyone who deals with her feels the effect of her resolve "to defeat materialism by getting people to work for nothing" (11). But this con artist who sets her junior colleagues against each other if she can profit from it also has a gentle, loving side. Rather than push a student she has been coaching to recite a jawbreaking line of verse, she knows when to back off and wish him luck.

She needs to have all her energies working at top form to traffic with "dark and dapper" (50) Joey Blatt, a businessman who has developed an interest in the school. Blatt soon wants to buy a share in Freddie's. In view of a growing demand for children in television, he hopes to turn Freddie's into a training school for TV acting. His plan makes sense. The performing arts are changing. TV and TV advertising have created the need for young actors with skills different from those the Temple School has been teaching for decades. To meet this need, the school will have to revamp its curriculum. Pupils will learn how to act for the small screen rather than for the stage, which uses techniques shaped by the need to touch viewers two hundred or more feet away ("Freddie's heart was always with the cheaper seats" [56]). But Freddie ignores practical matters like this during her first meeting with Blatt. She tries, instead, to throw him off stride and to jar his poise so she can gain control of the meeting. Like King Lear, she wants to retain power as long as she can. Thus she changes the subject when Blatt mentions the importance of generating a positive cash flow, keeping balance sheets, and maintaining a margin. But while letting him know that her rules for running the school clash with his, she also allows him to hope that she will accept him as a business partner. This hope beckons him. First of all, he enjoys the challenge of transacting business with someone as deft as Freddie in the invisible swordplay of negotiation. Next, this ex–slum brat turned millionaire wants a stake in the arts.

And this is where Freddie strikes. The chapter that shows the first meeting with Blatt ends thus: "And Freddie continued to withhold . . . the insult that might part them forever" (54). Perhaps this insult comes in the book's closing chapter. It would follow from her shrewdness, her love of power, and her fine sense of timing both to delay her boldest maneuver as long as she can and to risk her future on one toss of the dice; the insult that does not "part them forever" could insure Blatt's submissiveness if properly delivered. The stay-at-home Freddie accepts a dinner invitation from Blatt. Once seated in the chic restaurant where he has booked a table, Freddie announces that she has "done enough for Shakespeare" (156). The Temple School will stop training young hopefuls in Shakespearean drama in favor of teaching them how to do TV commercials.

Blatt is stunned. This crone who has been mocking his sound advice has suddenly given him what he has been waiting for—and without his even asking for it. But the gift carries an unexpected surcharge. Buoyed up by his coup, he bares his soul to Freddie. He tells her that he was thrilled by a recent production he had seen of *King John*. The brilliance of the boy actor cast as Prince Arthur touched the heart of this stranger to the theater. It decided him immediately to invest heavily in the School. His witnessing of the play was thus a major breakthrough to him, as is his recounting it to Freddie. But Freddie, rather than sharing his euphoria, mocks it. Faulting his artistic taste, she indicts him for being blind to bad acting (159). The scene breaks here. Why? Blatt might have reacted to Freddie's long-deferred insult by retracting his offer. Yet the season is winter, the time when people, gripped by cold and darkness, most need, as in Christ's birth, a redeeming miracle.

But what redemption could Freddie's broadside have unleashed? Her recent stay in the geriatric ward of a hospital sharpened her awareness of the ravages of time, a process she had always believed the school exempt from. Why else would she neglect the school's physical maintenance? And since this old ruffian knows how to get what she wants, she has also seen herself, the school's founder and guiding force, as indestructible, too—until recently. The loose, cross-hatched skin, rheumy eyes, and shaky, mottled legs she saw while in the hospital showed her the need to adapt to change. "There mustn't be a future without Freddie's" (157), she tells Blatt just before blasting him with the worst insult she can imagine. The school must survive. Just as Chekhov's Mme. Ranevsky cedes her cherry orchard to an ex-lackey, so will Freddie take money from Joey Blatt to redo her acting school as a TV training center in this novel that mentions Chekhov (92). Both women emit splendor in their downfalls. Mme. Ranevsky rejects the champagne Lopakhin offers her to celebrate his purchase of the cherry orchard, and Blatt, though jubilant about his new tie with the arts, suspects he will always be scorned as a philistine by those whose approval he craves.

Freddie's salvo not only denies him the fun of showing off to himself. It also distances her from an oaf who once lived in the same neighborhood as she and whose money will revamp the school while she is still living there. But her coup de théâtre eventually loses its color. The following passage records the assurance with which she rules over a realm that enjoys the same honor as London's most hallowed institutions:

> Like Buckingham Palace, Lyons teashops, the British Museum Reading Room, or the market at Covent Garden, she could never be allowed to disappear. While England rested true to itself, she need never compromise. (42)

But all the Lyons teashops disappeared from London four years before the publication of Fitzgerald's 1982 novel—as she reminds us (145). The novel's readers thus know that Freddie's pride will defeat her. Any reprieve that Freddie and Freddie's enjoy takes a form she neither recognizes nor approves of.

Though money does not drive Freddie, it does bring out her true nature. And the person she is likeliest "to Freddie" is a job applicant. Because the law requires her pupils to study geography and French in addition to being trained in music, dance, and top-hat-and-cane, Freddie needs teachers of academic subjects on her faculty. She interviews two candidates in chapter 2 and hires them both—on her terms. The first, Hannah Graves, comes from northern Ireland. Wholesome, sane, and eager but adrift, she wants a theatrical career, but not on the stage. She has thus handed Freddie an opportunity to pounce. Seeing in this "nice-looking girl of twenty" (19) a love of theater that might blind her to more pragmatic concerns, Freddie grabs the chance to underpay her.

She is more ruthless still with her second hire, Pierce Connell. The sorriest sad sack in all of Fitzgerald, he is referred to in the book's narrative passages by his last name, a rare if not unique practice in the canon with someone his age. Maurice, who is also about thirty, goes without a last name in *Offshore,* while Jeff Haggard and Sam Brooks of *Human Voices,* though fifteen years Connell's senior, are always referred to in narration by their first names. Pierce Connell's first name calls forth the activities of penetrating, poking, and stabbing, and he does act in keeping with these activities by having sex in the book. But this rut is out of character for him. It is offered to him, and he responds to it so oddly that it is never repeated. Fitzgerald deliberately avoids calling him Pierce because his hangdog, self-disparaging ways have blunted his edge and incisiveness. For instance, he wants to write. But preparing his writing desk saps so much of his verve that he has none left for the writing itself. He claims that the sin to which he would adapt most easily is sloth; the slothful are happy, he believes. He will not join their ranks, though. His Protestant respect for duty and responsibility have shown him the need to define himself through action. His ambition to become a drainage engineer (93) hints at the grief his search for self-definition will bring. The inept Eddie James of *Offshore* has an engineering degree (just as Desmond Fitzgerald qualified as a lawyer). Like Eddie, Connell lives in a world of diminished expectations. In fact, he apologizes so often that he seems guilty about his very existence.

It is his lack of a degree that empowers Freddie to offer him a lower salary than she does the much younger Hannah. But rather than balking, he justifies the low value she has placed on his services. In fact, by saying that he has no interest in either the theater or teaching, he seems to be talking Freddie out of hiring him. What he wants is a job on his own terms. He does not try to make a favorable impression on Freddie because he knows that, once hired, he will not be able to live up to it. But she has her own agenda. In her last recorded words spoken at his job interview, she says, "I'm doing you down, dear" (22). Her meaning is clear. Once he accepts being underpaid, he forfeits the chance to complain about being cheated. Freddie is betting that he will let her wrong him because he doubts that anyone else would hire him. It is a safe bet. His pawn complex runs so high that he will often do the reverse of what he feels like in the hope that he will turn the odds for success in his favor.

Freddie has to live with some unexpected offshoots of her decision to hire him. After failing to grab, let alone hold, his pupils' attention, Connell stops trying; he cannot teach people who refuse to listen to him. Hearing this news forces Freddie to rethink the advantage she has over him. A byproduct of his self-doubt is a rare honesty. Connell is drooping and his outlook is bleak. But because this Irishman would never try to sell himself to anybody, he remains his own man. Secure in his self-image, he will not puff himself up in the eyes of someone who will soon be disappointed to find him the nobody he is convinced he is. His haplessness gives him a freaky kind of inner strength. Having renounced received standards of success, he has only himself to satisfy. He asks so little from life that he cannot be compromised or corrupted.

His colleague Hannah relates differently to him than does Freddie. In chapter 4, she interrupts one of his litanies of self-disparagement by saying, "You're too much alone, Pierce" (26). She means that he needs a wife, namely her. Later, she tells him that he is too hard on himself (43). And whereas she even asks him to stay the night with her, she soon sees that he would be a dangerous partner, his hangdog ways sidetracking him from the work of bonding. But her head is soon turned by one Boney Lewis, "the wreck of a blue-eyed grey-haired man" who seems to her "only just able to make ends meet" (81, 84).

She meets this "charming drunk" (67) of forty-three at the fictional Nonesuch Theater, where he has a part in *King John*. She has gone there to instruct twelve-year-old Mattie Smart, another cast member. Mattie and Boney share a dressing room, probably because they play an important scene together. As Hubert de Burgh, Boney has been told by the king to kill Prince Arthur, the legitimate heir to the throne and also the king's nephew. But a deeper, darker force has also brought these two actors together. Like Mattie, who plays the role of Arthur, Boney is a brilliant amateur, someone to whom "a certain level of performance came so readily . . . that he might have felt it ungrateful to Providence to work harder" (71). Fitzgerald has put two more underachievers into the novel. She has also made them alter egos. And by having them share a dressing room, she forces the older Boney to confront his professional failure. This he does straightaway. And the confrontation makes him hate Mattie, whom he cannot discuss without saying how much he would enjoy making him wince.

Hannah knows nothing of this aversion. And it would not matter if she did. She overlooks Boney's scruffiness and the sense of decline he projects. When Connell says that he looks like he drinks (97), she changes the subject quickly. What matters to her is that Boney does not mope or pity himself like Connell does. She needs a better reason to close with Boney even though she may not look for one. Hannah had sex before she entered the book, and the experience soured her. She and a Belfast boyfriend were vacationing in London. But a mishap with her dress (prefiguring the one in *Innocence*) and the departure of the boyfriend, John Brannon, to the United States to study medicine show her to be unlucky in love, a problem that neither Connell nor Boney can help her solve.

The turning point of her bond with Boney comes when she sees his coat, "a Donegal tweed so fine that she felt like stroking it" (84). Eroticism has burst forth quickly, as it usually does in Fitzgerald. The coat gives Hannah an excuse to fantasize about its owner, whom she would have written off had she met him in the shadow of her parents' Belfast home. The thought of her mother's objection to Boney as a suitor (84) stimulates her so much that she forgets the lesson she is trying to give Mattie. Then Boney enters the dressing room where the lesson is taking place and, with his usual flamboyance, embraces her thighs "energetically," an act that leaves her more "interested" (86, 87) than shocked. Reflecting Fitzgerald's insight into the auras people project, any advance Boney made on Hannah, he knew she would welcome.

But if Hannah is not ready to acknowledge her interest in Boney, her unreadiness wanes quickly. When, in the next chapter, she asks Connell if she has mentioned Boney to him, he says that he has heard her say Boney's name more than ten times in the past two days (98). She is still denying her heart, though, an hour later when she invites Connell to spend the night (98). Boney has roused in Hannah a lust that she is willing to sate with Connell. Though conventional, the book's sexual symbolism both helps carry and underscores the action. At the end of chapter 15, Boney comes to her late at night both uninvited and unannounced—but not unwelcomed. Forget Hannah's claim that she forgot to lock the door of her bedsitter and her surprise that Boney knew where she lived. She made sure he knew how to find her. This knowledge he implements quickly. After climbing into bed, he releases the hair she had bound up with a rubber band and then spreads it on the pillow. The next chapter opens with her making another key to her bedsitter, presumably to give Boney, whose name puts forth a matching phallic ambience.

She might regret welcoming him into her bed. At the start of chapter 13, Fitzgerald summarizes an episode from the Old Testament found in 1 Samuel 1: 2–20: "Hannah was the mother of Samuel the prophet, and for many years she had been barren" (99). What happened in the biblical story is that a priest who had seen her moving her lips while praying in a temple thought her drunk. Realizing his mistake, he gave her a blessing, the effect of which was the son she later had. Hannah Graves has no son in *Freddie's,* and her palindromic name, with its double *n* in the middle, suggests she never will. Nor is she ever mistaken for a drunk. But her lover Boney, who, at forty-three, could be her father's age, has been boozing for years. Herself the widow of a long-term alcoholic, Fitzgerald would warn Hannah off Boney if given the chance. Boney's inviting Hannah to Venice (131) clinches the point. Venice symbolizes sexual disappointment in Fitzgerald. In *Offshore,* Maurice decorated his barge in a Venetian motif in response to the hope, which never materializes, that one of his johns will make good on an offer to take him to Venice. Hannah has gravitated to casual, convivial Boney because he differs so sharply from the hand-wringing Connell. But what does this inertia say about her prospects? In John Brannon, Connell, and Boney, she has slept with three men a decade apart in age. Her last name, Graves, suggests wryly where her practice of bedding progressively older men will land her if sustained.

Yet she cannot be faulted for turning to Boney after shouting herself hoarse trying to silence Connell's self-abasing bleats. The morning after she sleeps with Connell, she wakes up to find him gone. This ditherer has taken charge, but only to reinforce his shamefaced ways. He has gone to his family property in Ireland. What took him there was his innocent assumption that, having slept with him once, Hannah wants to marry him. He has gone to secure some land on the property where they can live in comfort. But characteristically, he argues so weakly for himself as a breadwinner and a protector that he sounds as if he is asking her indirectly to reject his proposal—if he is, in fact, proposing: "Teachers have wives, of course, and they support them, but I think we should admit that most teachers are a good deal more competent than I am. Promotion would pass me by" (115). On the other hand, this self-assessment, bleak as it is, has a heartbreaking honesty and clarity that could sway Hannah in his favor, what with her penchant for picking unavailable men to close with; like Boney's age, John Brannon's trip to the United States put him off limits as a prospective mate. When Connell tells her, "I know there's nothing you can't do well. . . . Wherever you are, people take notice" (105), he is framing an appeal many young women would have trouble rejecting. But Boney's "heartwarming shifts and evasions" (144) prevail over Connell's endless wash of sincerities. Living away from home on her own for the first time, she wants to have fun without fretting over moral consequences.

Her farewell scene with Connell occurs mostly at a Lyons teashop, a setting that kindles Fitzgerald's comic imagination. The Lyons teashops, or corner shops, began in the 1920s as an upshot of the temperance movement and stayed in business until 1978 (145). Working people could stop at a Lyons for tea and scones (fish and chips were added later) as a midday snack during the work week or on a Saturday shopping trip. Fitzgerald injects some fun into this last recorded meeting of Hannah and Connell. Her purpose: to develop the encounter, to preserve evenness of tone, and to show how context colors social experience. Recognizing the need to observe Lyons decorum, Hannah and Connell both speak at an "acceptable teashop pitch" (146). They are bound to observe this constraint. Like Annie Asra and Sam Brooks of *Voices,* Connell talks about quitting his job, as will Daisy Saunders and Fred Fairly in *Gate of Angels,* after being jarred by the clash of sex. Apparently, the promise as well as the actualization of sex in Fitzgerald packs such force that it threatens our livelihoods. *Offshore* also gives insight into the dangers hedging the Lyons episode in *Freddie's.* Like Nenna and Eddie James, Hannah and Connell are former sexual partners who have become estranged. Their conversation covers a gamut of emotions, any of which could lurch out of control in a heartbeat if not for the restraints imposed by Lyons protocol.

But still another "check on [the] . . . intimacy" (145) and the barely controlled frenzy comes from the hour when the conversation is taking place (i.e., just before closing time), when the help wants to clear the shop so they can finish their work and go home. Thus Lyons patrons who want to keep their tables have acquired "the art of keeping a statutory amount of cold tea in their teacups" (149). No distraction, this segue into closing-time etiquette heightens dramatic tension since Connell wants to lengthen his time with Hannah, whereas she is just as anxious to say goodbye. Wanting a fast, clean break, she delivers what she thinks is a parting shot when she says that she has "become fond" (148) of another man. As will happen in Fitzgerald, the words that convulse a speaker—because she suspects that the "enormous moment" (*Voices,* 112) they create could change her life—fall flat. Connell's foreknowledge of this man's identity has defused Hannah's pronouncement. But Connell has his own bombshell to fire. Without irony, he thanks Hannah for consoling him with the knowledge that, rather than having replaced him with a bright or handsome man, she has picked in Boney another loser—someone like Connell himself.

Very little, if any, of this is spite. But Connell, always ready to run himself down, grumbles about having failed to tell Hannah that he loves her and wants to spend the rest of his life with her. His belief that Boney must love her desperately to have won her heart, though, falls wide of the mark. Boney, with his reckless disregard of her feelings, is a neglectful lover. But even if he is also the "aging failure" (151) Connell claims he is, it does not matter to Hannah. Connell's gibe whets her love of Boney. The extra pint of milk and the cans of beer she orders after Boney's first visit to her bedsitter show that love to have roused her nesting instinct. She need not admire Boney to want to spend time with him.

Having tea together at Lyons opens a great divide between Connell and Hannah. But, absurdly, it also keeps faith with the deconstructionist premise that even the most seemingly lucid texts contain covert meanings and contradictions. The psychological accuracy of the motivation, the control exerted on the motivation by the teashop setting, and the influence of events that have taken place since Hannah's last meeting with Connell all fuse in a climax that is sad but funny, logical but emotionally wrenching. An effect like this, one that expresses what is both vital and inexpressible, can only stem from superior writing, not the antiwriting beloved by deconstructionists. The legacy of social comedy identified with Jane Austen has rarely glowed as brightly and as proudly as it does in the Lyons teashop in chapter 17 of *Freddie's*.

But the teashop scene, though coming in the book's closing chapter, does not close the book. The finale of *Freddie's* belongs to the Temple School's best pupil, nine-year-old Jonathan Kemp. Jonathan's last name recalls that of Will Kemp(e), the leading comic actor in Shakespeare's Lord Chamberlain's Men (later the King's Men), who would be replaced by Robert Armin. Fitzgerald makes Jonathan an orphan to free him from the duties of family, to infuse in him the orphan's need to prove himself, and thus to make good on his genius. She also contrasts him with twelve-year-old Mattie Stewart. Mattie bids fair to build on the theatrical success he has already won. But besides being older, taller, and better looking than Jonathan, this "completely finished personality" (35) lacks Jonathan's promise of artistic growth and fame. It shows. Whereas Jonathan is unruffled and self-contained, Mattie strains to impress others. Nor does he resent Jonathan's genius. If he wishes Jonathan ill, it is only because he has been hoping for the chance to help him and thereby gain his favor.

Jonathan, though, seems to need nobody's help. Introduced as "a very small preoccupied boy who did not speak" (27), he prefers silence because his future is clear to him; he would rather learn his art than chatter about it. He knows both where his genius lies and how he will have to develop and refine it. Having simplified his life, he will not waste energy. For instance, rather than try to charm adults, he tells them, as succinctly as possible, what they want to hear. And why should this orphan seek the favor of an adult world that has turned its back on him, anyway? He does not write a letter to the *Times* for Freddie because, having poured his virtue into the stage, he is loath to divert it in an act irrelevant to his career.

He holds back often, even in his chosen field of stage performance. Not satisfied with a comic routine he has been practicing, he refuses to display it for a visitor as august as Noël Coward. His high standards serve him well. While watching a scene from *King John,* he brainscreens a version of it with different physical gestures and vocal inflections from those he has been witnessing. He is a dramaturge as well as a player. Going beyond Konstantin Stanislavski's method acting, he would rather convey an emotion to an audience than internalize it. The confidence he has in his stagecraft pays dividends. After an injury to Mattie vaults him into the role of Prince Arthur, he improvises a pose that wins the director's praise. Jonathan relishes the moment. Having enhanced the effect the director wanted to create, his pose also confirms his faith in his stage instincts.

Strikingly, the first person he is seen speaking to in the novel is Pierce Connell. Jonathan's aplomb matches Connell's self-doubt in both its intensity and persistence. Would that he had reined it in. Arthur's big scene in *King John* is "the Jump," in which Arthur tries to flee the jail where the king has stowed him. But the leap from the prison wall enacted to bring him freedom kills him instead. Advisedly, the accident that forced

Mattie out of Arthur's role occurred while Mattie was practicing the Jump. But Jonathan, buoyed up with the artist's pride that is always punished in James Joyce and Thomas Mann, ignores this warning. Jonathan is special. He will surpass the requirements posed by the play's director for the Jump, even if his sterner reading of them puts him at risk. He is compelled to act the scene he has choreographed in his mind. He does not need supervision; his craft and dedication will overcome the dangerous conditions in which he will perfect the Jump.

To preen her vanity, Freddie has been rejecting offers to rent a small yard adjoining the school; having "a coveted empty space in the thronged city's heart" (133) means more to her than money. This same dark, snowy yard is where Jonathan practices the Jump. Pride has met pride. Fitzgerald told Joan Acocella in 2000 that Jonathan dies "accidentally, leaping off the wall" while practicing the Jump.[5] Like the two drowning victims at the end of *Offshore*, he succumbs to a fluid medium. But his death hits us harder. He is alone, he is only nine years old, and he has lost a future brighter than those of Maurice and Eddie combined. Also, the snuffing out of his budding genius makes his loss our loss, Freddie having forecast for him a career that might have changed the British nation (35). It is an ironic vindication of her forecast that his devotion to a stage death causes a real death. The death spells out both his tragedy and his triumph.

As a pro, he had vowed to practice the Jump until he had it right. Repeating the same act imparts the warm assurance that practice makes perfect. Repetition is part of our nature, and we succeed in our endeavors by mastering them. Once attained, mastery reassures and comforts us. But the words in the book's final sentence, "again and again and again" (160), also evoke Freud's equation of repetition with the death wish. Ending in darkness and snow, the novel has been moving toward death. Each of the two previous episodes in its last chapter show a man and a woman in an eating space, Hannah and Connell and then Freddie and Joey Blatt. Both the Lyons teashop and the smart Italian restaurant where these episodes take place serve food. Strikingly, no food is seen being served or eaten in either episode. This omission is intended. Though unfolding indoors, the teashop and restaurant scenes in chapter 17 of *Freddie's* foreshadow the last one, where Jonathan appears alone amid falling snow, a caution to all jumpers as well as a symbol of death.

Each of the crucial subchapters in chapter 17 ends in futility. The discussions of the future depicted in the teashop and the restaurant clash with the actions of someone who is denying himself a future. Freddie's words to Blatt, "You don't know bad acting when you see it" (159), segue to an example not of good acting but of the rigors upon which good acting depends. Whereas Mattie, the boy whose acting Freddie denounced, breaks his arm performing the Jump, the one she hailed as a genius, having invested much more in his art, dies. Jonathan sees no difference between stage acting and reality, his art having taken on a life of its own. The inevitability of his death is both aggressively prosaic and surreal, dovetailing each moving, well-imagined scene featuring him with all the others.

Freddie's divulges, along with the danger, the eroticism hidden in ordinary life. As the Connell-Hannah-Boney love triangle shows, sex turns out to be as much of a trap as Jonathan's artistic devotion. Fitzgerald's pessimism recurs in the dead marriage of Eddie and Nenna James in *Offshore;* in Annie Asra's belief that her love for Sam Brooks in *Human Voices* will result in nothing (98); and in Charlotte Mew, the real-life lesbian subject of Fitzgerald's next book after *Freddie's*, who falls in love with two straight women. Sex in all her work is not just whimsical but deeply disruptive, not life enhancing but life shattering. What is broken cannot be fixed; the fling cannot be unflung. The speed with which her people who fall in love talk about quitting their jobs tallies some of this damage. Fitzgerald is not a sensualist. Her observations about sex deal more with misunderstanding, regret, and loss than with the joys of physical connection. This distrust labels her a modernist. Although her Catholic faith urges unity, her imaginary world is fractured —humanity broken into as many shards as the bomb damage has strewn around London in *Human Voices*. She mocks the assumption that just because two people from the north of Ireland work together in London, they must fall in love. The common ground Hannah and Connell share rests on a cliché. This makes bad fiction. Their isolation, not their connection, makes their story worth telling.

And it is the theatrical context furnished by Freddie's that makes it resound—all the more remarkably because neither Hannah nor Connell has any stage ambitions. The context is carefully foregrounded. En route to Freddie's, which stands on Baddeley Street (23), perhaps chosen to honor the actress Hermione Baddeley (1906–86), one inhales the vegetation of Covent Garden while wading through a litter of straw, crushed cardboard boxes, and trampled greens. The school itself provides glimpses of sets and costumes in varying degrees of serviceability. Anecdotes told of famous actors like Laurence Olivier and Peter O'Toole (91, 8), are distorted by time, if they were ever true in the first place. We are also reminded that the theater is a business that, like all others, needs to make money. A theatrical agent, for instance, has to decide which of his young prospects is worth investing in. And raw talent is not the only factor to weigh while assessing the future of a child actor. Freddie's pupils, scarcely any of whom will act professionally between ages twelve and sixteen, check their height and weight often to gauge their chances for the stage roles they covet; as Jonathan learns, being short has both drawbacks and benefits. The skill with which Fitzgerald creates Freddie's validates the appearance there in chapter 8 of its friend and stay, Noël Coward, who eulogizes his beloved old rascal of a teacher (62).

Away from Freddie's, Fitzgerald's portrayal of the theater rings just as true. By 1963, the book's time setting, the kitchen-sink school of English drama, exemplified by John Osborne's *Look Back in Anger* (1956), Shelagh Delaney's *A Taste of Honey* (1958), and Harold Pinter's *The Caretaker* (1960), had already recharged the London stage with both its working-class characters and speech and an acting style that made up in force what it lacked in polish. Kitchen-sink aesthetics, though, affect the production of *King John,* which starts in chapter 9, the book's midmost chapter, less than does the theater of the absurd. The actor who plays the title role, William Beardless, refers to George Arliss (1868–1946), who, amusingly, sometimes wore a beard, as in his only Shakespearean role (viz., Shylock in *The Merchant of Venice).*[6] *King John*'s director, Ed Voysey, whose name comes from the 1905 problem play, *The Voysey Inheritance,* chides an actor for pretending to grope for his next line. The "naturalism" (70) mistakenly noted by Ed refers to Samuel Beckett's *Waiting for Godot,* which debuted in English in London in 1955 and which often gives the impression that its cast members have not learned their parts. From the theater of cruelty of Jean Genet and Peter Weiss comes Ed Voysey's idea of having the role of King John's ten-year-old son Henry acted in the manner of a doddering old man. Canadian-born culture critic Marshall McLuhan, whose popularity peaked in the 1960s, supplies the idea of using real gas footlights for the production with his belief that nobody moves forward without also checking the rearview mirror of the car they are driving.

And why should these ideas not come to Ed Voysey? The author of *The Voysey Inheritance,* Harley Granville-Barker (1877–1946), revolutionized Shakespearean production besides writing long analytical prefaces to the plays. Ed, no great reader (66), may have ignored these prefaces, but he *has* braced himself for the chore of shepherding *King John* into production while also protecting the fragile egos of his actors. *King John* was the play chosen by Fitzgerald for him to direct for several reasons. The title character's weakness, indecisiveness, and impressionability evoke the same traits in Connell. The play also includes a character named Lewis, who calls to mind Boney Lewis. Lewis, heir apparent to the French throne, calls forth, in turn, the motif of usurpation; John snatched the English crown from its rightful heir, Arthur, just as Boney appropriated Connell's place alongside Hannah and Joey Blatt is preparing to take charge of Freddie's. Arthur's death, finally, is as gratuitous and thus wasteful as that of Jonathan, the boy actor the role was assigned to. Hubert de Burgh (Boney's role) spares Arthur, despite having been told to kill him. Already free, Arthur has no reason to jump from the prison wall to his freedom. His needless jump ends his life in the same wasteful way that Jonathan's jumping does *his*—in a conflation of life and art reminiscent of Pirandello.

Fitzgerald's intellect and instinct work together to avoid a dull, flat one-to-one correspondence between Shakespeare's early history play and her novel. Her mosaic distributes traits she saw in her husband Desmond and King John among Boney, Mattie Stewart, and Connell, all of whom underperform in their own ways. But the mosaic does not merely extend her range of allusion and reference; rather, it energizes one of the book's most riveting effects—the enchantment created by a stellar dramatic production. *Freddie's* shows how a few actors helped by a handful of props, some notes of music, and clever lighting can grip an audience: "They [the actors] were creators in their own right, each performance coming to life, if it ever did, between the actors and the audience, and after that lost for eternity. The extravagance of that loss was its charm" (56). Its brevity constitutes a play's glory. Actors and audience have forged a union of beauty and loss. Fitzgerald is speaking of that stage magic that can enchant an audience. The enchantment is unique; it belongs to the theater alone. It also explains why some of Britain's greatest stage actors like Gertrude Lawrence (1898–1952) and Katherine Cornell (1898–1974) avoided making movies. Hardly anyone born after 1950 knows either of these stars. But perhaps neither one would have fought obscurity if it meant sacrificing those rare moments of sublimity they helped create before live audiences.

At Freddie's lines up well alongside its predecessors. There *is* the odd lapse. John Brannon, Hannah's Belfast beau, allegedly took his medical training in Galveston, Texas, as clearly impossible in 1963 as was John McVitie's alleged New Jersey accent in *Human Voices* (93, 48). Such flubs are rare, though, a trifle to pay for a novel whose dizzying moral ironies, smart pace, and deft set pieces give it a real grace.

CHAPTER 9

Stumbling into Geopolitics

Fitzgerald set *Innocence* in 1955 and 1956 because its Italian characters, who now move about freely, recall German troops occupying the public offices of their cities and setting curfews while also refitting factories for wartime production. Most of the traumas of postwar reconstruction have waned—but only to give way to new ones. Though Mussolini is mentioned (112, 197), the Italy of *Innocence* faces anxieties created by the cold war. A character's reference to "a third world war" (190) stands as just one example of the impact of Soviet imperialism. This impact pulsates through *Innocence,* a work that unfolds midway through the period from 1953 to 1958, in Giuseppe Mammarello's words "one of the most difficult . . . of Italian political life."[1] Ordinary people felt blocked by a bureaucracy both inept and corrupt, and the rules put in place to ease the blockage caused only conflict, both between and within contending parties.[2]

Fitzgerald's knowledge of this turmoil (206) shows in the early working title for *Innocence*—"The Same Mistake."[3] In fact, one of the meanings of the title she settled on for her 1986 novel stems from her belief that the solutions to ease Italy's distress put forth by civic leaders and economic planners amounted to little more than innocence or naivete. She voices her skepticism with her usual offbeat wit. Though Stalin's 1953 death is ignored in the book, both the Twentieth Congress of the Communist Party of the USSR (in which Stalin was denounced) and the Hungarian Revolution of 1956 provide topics for talk (63, 206). But the talk is brief, and the communists seen in the novel are all pathetic. Two of them who failed to find work in Turin in the far northwest of Italy had to slog 750 kilometers to their home in the south (36). One of them, long dead before the novel's present-tense action unfolds, exposed his son to a horror so brutal that it twisted the boy. His friend and co-trekker, "a part-time book-keeper, one of those not born to succeed" (35), calls to mind other underachievers and nonstarters in the canon based on Desmond Fitzgerald. A third communist is the real-life journalist and agitator, Antonio Gramsci (1891–1937), who staggers into the book as a "tiny, crippled" (37) convict, toothless, reeking, and dying.

Yet the book takes place during "the years of the Italian economic miracle" (59–60). Miraculous these years were. By 1949, the year Italy joined NATO, the country's economy had recovered from the havoc of war. Rapid growth in the steel industry helped build much-needed roads, bridges, and railroads. Per capita income grew along with investment.

Driving much of this growth was the Marshall Plan, a European relief program developed in the United States to curb inflation, promote employment, and help farms and factories expand.[4] Public health improved, too, as is seen in heretofore empty clinics now being thronged by Italians requesting antibiotics "paid for by the Americans" (60). But American pharmaceuticals and cash brought obligations. A number of military bases opened in Italy as a spinoff of a political ideology that opposed, together with Rome, the red threat.[5] This anticommunist coalition pithed trade unionism and slowed legislation in the areas of hospital insurance, welfare payments, and pensions. But the sound of Fiats and Olivettis (106) rolling off assembly lines silenced most of the groans. Even one of Fitzgerald's die-hard communists admits, "Things are getting better, production is up, the standard of living is higher, people are earning more money" (117).

But this affluence had made Italy a client state of America. Federal outlays in the United States like the GI Bill had been providing both college tuition and mortgage money. The newly educated Americans who rushed to the suburbs soon developed a taste for foreign travel. By the mid-1950s, Italy had snapped to this development. The advertising and market research that fueled America's new prosperity would also upgrade Italian merchandising. Italy had culture to market. Thus Fitzgerald portrays a writers' conference taking place in the Roman studio of a princess with the Evelyn Waugh–sounding name of Billie Buoncampagno (102). Matching this event is a meeting of art historians near Florence, which includes an American (170). But Italy is not trying to lure foreign scholars and writers alone. The intellectuals drawn there by sites like Bernard Berenson's villa I Tatti and Max Beerbohm's Rapallo formed but a small part of the tourist base the country could support. Tourism boards ordered families like the Ridolfis of *Innocence* to open their ancient estates to foreign visitors. To attract visitors, they would even embellish the centuries'-long legends connected with the estates.

Any worries about a national identity crisis on the part of Italians soon vanished in the fun. The American tourism and cinema that leveled Italian manners, breaking down old forms of group loyalty and discipline, also impelled self-awareness. Though Grace Kelly is mentioned in *Innocence,* so are Ingrid Bergman and the out-of-wedlock twins she had with Italian film director Roberto Rossellini (32, 139). And the appearance of movies like Vittorio De Sica's *The Bicycle Thief* (1948) and Frederico Fellini's *The White Sheik* in 1952 had won friends for Italian cinema worldwide. In fact, Fellini is mentioned twice in *Innocence* (62, 106), and Antonio Gramsci, when he appears in chapter 11, looks as hideous as a Fellini grotesque seen close up in one of the later films while also reflecting Fellini's practice of putting real-life celebrities in his work.

This windfall, though, had limits. Italy's preeminence in film and the postwar developments in rubber, fertilizer, and petrochemicals that made her a major economic force tipped north. Speaking of the "grave disequilibrium between North and South," Paul Ginsborg tells how southern Italy never took to industrial expansion nor, hampered by poor soil, profited from land reform.[6] Thus the south stagnated, and the economic gap dividing it from the north grew. Laborers looking for work fled the land to take jobs in both public works programs and construction;[7] in Luchino Visconti's 1960 movie, *Rocco and His Brothers*, a family moves from Sicily to Milan. Near the end of *Innocence*, a southerner talks about some of his neighbors leaguing together to build a new hotel in their hometown (202). But such activity was rare. Most gifted, ambitious southerners headed north, like Fitzgerald's Salvatore Rossi. Raised in the small fictional town of Mazzata—in the province of Campagna between Naples and Bari—Salvatore qualified as a medical doctor in Bologna before practicing as a neurologist in Florence.

But the northward migration of bright hopefuls like Salvatore tells only part of the story. When an elderly Florentine hears a young man described as "clever, very hardworking" (12), she assumes he is a southerner. As is seen in the loss of American pioneer sinew in Edwin Arlington Robinson's "Richard Cory" and Eugene O'Neill's *Hairy Ape* (1919), any elite body must beware of internal rot. Aunt Maddalena assumes that her longtime neighbors in "the city of the mind" lack the pep to succeed professionally.[8] Her assumption enriches the novel. The counter-rhythm set going by the interaction of the haves and the have-nots had already caused some shocking reversals in works as different as Theodore Dreiser's *Sister Carrie* (1900) and Jean Genet's *The Maids* (1954). A. S. Byatt might have had Fitzgerald's appreciation of the reversibility of personal fortunes under capitalism in mind when she praised *Innocence* for "the completeness of its Italianness."[9]

A character in *Human Voices* says, "I've never met a man . . . who didn't have to work hard" (102). What has kept him from meeting slackers like Milo North of *The Bookshop*, Maurice of *Offshore*, or Boney Lewis of *At Freddie's* is chance, given their frequency in Fitzgerald's work. More important to note here is that even though these ne'er-do-wells take life from Desmond Fitzgerald, they all look and act differently from each other. The same may be said for Giancarlo Ridolfi, whose noble Tuscan family Emily Leider calls "long in lineage . . . but short in cash."[10] Giancarlo might have dodged this plight. Though sent to England and Switzerland to study business, he never made money. His American wife left him and their two-year-old daughter fifteen years before we meet him (in a parody of *Madam Butterfly*, which he saw as a boy [12]). Everything is slipping away from him. The prestige he enjoyed both as a cavalry officer and a count is long gone. At the time he comes before us, at age sixty-five, he has lost so much faith in himself (like that other time-waster, Pierce Connell of *Freddie's*) that he directs most of his efforts to avoiding trouble; any clash of wills, he fears, will cave him in. It is apt that he lives in "the second-floor flat of the decrepit palazzo" (15) called Limbo. This half-lifer shuns moral decisions. Instead, he does what comes easiest, choosing lines of action that tax him the least.

The Count, as he still likes to be called, lives with his older sister, Maddalena, largely because, like him, she made an international marriage that went bust; her effete English husband dropped her when he discovered she was not rich. This loss led to another. Mad is missing two fingers. A thief sitting behind her in a bus cut off the third and fourth fingers of her right hand to steal her diamond ring. Fitzgerald's keen sense of the absurd, as is conveyed by this jarring note, also fuels one of her leading ideas: that Mad's stolen ring came from her birdwatching husband and that its theft gave her a bird-like claw knit with the dismemberment motif dominating *Innocence*. People are cut off from the people, places, and things that define them. Neither Mad's husband nor the Count's wife (divorce being forbidden in Italy) will come to the wedding of the Count's daughter to Salvatore, a man severed from *his* roots in southern Italy. The severing of Mad's ringless finger serves another thematic end. It shows that cruelty, though a natural, if regrettable, human impulse, must be held in check. Once loosened, it will strike out wildly, flouting not merely decency but even humanity.

Fitzgerald's use of the phrase, "good intentions" (165), recalls Bernard Shaw's saying in *The Revolutionist's Handbook,* his epilogue to *Man and Superman* (1903), that good intentions comprise the paving stones of hell. Fitzgerald ascribes much of the damage performed in the novel to innocence (the Contessina Chiara Ridolfi attended the Holy Innocents Convent School in England). Never a concept-driven writer, she always seeks realism's patient surfaces and its immersion in verifiable details. She also knows when to probe. The book opens with a legend about some sixteenth-century owners of the Ricordanza, the Florentine villa that still belongs to the Ridolfi family. The sixteenth-century Ridolfis were midgets. To convince their daughter that she was normal, they miniaturized the villa, redoing stairways, doors, and tables to midget scale. All the visitors to the villa, moreover, like the governess, the doctor, and the notary, had to be midgets, as well, and, in still another love-driven ruse, the girl could not leave the estate.

To amuse her, a dwarf came to the villa to perform as a clown. But he cracked his skull trying to make her laugh; to define a person or a family by their most glaring abnormality causes pain. But this lesson was lost on the Ridolfi parents. They soon invited to the villa "a little midget girl" (9) named Gemma da Terracina as a playmate for their daughter. A sudden, unexpected growth spurt on Gemma's part tallies the cost of denying the truth. To maintain social harmony, her host family decided to blind Gemma, who might have already been deaf and dumb; she could never know how much she differed in size from her daily companions. Now Fitzgerald never says that Gemma's eyes were put out or that, in another innocent, but vile, attempt to protect her, her legs were severed at the knees. But she *does* reaffirm in a different key her belief, first stated in *Bookshop* (in a paragraph that opens with the words, "She blinded herself"), that the world consists of exterminators and exterminees (34).

This division is handled with greater detail and depth in *Innocence*. Since the 1978 publication of *Bookshop*, Fitzgerald's imagination had grown more subversive, and the ideas it serves hit in at oblique, often painful angles. Joan Acocella noted this change when she called the biography, *Charlotte Mew and Her Friends* (1984) "a break in Fitzgerald's career": "Suddenly in the late novels," the first of which is *Innocence*, "there are scenes not just of defeat but of actual horror."[11] The horror Acocella has noted rankles all the more for several reasons: it is often enacted to promote harmony; it is more natural than abnormal; it is thematic as well as scenic. In *Innocence,* which features a character who works at S. Agostino's Hospital in Florence (40), Fitzgerald never endorses outright St. Augustine's belief in original sin and human depravity. A tacit endorsement, though, seeps through her trademark combination of subtlety and shock. And the seepage starts in the book's first chapter. A sixteenth-century doctor is paraphrasing Machiavelli to the midget-size Count Ridolfi: "Nature has implanted in everything a hidden energy which gives its own resemblance to everything that springs from it, making it like itself" (8). Effects follow relentlessly and inescapably from the causes they always resemble. An organism's origins, says Machiavelli, pervade its every aspect; every feature of the organism reveals its parent stock. Machiavelli uses as his example of genetic descent the lemon tree, the twigs and leaves of which all smell lemony. He might have visited the Ricordanza, a place memorable for its lemon trees; as in 1568, when the book begins, the Ricordanza of 1955–56 swarms with lemon trees and "their bitter green smell" (65).

This same bitterness suffuses both the property and its proprietors. The Ridolfis have lost their money. Giancarlo drives an ancient Fiat, and the marble statues in his rundown flat look "yellow as old teeth" (15). The wine from the family vineyards has never regained the classico status it lost in 1932 in a ruling that cut its market value by twenty-five percent. This loss is still felt. As in *Bookshop,* an early chapter of *Innocence* shows a dressmaker insulting a woman. A Florentine couturier whose "ramshackle factory" makes dresses so elegant and exclusive that it has no nameplate or doorbell refuses to design the Contessina Chiara's wedding dress, a setback that leaves this beauty who savors the "cold bitter green smell" of her family's lemon grove "crying bitterly" (27, 109, 140). The bitterness spreads. The aristocratic Chiara's marriage to a doctor with "the commonest name in Italy," whose southern hometown "was not beautiful and could never have been visited by anyone in search of beauty" (82, 112), harks to postwar Italy's social mobility and democratic mind-set. In the new meritocracy, a hard worker of humble roots can renew a faded blueblood family that will, in turn, exalt *him*. But this process never occurs in *Innocence*, proof of which is the death of the baby conceived by Salvatore Rossi and Chiara. Machiavelli's statement on the spread of essences (8) has ramified. The attributes of organisms stay within their bounds. They also obey fixed laws. Grafting a lemon branch upon the trunk of an apple tree will yield only death. A character in *The Beginning of Spring*, Fitzgerald's next novel after *Innocence*, says, "It's unkind to ask anyone for more than they have to give," and, in *Innocence*, Chiara will worry about harming people "by wanting them to do what they couldn't" (154, 191).

She and Salvatore remain dazzled by the sexual magnetism that first brought them together. Like Flaubert's Emma Bovary and Natasha Rostov of Tolstoy's *War and Peace* (1865–69), Chiara falls in love at first sight in the presence of music. Meeting the twenty-nine-year-old Salvatore during the intermission of a Brahms concert, she is gripped straightaway by a force that tramples her civilized reserve:

Chiara gave the doctor her hand.
"You enjoyed the Brahms?" he asked.

She looked at him politely, but in wonder.
"Of course not." (32)

Her avoidance of the safe, socially correct answer emboldens Salvatore. Minutes later, he invites her to step out with him into the "warm rain." He frames his invitation in terms harsher than her Berkshire convent school education had prepared her for: "Come outside, put out your tongue, taste it [viz., the rain]" (33). Come outside she does. But the dampness of the dress she wears for the second half of the concert vexes her to the same degree that Hannah Graves felt vexed wearing a "limp dishrag" (90) of a dress to a London playhouse in *Freddie's*. That the vexation "stayed with her [viz., Hannah] longer than the memory of her boyfriend Johnny [Brannon]'s lovemaking" (*Freddie's*, 90) displays once again the grief provoked by sex in Fitzgerald.

It also looks ahead to the grief that will pound Chiara. She and Salvatore are introduced by a patient of Salvatore's called Mimi Limentani. In line with the relentless causality driving the novel, Mimi will also attend their wedding (147). The bitter green smell exuded by the Ricordanza's limonaria, or lemon grove, both carries a great distance and settles into whatever it touches. This vigor must be dealt with; the phrase, "bitter green" (65). conveys a force reminiscent of Keats's mingling of sense experiences in his "Ode to a Nightingale." A creature of instinct as well as a convent-schooled blueblood, Chiara thrives in the lemon grove. She spent her happiest childhood moments there (109), and its tang sparkles her blood. Rather than enter the villa directly with Salvatore to have sex with him for the first time, she takes him on a roundabout course through the lemon trees.

The sex that follows the couple's passage to the upstairs bedroom is not depicted. In fact, the couple is not seen entering either the bedroom or the villa. They need not be. The narrative of Chiara's deflowering has already been conveyed by the lemon symbolism. Fitzgerald does depict the deflowering's aftermath. Brief as it is, this scene portends the sadness of the marriage that will follow it. Just as Chiara savored the sharp smell of the lemon grove she walked through with Salvatore en route to her bedroom, so does she bask in "a sensation of purity and calm" (113) during the afterglow of sex. She resembles that other seventeen-year-old, Annie Asra of *Human Voices*, in being on easy, comfortable terms with her heart. No mistake or stain upon her honor, her lovemaking with Salvatore chimes with both her private and her ancestral past. Salvatore, meanwhile, "unsettled" (113) by her serenity, has been thinking about real estate; he must sell some property in Mazzata before building a house for himself and Chiara in Florence. The beauty of the moment has fled. Sex, even love, he has redirected to a series of other exchanges, many of them financial. No sooner has love touched him than money cheapens it.

No surprise, this. Salvatore has never equated sex with joy. As accomplished as he is, he lacks the self-acceptance to enjoy life's greatest blessings. For the past three years he has been spending one night a week with a local dressmaker. The arrangement pleases him. Because Marta lives near his clinic, she is convenient. Like her humble job, her being eight years his senior also disqualifies her as a wife. His affair with her, regardless of its heat, takes place within brackets. The money he dutifully gives her, finally, ratifies his immunity to her, downgrading the raw primitive force of their bond to a financial deal. He feels safe. He can enjoy sex with Marta because he has tamed it with both money and that trusty foe of spontaneity, a fixed routine. But barriers can fail him. A poem inscribed on the stone gates of the Ricordanza conveys the self-contempt the lovesick Salvatore feels after dawdling outside of Chiara's home instead of treating patients:

> Maggior dolore è ben la Ricordanza
> Senti' dir lor con sì alti sospiri—
> O nell' amaro inferno amena stanza?

The tercet is a weak *contaminato* from Dante's *Inferno* 5.121, and *Purgatorio* 19.74, the latter verbatim. The third line, with its incongruous sarcasm, comes from a Dante imitator. Here is a translation of the lot:

> A greater pain indeed is to remember—
> I heard them say with resounding sighs—
> Or rather a pleasant room in bitter hell?

"La Ricordanza," besides being the name of the Ridolfi estate, also means remembrance, memory, and reminder, which explains Fitzgerald's reference to bitterness ("amaro," which sounds like "amore," the Italian word for love, in the tercet's last line). Salvatore's awareness of the "bitter green smell" (65) drifting from the nearby lemon grove as he reads the inscription restates Fitzgerald's warning of the dangers of sexual love. Eros sustains life. But it has also put the self-denying Salvatore at odds with himself. And the ascendancy of lemons, with their caustic jungle shimmer, makes us wonder if the cost of sustaining life can be too high. Later in the action, a gardener, speaking of lemons as a friend to the stomach, says, "Cannibals . . . use lemon juice, without it they could not digest human flesh" (199).

What is to be gained by supporting cannibalism? The tiny obscure detail that invites this question evokes the shakiness of life's moral foundations. The same inoffensive, prosaic lemon juice found in nearly every kitchen also fosters one of mankind's most shocking taboos. Salvatore's use of reason and duty to stave off such awkward truths is breaking him down. Like Dostoevsky's Ivan Karamazov, he indulges the wild, infantile, murderous impulses of the unconscious. His energy, mental quickness, and dedication no match for his demons, he is the perfect hero of his paranoid age. This hero of his own drama soon finds himself playing the villain in someone else's. So much for the bloom of innocence. Even his heroism runs the reefs of self-disgust. Freud's *Civilization and Its Discontents* posits guilt as the outcome of suppressing our aggressive instincts in order to live in society. We redirect our aggressions inward in the form of a punishing superego. Thus the emergence of the inhibiting, sometimes paralyzing guilt that makes us feel like helpless misfits.

Nor do the repressed always return to the fold. Even though Salvatore has a prestigious job and a comfortable fixed residence, his exile is chronic. The passage of time has deprived him of a home to return to. He last appears before us in transit. He is preparing to visit the convalescing Chiara. But his preparations rankle. His reunion with the wife he has been living apart from for several weeks—itself a danger sign—may never take place. The following entry from Fitzgerald's research notes to *Innocence* infers that he flew in the face of his deepest needs by sending her away, to begin with: "They [Salvatore and Chiara] loved each other to the point of pain and could hardly bear to separate each morning."[12] Weak of purpose, he has already set out for the rest home where Chiara was staying but lost sight of his goal when an imagined slight convinces him to kill himself instead. Fitzgerald sums up his anxiety thus: "Things might upset him which simply wouldn't be noticed at all by the rest of the world" (181). Had he developed the social conscience of his Marxist father, he would be less self-absorbed (though he might have balked at his government's support of the Soviet invasion of Hungary in 1956).[13]

A possible direction for this smart, prickly outsider lies in his foil and confidante, Gentilini, a fellow doctor of forty-five whose job, wife, and four kids sap so much of his vim that he has none left for the devious motive-seeking that is chewing up Salvatore. Salvatore never calls him by his first name, perhaps because he does not know it. His "one reliable friend" (139) may not be all that reliable—or close. Salvatore does keep people at bay. Despite his medical degree and thriving practice, he has remained, in his mind, a provincial southerner whose guard stays up because he does not have much to give. Perhaps he doomed himself to loneliness by rejecting his roots, always a danger according to Gramsci (120). His low self-esteem, melancholy, and unconscious sadism having descended from the Jewish Joey Blatt of *Freddie's* (whose parents, like Gemme da Terracina, may have been deaf and dumb), he has been masking his truculence behind a rigid sense of right and wrong.[14] His persona serves him well in his clinic. With his patients, he is always comforting, caring, and reassuring. But this warmth deserts him away from the job. Taking one step outside the door of his clinic bares this neurologist's frayed nerves. So conflictive is he that he subverts his best chances. Disobeying his deepest wishes, he insults Chiara when she visits him. Although twelve years his junior, she surpasses him in patience, balance, and heart knowledge. Her nerves are also steadier than his, as makes sense in someone well attuned to her ancestral past. When asked if, despite having sent her away, he wants to see her, she answers, "He doesn't know that he does" (71).

His decision early in life to do the opposite of what is expected of him has been tearing him apart. First of all, the contrarian lives by dumb opposition rather than by judging options on their merits; he cannot choose creatively. Next, he wears himself down bucking the flow of life. The simplest decision ties him in knots: "Everything that he had done since he had met Chiara had run counter to his own resolutions for the conduct of his life, which, in turn, had been specially designed to run counter to what was expected of him" (63–64). Frustrated, he smashes everything capable of being smashed, including himself. Praise offends him (175). That he is a neurologist suffering from bad nerves defines his innocence. Unluckily for Chiara, he occupies the outer arc of passion, where eros and violence meet. Twice during her association with him she is without a key (72, 177). At book's end, she is living away from home by herself. As the death of her baby with Salvatore shows, their rickety union threatens Italy's rich history and established traditions. Perhaps she is safer at her rest home. His puritanical aversion to life has made him a desperate combination of superiority and self-loathing. It may have also put him closer to cannibalism than he suspects.

His crisis emits shock waves. As if Chiara's stay in a rest home has caused a virus of homelessness at a time when Italy is enjoying a building boom, a shelter for the homeless later loses all its inhabitants (211). Even though not rationally traceable to Salvatore, this evacuation hews to the spirit of discontinuity and desperation he whips up around himself. It also has religious overtones. Three times in the course of the book, he walks away

Stumbling into Geopolitics / 199

from a meal he was invited to share with others (56, 108, 176). As in Virginia Woolf's *Mrs. Dalloway* (1925) and *To the Lighthouse* (1927), the meal symbolizes the feast or communion, in which the sharing of food sustains life. Salvatore is a doctor who cannot heal himself. His rejection of the feast reflects the same apostasy he displayed when he scolded his beloved Chiara for coming to his clinic at closing time to have dinner with him. His demons have swamped him, as is seen in the frenzy with which he refuses the prize he covets most, a pathology only heretofore dramatized in English fiction in Rebecca West's *The Fountain Overflows* (1956).

His life soured when, at age ten, he visited his father's idol, Antonio Gramsci, in the Roman hospital where the communist leader, "always under guard"[15] since his arrest by Mussolini,[16] had been placed. The sight of Gramsci repelled Salvatore. Wasted by tuberculosis of the spine and chronic illness, this puny crippled author of *The Prison Notebooks* (1975) is both uglier and more deformed than any animal or corpse Salvatore had ever seen. John Gross of the *New York Times* has described the effect of this shocking encounter upon the boy: "He decided there and then he would never have anything to do with politics. He also resolved to become a doctor, and to avoid becoming emotionally dependent or wholly committed to another person."[17]

Politics he can shun. Chiara he can't. But when his colleague Gentilini offers to arrange a meeting between him and her, he recoils, hiding behind the bogus romantic idea that if he and Chiara are destined to meet, no practical steps need be taken to bring them together. To actively pursue a love bond would violate its purity, even though he knows how much he needs one. His taking leave from Gentilini in part one, chapter 16 conveys his conflictiveness: "Salvatore broke off, and abruptly held out his hand. 'Think of me as a cripple, if you like, don't turn from me, take my hand'" (53). Rattled between an angry pride and the urge to surrender, he speaks more truly than he knows. The crippled Gramsci had shaken his hand in Rome's Quisisana Hospital twenty years earlier (43). By offering his own hand to Gentilini, he has identified with the most repulsive man he has ever met.

How can he expect to be happy? A handshake later forced on him by an elderly disciple of Gramsci gives him the nerve-racking sensation of holding something "as cold and dry as a hen's foot" (117). But Chiara's Aunt Mad's right hand, with its two missing fingers, also resembles a hen's foot. The ties joining the people in *Innocence* are shown again and again to be more problematical than we had thought. The mutilation or dismemberment motif that joined Aunt Mad to Gemma da Terracina, the child whose visit to la Ricordanza might have cost her her eyes and her legs, has metastasized. The "hidden energy" (8) Machiavelli found in lemon trees back in chapter 1, where Gemma was also introduced, is claiming new victims. Less than five feet tall, the toothless hunchback Gramsci harks to the midget owners of la Ricordanza.[18] But rather than inflicting pain, he is savaged both internally by disease and externally by a government ruling that has forbidden the doctors at Quisisana Hospital to treat him.[19]

A potential force for good in this grimmest of all Fitzgerald novels to date is Cesare Ridolfi, manager of Valsassino, the family vineyard. Like Ed Voysey of *Freddie's,* he does not read much. And even though he speaks English, he prefers silence. He spurns an offer to speak at his cousin Chiara's wedding, and, equally reluctant to express himself in writing, rather than send a letter he has composed he tears it up. First seen "sitting absolutely motionless and solid in front of two piles of paper" (19), he also has a deliberateness that contrasts admirably with Salvatore's fret and frenzy. This vintner who is usually seen either sitting at his table or working in the fields (e.g., 185) is a Tolstoyan man of the earth who disdains intellectual systems. He has aligned himself with the cyclical rhythms that govern his routine. When he does talk, he cuts to essentials quickly and uses few manual gestures. The productiveness and efficiency that stem from his personal economy make it apt that he turn up whenever he is needed, such as when he helps revive a fainting victim at Chiara and Salvatore's wedding.

Also on hand to help Mrs. Gentilini is Chiara's friend and confidante, Lavinia Barnes. An English classmate of Chiara's at Holy Innocents, Barney, like Florence Green of *Bookshop* and Annie Asra of *Voices*, is the voice of truth. But whereas Annie and Florence were small, Barney towers over everyone. In fact, she rarely enters a scene without some reference being made to her bigness (e.g., 80, 154). This bigness, which gains emphasis from the midget heritage of the Ricordanza, taints her honesty. She is a big woman with a loud mouth. Her innocence inheres in the right she has arrogated to herself to judge people to their faces, to give them unwanted advice, and to tell them where they come up short. No subject is off limits to her; no sensibility too tender to be spared. She is forever reminding Chiara that her family is broke, and she accuses the Count, now that the Italian cavalry he served with has been disbanded, of redundancy. It is no wonder that the Count, "not used to quite so much straightforwardness" (81), leaves town during the time Barney is Chiara's houseguest. "Innocence is a quality Mr. Trevor highly prizes," says Fitzgerald in her review of William Trevor's *Excursions in the Real World*.[20] She, in opposition, follows in the tradition of Henry James, Elizabeth Bowen, and Graham Greene by writing a novel she even calls *Innocence* that shows the havoc innocence can cause. To underscore her moral position, she sets her novel in Italy's premier center of learning and artistic activity, a place whose residents might be expected to have shed their ingenuousness.

In Barney's case, she even yokes the dangers of innocence to those of feminism. More is the pity because of women's subordinate place in 1956 Italy. Many Italian men at the time clung to the Latin schoolboy machismo that preens itself by downgrading women. One grumbles that women are so rearguard in their thinking that they would have us living in caves, an idiocy repeated by Salvatore when he sees himself being bested in a duel of wits with a woman (120, 139). Even Gramsci, that champion of social equality, allegedly believed that "all Italian men look for in marriage is . . . a hen with something substantial in the Post Office Savings" (202). Belittling women may even be a national pastime. Chiara's appearance in two crucial scenes without her house key (72, 177) implies female powerlessness and disenfranchisement. Yet hens have claws, which can scratch away at male self-esteem. Women prove their value in *Innocence*. When Chiara claims that Salvatore wants her even though he "doesn't know that he does" (73), she is seeing past the fury that wrecked his judgment when he scolded her for coming to his clinic. The nerve-racked Salvatore has forgotten the healing power of female gentleness and compassion he knew as a boy. In a Roman hospital full of male doctors, he had intuited that "a woman was needed" (45) when he saw a collapsing Gramsci spilling body fluids.

But no help would have come from Barney. Even when asked to lift Mrs. Gentilini to her feet after her fainting spell at the wedding, Barney must first moralize on the evils of drink (152). Cesare, on the other hand, diagnoses Mrs. Gentilini's problem (she drank no alcohol) and then treats it quietly and efficiently. This contrast describes Barney's self-righteousness as an exaggeration of faults commonly ascribed to men. Barney has been outdoing Sir John of *Golden Child* and Joey Blatt of *Freddie's* in acquisitiveness and self-promotion. But this voracity has not starved her heart. Having shared with Cesare the toil of carrying Mrs. Gentilini to a place where she can rest, she soon falls in love with him. Just as the ten-year-old Salvatore knew that Gramsci's survival depended upon a woman's help, so does Barney value in Cesare qualities she herself lacks, like patience, generosity, and the ability to suspend judgment in a crisis.

He shocks this termagant by not responding to her declaration of love. Whereas the smallest trifle upsets Salvatore, Cesare's composure will quiet any flap. But it is little more than an animal composure, as if Fitzgerald, the widow of an alcoholic, would give a vintner heroic stature. She says of Cesare, while he is listening to Barney's marriage proposal, "There he sat with his hands on the [dining-room] table, as though locked to the wood" (185). She carefully avoids making him a Lawrencian primitive whose dark virility will revive the sleeping beauty. Cesare tends his farm well, and he has the social instincts to divert a crisis. But at times his stolidness invites comparisons to the wood he seems continuous with. Part two, chapter 32, begins thus: "Cesare was sitting at one end of the dinner table . . . the same end as usual, doing nothing . . . and appropriately thinking of nothing" (218). For all his skills, he prefers to idle his time away, Fitzgerald having avoided seating him at his workbench. His listening to a radio broadcast of the music of the early composer Monteverdi (1567–1643) implies an indifference to what passes for progress in the arts, and his impassiveness recalls Tolstoy's statement in *War and Peace* (Tolstoy is mentioned twice in *Innocence* [105]) that the true Russian knows nothing and wants to know nothing because the truths governing life, though capable of being lived, defy thought.

Another dinner-table scene, advisedly placed in the book's last chapter, again uses contrast to sharpen dramatic action. The same furniture that comforts Cesare vexes his visitor, Salvatore. Salvatore is shocked to find his host content and comfortable sitting by himself. But Cesare has always enjoyed the place where he has worked and lived for decades. His opposite number, Salvatore, having moved from Mazzata to Bologna and then to Florence, cannot relax anywhere. So stressed is he, in fact, that he believes his death would help Chiara. Ignoring this hysterical outburst, Cesare tells him not to worry; he predicts that Italy's coming membership in the European Union will legalize divorce in Italy in twenty-five years. Again he uses humor to divert the dramatic drive instigated by Salvatore by discussing whether insurance firms pay benefits to the survivors of suicides. But, thinking beyond the diversionary tactics he has mustered to calm Salvatore, he silently agrees with his guest that his cousin would be better off without him. He gives Salvatore a shotgun, advisedly one used to kill "vermin, rats, and snakes" (277), loads it, and walks away.

A phone call from Chiara—playing the interceding female of myth—stays Salvatore's hand. As in the fiction of Henry James, a great act has been contemplated and then renounced. The call, from Chiara's rest home in Riomaggiore, reroutes Salvatore into the mainstream of life. But he is still fighting the flow. For the first time that day, he had forgotten to make his daily phone call to Chiara. Then he tells Cesare, "We can't go on like this" (224), alluding to the doubt, contradiction, and desperation lacing daily life. Cesare, having already unloaded the shotgun he had given to Salvatore, replies, "Yes, we can go on like this. . . . We can go on like this for the rest of our lives" (224); life's mess and muddle has to be taken as a given. The effect of this wisdom upon Salvatore is unclear. He is still apart from Chiara. Though he is planning to see her the next morning, any trifle could distract him from making the trip. And even were he to rejoin her, his petulance could spark the same rage that marred the Jameses' reunion in *Offshore* and parted them forever.

Naturally, such a blow—if it is a blow—could not be blamed on Chiara. Salvatore has not learned to take life as it comes. Accustomed to imposing himself (Fitzgerald keeps him off the page with Barney, lest one of them kill the other), he has overlooked the value of silence and inaction. Cesare outpaces him in this regard. But solitary, reluctant to speak or write down his feelings, and even monkish in his devotion to the farm (a relative sees him "joining a contemplative Order" [101]), he lacks political force. He sustains the status quo rather than pressing for change. A Marxist's nightmare, he disregards questions of social justice and reform—no idle observation since Fitzgerald's next novel, *The Beginning of Spring*, takes place while Russia's communists are discussing revolution, some of them within earshot of the book's main figures.

He stays a bachelor, too, even though he does not take monastic vows. His inverted mirror image, Barney, the only person in the novel taller than he (150), might profit from heeding his tranquility. (In 1999, Fitzgerald contrasted idleness with the "busy tranquility" she found in Jane Austen's *Emma*.)[21] Bossy, carping, and always ready to take charge, Barney would crush the self-image of anybody if given the chance. Nobody is safe in her presence. In a heartbeat, she would shrink all of her associates into moral versions of the midget-owners of la Ricordanza in the sixteenth century.

An idiosyncratic book, *Innocence* is sometimes whimsical and often shocking and perverse. Its densely connected plot also gratifies our desire to be told a story, to be held in suspense, and to know what happens. What makes it such a complex, knowledgeable, and readable study of the darker motives is Fitzgerald's attunement to the subtle inflections of personal styles of thinking. She has the intuition, the vocabulary, and particularly the syntax to record highly instinctive drives that border the unconscious. As D. M. Thomas showed in *The White Hotel* (1981), Freud read human history as a tug between Eros and Thanatos, the urge to create and the urge to destroy. These drives, Freud contends, are always linked. In Salvatore Rossi's case, they are also kindled by a motif used in Dickens's *Bleak House,* the human subtext of financial exchange. Now Fitzgerald knows Tuscany's weather and topography, its soil and architecture, together with the streets and districts of its capital, Florence. But she also understands that 1956 Florence was a small town as well as a cultural mecca. As has been seen, Salvatore has been waging an affaire with the local dressmaker Marta on his own terms. But if the money he gives her in exchange for weekly sex voids any claim she may have on his heart, it still leaves him prey to the upsurge of negative energy.

His one recorded visit to Marta is sexless. He has come to break with her because of his recent engagement to Chiara, and, to show his goodwill, he makes her a generous parting gift. To his shock, she counts the money twice, confirming his view of the three-year affair as a financial arrangement. He feels flat-footed and outclassed. His dismay builds. Nowhere near tears and with her lovely hair gleaming seductively, Marta recalls seeing Chiara "crying bitterly" (140) on the day she and Aunt Mad left Parenti the couturier in distress after hearing his refusal to make the Contessina's wedding dress. A part-timer at Parenti's, Marta happened to be working there the day of the Ridolfis' visit.

But if Marta's witnessing of this episode stuns Salvatore, her telling him that she apprenticed for Parenti twenty-one years earlier, when she was Chiara's age (140), might have sent him through the roof. Marta, though, has followed those other wise Fitzgerald heroines, Annie Asra and Freddie, in withholding vital knowledge, perhaps to keep a weapon in reserve. Suffice it that she has dissolved the distance between the paid sex she had with Salvatore and the sacrament of marital sex. Her silence wins her another victory. Not only does the unwelcome identity that Marta pointed out to Salvatore vex him; it also snags his memory. When he learns on his wedding night that Marta made Chiara's honeymoon dress, he loses grip. Or, rather, he redirects his grip to the dress, which, by dint of Marta's sturdy needlework, resists his attempt to shred it. The eventual destruction of the dress takes the place of sex, as is seen in the following exchange between the honeymooners as they view the scraps of cloth littering the floor of their room, Salvatore sounding like a bridegroom who fears he may have been duped:

> Salvatore looked at her. "Your hand is bleeding."
> "I know. I don't mind."
> "Why don't you mind?"

"It doesn't hurt much."

"Why doesn't it hurt much?" he asked furiously. (157–58)

More comes apart on this wedding night than Chiara's dress. In another fateful denial of the feast, or sacrament, the couple cannot take their wedding dinner; the destruction of the dress has left Chiara with a wardrobe of clothes, all of which would violate the dress code of the hotel's dining room. The miscarriage that follows and Chiara's ensuing trip by herself to the riverside (Fitzgerald's mother, Christina, also vainly sought health near water [*Knox Brothers*, 208], as did Charlotte Mew's sister Caroline Anne [*Charlotte Mew*, 202]) both stem logically from the wedding-night debacle. The newlyweds do not appear on the page together during the last fourteen chapters of *Innocence*. But Chiara may need still more time away from Salvatore. His deriding of the sixteenth-century legend of Gemma da Terracina as "superstition" (161) betrays his ignorance of her. Formed in large part by the spirit of the Ricordanza, Chiara is a creature of legend. She might have even chosen the "giantess" (80) Barney as a best friend because she identifies with tiny Gemma. Or perhaps with her forebears, Gemma's supposed oppressors? Healthy eighteen-year-old women do not usually miscarry. If inherited guilt prompted Chiara to connive at her own miscarriage, then Salvatore may have as much to fear from her as she does from him in what looks increasingly like a marriage from hell.

The lack of hard evidence to support this reading should not rule it out. *Innocence* abounds in good moments, many of them reaching us indirectly or exploding without warning. Richard Eder has discussed this highly original, thematically right technique: "Dialogue consists of simultaneous monologues. Every voice has to make itself heard against enormous competition: the weather, the state of the crops and whatever else is going on in a person's mind."[22] As in Samuel Beckett, the discontinuities and disconnects pitting Fitzgerald's 1986 novel turn the mind to apocalypse. The mind remains active and engaged. An epigram fueled by parallel phrasing sends an episode in an unforeseen direction: "Politics and business can be settled by influence, cooks and doctors can only be promoted on their skill" (49). There is also the good joke to remind us of God's sense of humor. Of an orphanage run by the elderly Fitzgerald says, "The toothless . . . co-exist with the toothless" (14).

More dramatically, scenes and even chapters stop before rounding to resolution. In fact, *Innocence* shows Fitzgerald learning and then mastering the device of the strident, off-key tag line in both narration and dialogue. By chapter count, the book reaches its halfway point at the end of part one, chapter 37. Barney has just recounted the sad tale of her breakup with a man she thought she loved (which took place, interestingly, over dinner). Her grandmother, speaking from outside the room in which Barney is confiding in Chiara, mentions the laughter she thought she heard on her side of the closed door. Then, in the chapter's last sentence, Chiara says, "We're not laughing, I promise you" (127). The conversation that ended a moment before, in which she witnessed "the fall of the great Barney, whose judgment had for so long seemed beyond dispute" (126), *was* no laughing matter. Barney has ignored the advice she had been peddling so freely, leaving Chiara without a reliable confidante with whom she can discuss her puzzling, sometimes painful bond with Salvatore. She is now on her own. Her off-tone concluding words to the chapter that peaks in her revelation point the action in a direction different from the one where we thought it was heading.

Throughout, narrative selection keeps sharpening our attention. Instead of describing the wedding of Chiara and Salvatore, for instance, Fitzgerald displays some photos of bygone wedding dinners before cutting, more ominously, first, to a discussion between the bride's father and a friend about their bowel habits (146, 150) and, next, to Mrs. Gentilini's fainting spell. The denial of cohesiveness and follow-through will continue to slow or divert narrative drive. A character appears for the first time on the book's last page (224), and, thanks to a non sequitur he voices, saves Salvatore's life. Fitzgerald's flair for the jarring detail once again reaffirms life's resistance to rational formulas, laws, and, as is seen in the broken international marriages of the Count and Aunt Mad, literary models.

It is this same jumbled, recalcitrant life that Fitzgerald revels in. Like a Chekhov play, *Innocence,* with its occasional time glides, eschews a clear beginning, middle, and end, focusing instead on the shapeless, fragmented middle. The love interest is played down, discussed from a distance, or refracted through an encompassing cultural drama of which it is symptomatic. The lovers spend little time together on the page. Climaxes are shunned. Thus Chiara and Salvatore are shown walking through the limonaria en route to her bedroom, and they do not reappear to us until she annoys him with a postcoital laugh. Nor should we feel cheated. The fuck that Fitzgerald does not describe interrupted but briefly an ongoing, deep-rooted reality defined by the green bitterness of the limonaria and Salvatore's surliness. Salvatore's grump represents an outer edge of this reality—if it is on the chart at all. Having renounced his own heritage by coming north only to discount the heritage of his wife, he has put himself out of step with life. Edge and center have switched places on him. Yet his marriage has also swept all of the book's other characters into the force field created by his neurosis; as in the poltergeist scene in *Bookshop,* two of them are bracing for whatever shocks may follow. Complex and strange, absurd and painful, *Innocence* provides a revealing, if unsettling, back entrance into the human condition.

CHAPTER 10

Degrees of Exile

The Beginning of Spring carries forward from *Innocence* Fitzgerald's growing interest in foreign cultures, an interest that will crest in *The Blue Flower,* which takes place in Germany in the late eighteenth century. Unfolding in 1913, *Spring* depicts a world more familiar than that in which the poet Novalis (1772–1801) spent his youth because, among other things, it frames anew a question that has been puzzling westerners for some two hundred years, since Peter the Great's (1672–1725) conquest of Sweden made Russia a major power. Namely, is Russia part of Europe, or does it have its own special outlook and mission? Fitzgerald's 1988 novel poses the question thoughtfully. While including examples of Russia's storied simplicity and intrinsic goodness, it also portrays in mystical terms "the magnificent and ramshackle country . . . where nature represented not freedom but law" (177). The notorious Rasputin is discussed (49, 61), and the annual rituals impelled by the beginning of spring forge bonds tighter than those imposed by social or political change. At the same time, change must be dealt with. Fitzgerald's nuanced, historically correct portrait shows business crossing international frontiers as her Frank Reid, the owner of a Moscow print works, deals with firms in Finland and Japan. Frank even has to hire the company's first cost accountant to keep pace with new developments in bookkeeping.

But he still has a powerful, inscrutable bureaucracy to appease. Like Great Britain, Russia stands apart from Europe. But whereas Britain has a history of greatness and a tradition of civilized, parliamentary government, czarist Russia's blend of barbarism, cheap mysticism, and upperclass corruption made it a perfect target for the lunacy of foreign-imposed communism. The major crises in the politically stable worlds of Balzac, Dickens, and Flaubert were private. Russia, on the other hand, faced threats that could shred the fabric of society, crush family life, and rend a longstanding religious cohesion. Not that the Romanovs built a healthy organic society around religion; czarist Russia never developed an educated middle class with political rights. Instead of building an open society nourished by a spirit of cooperation, compromise, and mutual respect, Russia always put her imperialist goals first. This hegemony blocked the formation of an open society. Nor will economic efficiency and civic leadership come from a church obsessed by apocalyptic hopes or an intelligentsia seeking salvation either abroad or in the peasantry. Survival in such a milieu demands cunning. Anyone dealing with the Russian bureaucracy had to learn one important lesson—to observe the canons of protocol and guile. A slip or a misplaced word could spark an incident. Thus Frank, a dab hand at the art of self-protection, keeps a bottle of caraway-flavored vodka in his office desk "exclusively for the use of the police" (113).

Fitzgerald, though, sides with history against the Marxist belief that free-market capitalism would banish (rather than resurrect under a different name) the corrupt old regime. The workers' revolution broke in a nation that lagged behind Germany and Great Britain in factory production. And it failed to replace the traditions it had overthrown, like the blessing and baking of cheesecake on Easter Saturday (164). The Bolsheviks who promised freedom and equality delivered torture and death instead; in the 1930s, Stalin would engineer a famine to wipe out landowners. The Fitzgerald of *Spring* follows her usual practice of siting her action on a border. But she introduces a new urgency. By setting *Spring* in 1913, she drops her characters both in the shadow of the First World War and between a selfish regime that ignored their civil rights and a Soviet killing machine that would equal Nazi Germany in cruelty.

Some would withstand the pressure. A proper sense of community and a respect for family values still prevail in Moscow, Fitzgerald's treatment of which won high praise from Anita Brookner: "The novel is about Moscow, and not only about Moscow, but about Moscow in 1913. With astonishing virtuosity, Mrs. Fitzgerald has mastered a city, a landscape, and a vanished time."[1] This praise was standard. Jonathan Penner hailed the novel as "a remarkably vivid portrait of pre-revolutionary Moscow."[2] The flavorsome period atmosphere Penner and Brookner both admire inheres largely in the long-established belief that the Russian character is basically feminine. "Dear, slovenly mother Moscow" (35), as Fitzgerald calls it, embraces all that Tolstoy prized as wholesome, comforting, and enfolding in the Russian folk spirit. About Pierre Bezukhov, who leaves glittering St. Petersburg for the shambles of Moscow during Napoleon's invasion in *War and Peace,* Tolstoy said, "In Moscow he felt at peace, at home, warm and dirty in an old dressing gown."[3] This dowdy, all-swathing ease would define Moscow a hundred years later, Fitzgerald saying, "there was nothing you couldn't get repaired in Moscow, a city which in its sluggish maternal way cared, as well as for the rich, for the poorest of the poor" (70). Like Joyce's River Liffey, the Moscow River can cleanse, heal, and protect; a pistol used in a break-in sinks to its dark, muddy floor, never to resurface as guilty evidence.

Fitzgerald's Muscovites have a lower standard of living and fewer economic opportunities than do Parisians or Berliners. Yet like all big towns, Moscow boasts a large, complex business community, crowded shops and markets, where piles of cash change hands, and dangerous slums. Most vitally, everything in it connects. It is a budding manufacturing hub, a capital city, and a metropolis that feels like a village. Lacking fixed edges, it is always on the go—toward spring, toward communism, and toward some new problem that requires fast thinking and, often, a wad of rubles.

Making this activated field resonate is Frank Reid. "Having always kept his life on an even . . . keel," Paul Stuewe says of Frank in *Quill and Quire,* he is "now forced to undergo the kind of fundamental self questioning . . . he has consciously avoided."[4] Tugging against his customary self-avoidance is a background that qualifies him as a guide to his milieu. Though his parents were English, he was born and raised in Moscow, where they owned the printery he is managing at the time of the book. His ten-year-old daughter has become more Russified than he; Dolly speaks English at home but can only write in the Russian language that is the medium of instruction in the school she attends. Yet Frank too speaks Russian all day long both with his workers and clients at the printery and his servants at home. He has also been wearing Russian-tailored clothes and eating Russian food for decades, and he has a Sherlockian knowledge of Moscow's streets, lanes, and byways. A servant who tells him, "You are Russian, you are used to everything Russian" (124), has judged him well. Frank feels at home in Russia. If he did not love his motherland, he would fret less about the direction in which she is heading.

Yet his English bloodlines, while posing no emotional bar between him and Russia, create some slippage between him and his native land. The cool English common sense and preference for simplicity and straightforwardness that divide him from his neighbors also sharpen his view of them. He warns an employee bent on working in England that, once out of Russia, he may not be readmitted (178). Frank's English point of view also helps him protect himself and his family. Alert and responsive to his country's charged politics, he knows that he may have to flee Moscow at a moment's warning. This prospect he views coolly. When a Russian university student facing deportation, echoing Dostoevsky's Dmitri Karamazov, blurts our, "A Russian can't live away from Russia, but to you it's nothing" (107), he remains silent.

Empathic and shrewd, Frank gives his family a comfortable life while doing a useful job, helping the unlucky, and satisfying a corrupt police force. This regimen holds until he suspects that he is on the wrong side of history. Born circa 1878–80, he married the schoolmistress Nellie Cooper in 1902 and then took her to Frankfurt, where he operated print machinery, where his first two kids with Nellie were born, and where, recalling Chiara Ridolfi Rossi of *Innocence,* Nellie lost a child to miscarriage (33).[5] In 1905, a year of "strikes and violence" (33) that saw both the end of the Russo-Japanese War and an abortive socialist revolution, both of Frank's parents died, and Frank and Nellie settled, presumably for good, in Moscow, where Frank would run the thirty-five-year-old family business. A third child was born in Moscow, leaving Frank and Nellie, like Desmond and Penelope Fitzgerald, parents of two girls and a boy.[6]

Much of this went according to plan. Heir to the family business, Frank studied engineering and printing at Loughborough before apprenticing in Nottingham. Unlike Giancarlo Ridolfi of *Innocence,* he had the drive to benefit from his early training. He also showed the resolve to deploy executive initiative his first day at Reid's after his father's death recalled him to Moscow. Taking charge immediately, he brings his workers together to deal with the dishonesty of a foreman. This caring employer and "decent . . . mild skeptic" will continue to draw upon the solid, foursquare virtues associated with the places he has lived.[7] London, Oxbridge, and the chic southern counties of Surrey, Sussex, and Kent play little or no part in the formation of his, or his firm's, character. His training was technical, not academic, and, appropriately, he meets Nellie in her native Norbury, in the midland county of Staffordshire. He continues to prize midland grit and steadiness over elegance and wit. His instincts serve him well. As if the chaos and confusion he is living through were not worry enough, a series of domestic shocks sends him reeling. These he tries to take in stride. Despite his anxiety over the whereabouts of his children, he comforts rather than scolds a waitress who works in the canteen where he was told to find them (16) after they had been abandoned by their mother. Later, punctilio will dissuade him from reading a letter not addressed to him, even though it came from Nellie, who has not written to him during the three weeks since she bolted home.

His restraint squares with his reluctance to judge Nellie. After her bolt, he writes to her every day, including in his letters postal money orders. Though he saw in her no sign that she was planning to leave him, he does recall that she was uncommonly quiet in the weeks prior to her departure (20, 6). He wonders if perhaps he lacks imagination, as an old friend claims (11). The self-inventory he is forced to take provides little balm. He feels uncomfortably like the clichéd husband who is the last to know of his wife's escapades. Compounding his woes is the fear that an innocent first misstep cost him the trust not only of Nellie but of the children, too. Did he connive at Nellie's defection with his foolish belief that she, a non-native, could be happy in a foreign country as foreign as preindustrial Russia?

He seeks refuge from guilt in no-nonsense practicality. A survivor, he has learned to deal with the Russian civil service, capricious and crooked as it is. The bribing of policemen, ministry clerks, and government inspectors to get electricity installed in his factory he accepts as part of the cost of doing business. Lacking illusions about man's innate goodness, he knows that his night watchman will not tell the police that a shot went off during his watch until he finds out how much Frank will pay for his silence.

The same shrewdness and quick thinking that helps Frank keep Moscow's justice system at bay steers him through other dangers, too. Harvey Pitcher explains that the chaplain of Moscow's English Church in the years leading to the 1917 Revolution was the "middle-aged, lively, and forthright" Frank North.[8] In *Spring*, he is called Cecil and then Edwin (13, 67) Graham. His wife, who "did both the seeing and the saying" (13) at the chaplaincy, has more color and dash. No figure of meekness and mercy, she is also dangerous. Likened to "a bird of prey which has not caught anything for several days" (63), she has an instinct for the withering sarcasm that can make an interlocutor feel suddenly beheaded. Her apparently full, accurate knowledge of all that goes on in Moscow's British community and the heavy smoke curling from the cheap shag tobacco she smokes lend her lucid, carefully nuanced verbal sideswipes a fearful mystery. Yet Frank stands up to her, rejecting her hint that he hire a woman who has come to the chaplaincy as a governess during Nellie's absence and matching her innuendo for innuendo in a later verbal joust.

Has wifelessness brought out some of his hidden virtues? He subdues and disarms a young intruder who steals into Reid's and then tries to kill him. Showing great presence of mind, he then shuts the safety catch on Volodya Grigoriev's automatic and gives the coughing, doubled-up Volodya a glass of water. But whereas this kindness and resolve both strike a chord with Frank's earlier behavior, his physical courage seems new and puzzling. But not for long. Losing Nellie releases inhibitions heretofore held in check by his duties as a husband, father, and employer. Though these obligations still rule him, the madness of Nellie's flight unleashes his tribal male instincts and prerogatives. The process begins quickly. After rejecting a middle-aged woman as a temporary governess, he hires dewy, voluptuous Lisa Ivanovna moments after meeting her. He was always physically disposed. His discovery in chapter 1 of his children's absence from home makes him feel "suffocated" (7). Later, with Lisa ensconced in the Lipka Street homestead, the deprivation he feels sitting a room's distance away from her grips him like "a physical pain" (130). The physical stays ascendant. When he closes with Lisa, "all the blood in his body" (167) tells him that she welcomes his sexual advances, even though he is her employer. It is no wonder that Fitzgerald's original name for him was Hungerford.[9] What follows his insight whets his lust for Lisa. He threatens to break the teeth of a man who accidentally intrudes on their foreplay. But the stallion in him does not swamp Frank's humanity. Following Lisa to her room, he knocks on the door and waits to be admitted rather than bursting in. Their lovemaking will be sweeter for being consensual. His restraint creates a moment of Keatsian poignancy. The assurance he wants does come in a vibrant chapter-ending image Keats would have approved of—the sound of Lisa's bare feet moving toward the door that temporarily divides them (167).

When Frank meets Lisa, she is selling men's handkerchiefs at the English-owned department store, Muir and Merrilees, "the Selfridges of Moscow"—"all Moscow shopped there."[10] Reticent and reposeful, she has a serenity that Nellie, "a jumper-up and walker-about" (83), lacks. But offsetting the "curious peace" (93) she brings to Lipka Street is her hair. Lisa's long, glistening hair is the first thing Frank notices when he meets her, and it disturbs him so much that he asks her to style it differently. Frank has become smitten, but, like many of Fitzgerald's love-crazed characters, he does not know it. The short locks Lisa displays the next time he sees her, rather than dimming her charms, highlight the beauty of her eyes.

Annie Asra of *Human Voices*, besides being placid and composed like Lisa, had *her* hair cut short after wearing it long. The shearing of these two women of about the same age also upsets the men they both work for. And the women respond with the same offhandedness to the disclaimers these men voice. Annie says, "It doesn't matter, it'll find its own level" (*Human Voices*, 86); Lisa, equally disinclined to grouse, says, "Well, if I made a mistake, it will grow again" (*Spring*, 93). The parallel runs on. Both Lisa and Annie, still in their teens, sleep with older married bosses who belong to a higher social class. This detail, though, not only sharpens the difference between the two lasses; it also confirms *Spring* as the Fitzgerald novel that most urgently signifies the darkness and inscrutability of the human heart. The oddly matched Annie and Sam Brooks face a doubtful future in a bomb-racked London, but they face it together. At the end of *Spring,* it is clear that Lisa and Frank have parted forever. The joiner's daughter has worsened the loneliness and apartness in her lover that the lover thought she had eased.

Worst of all, this grief is orchestrated. At the end of her job interview, Lisa asks Frank if he has a dacha (86). The question is not idle. After she takes the Reid children to the family dacha two weeks later to celebrate spring's onset, she never sees him again. And she knows she will not. Just before her interview, she had been seen crying at her handkerchief counter at Muirka's (the addition of the letter "k" makes it diminutive). She was lucky to be standing at her post. She needed a man-sized handkerchief to sop up her tears. Originally called Masha, after Chekhov's adulteress in *The Three Sisters* (1901), she feels exhausted by the complex dance she has been dancing (Masha played the piano) between the self she wants to be and the self she cannot escape.[11] Using her peasant bloodlines as her cover, Lisa is preparing to spy on Frank for the government or its enemies, a point noted by Mrs. Graham in chapter 18 (137) and discussed by Fitzgerald in her notes to the novel.[12] Her tears, like those of the vampire-like enchantress in Keats's "La Belle Dame sans Merci," convey her sorrow over an act of cruelty she is bound to inflict.

But the novel's original title, "Nellie and Lisa," besides foretelling the model employer and family man Frank's fixation on women, also gives his wife a prominence she deserves.[13] Absent from the present-tense action for all but the book's last sentence,

Nellie dictates most of the choices Frank makes after learning of her flight from Moscow in chapter 1. She has been compelling him from the start. When they met, she was living with her brother and sister-in-law in Norbury. She had been teaching for four years and singing in a choir in her spare time. Her first conversation with Frank, her fellow choir member, though slightly more guarded, has the provocativeness of the first words Salvatore Rossi and Chiara exchanged in *Innocence,* also in a musical climate:

> "I'm twenty-six," she added, as though it might as well be said now as later.
> "Do you like teaching?"
> "Not all that much." (25)

She soon adds that music does not mean much to her, either (27); she is ready for a change. A pattern has also taken shape. She repeats her age (29), as age counts a great deal in courtship, the goal of which is presumably marriage. Having spotted Frank as a potential suitor, she is feeding him information that will either speed his suit or, saving them both time and stress, thwart it.

This rigor, though, as Salvatore Rossi demonstrated in *Innocence,* often foils happiness. Nellie's resolve has put her at odds with her surroundings. Three times she tells Frank that she will not "be got the better of" (29, 31, 32) by Norbury. Her "practical good sense" (29) directs her choices, not the values and standards of her provincial hometown. Despite the spread of miles (some 1,600) it covers, *Spring* is as simple as the annual cycle in which its people wheel. What restores Nellie to Moscow at the end is jealousy, an urge hinted at by a reference to *La Belle Hélène* (98), Jacques Offenbach's light opera about the devastation wrought by the beauty of Helen of Troy (Nellie's name is a variant of Helen). Frank has told her in a letter that, in her absence, a "Russian girl" (96) has been minding the children. She may have also learned of Lisa's sexual charms. In this novel of veiled counter-narratives, news—even the most private kind—travels quickly among people divided by miles, years, and social standing. Finally, as was seen in Haggie Smith's fraught response to Dousha Vartarian in *The Golden Child,* English wives fluster when their husbands spend time with ample-figured Slavic women. The soothing, lulling qualities of these earth goddesses, they know, can beguile a man.

Perhaps Nellie's return to Moscow bears out the proposition, voiced earlier in the book by the sledge driver who took Frank to the train station where his kids were waiting for him, "Life makes its own corrections" (15). More markedly than in any of Fitzgerald's other novels, the plot of *Spring* plays on after a climactic finale, like that of Chekhov's *The Seagull* (1896), which resolves everything and nothing. Though the book completes an action, it also raises big questions it wants us to ponder. Frank and Nellie have been jolted into a new perception of life and love that demolishes their ways of thinking and feeling. They face a big struggle. Trapped by the past, guilty and at the same time innocent, loving, pitying, and resenting each other, understanding while not understanding at all, they want to forgive but find themselves doomed to remember.

Deepening their coming struggle is Nellie's brother Charlie Cooper. This novel that adopts Henry James's technique of building a complex, convoluted action, mostly interior, around a simple plot also uses the Jamesian device of the ambassador. Any discussion of Charlie might well begin with Simon Brett's description of him as "Frank's boring brother-in-law . . . who blossoms surprisingly in the alien atmosphere of Moscow."[14] Charlie has come to Moscow to discuss with Frank Nellie's flight from the nest. Ominously, he arrives on March 18, the Feast Day of St. Benjamin's (124), which honors the Persian martyr who was tortured and killed in 424.[15] Although no torment to Frank during his stay in Moscow, Charlie does try his straitened brother-in-law's patience. He says little about Nellie's activities in England and claims to know nothing about her state of mind. It is as if he has come to Moscow to collect information rather than to impart it.

Then, having lost his wife, who was advisedly named Grace, he gravitates emotionally toward Lisa. As an excuse to spend time in her company (and perhaps to soothe Nellie's nerves?), he suggests that she accompany him and Frank's three children to Norbury, where the kids can cultivate their English roots. Luckily, no rivalry or love triangle builds from Charlie's idea; at their most embryonic, Fitzgerald's love triangles sprout rue, as in Chekhov. But Charlie's asking Frank to convey his idea to Lisa for him in Russian invokes not Chekhov's *Three Sisters,* but Henry Wadsworth Longfellow's "Courtship of Miles Standish" (1858). The invocation is planned. When Frank first met her, Nellie was living on Norbury's Longfellow Road (25). Moreover, the choirmaster in charge of the concert version of Longfellow's *Hiawatha* that brought Nellie and Frank together is called Dr. Alden (27). This carefully chosen name torques on the poem's most famous line, spoken by Priscilla to John Alden, "Why don't you speak for yourself, John?" Lisa also favors the attentions of Frank over those of Charlie. But she cannot afford such a simple instinctive response. Her motives, only partly romantic, form another strand in a web of treachery that threatens to trap all the characters.

One of the builders of this web may be Selwyn Crane, the English bachelor who has long managed Reid's accounts. Selwyn's genius for life goes beyond the "reserve of good sense" (9) Frank credits him with having. This poet, hiker, and herbalist models himself on Tolstoy, whom he met several times before the great man's death in 1910. He follows Tolstoy by cobbling his own shoes (47), by seeking purity in poverty, and by renouncing violence. Nor does evil frighten this man "often thought to be touched by the finger of God" (84). A relentless self-improver, he lives in "a doubtful corner of Moscow" alongside "cholera suspects, military deserters, and wanted criminals" (148). The vice he might find in these down-and-outers he hopes to redeem through good example.

Yet much of the trouble recorded in the novel can be traced to this champion of underdogs, whom Frank finds as bland as "a drink of cold water" (77). Frank might have chosen his trope more carefully; the day before conjuring it up, he had read a news story about "a pair of dead lovers . . . frozen into the ice" (71) that had started to melt in a nearby river. The loss of love and life serve as a leitmotif for Selwyn, whom Tolstoy once heard sing. But this singer and concertgoer who invites Frank to a program of music by the most cacophonous Russian composer of the day, Igor Stravinsky (76, 179), has already yoked himself to discord. His having left the door of Reid's business unlocked, perhaps by design, enables Volodya Grigoriev to steal into the printery and destroy equipment belonging to the firm's chief compositor—on the eve of the feast day of the patron saint of printing, no less.

What brings Volodya to Reid's, though, are sexual, not political, motives; he wants to punish Frank for hiring Lisa as a governess. Analogously, Selwyn, who might have both ordered and facilitated the break-in, has women on *his* mind more often than might be expected in an alleged ascetic. The point can be developed. Most of the activities he performs center on women. After bringing Lisa to Lipka Street, he returns there mysteriously at the precise moment when Frank is getting ready to mount her. He sends the hapless Muriel Kinsman, the aspirant for the governess's job that went to Lisa, to a Tolstoyan community in England, where Nellie, who had learned about the place from him, will turn up, too (182). The news of Nellie's exit from Moscow also brought him to Lipka Street in chapter 1, supposedly to comfort Frank. Actually, Selwyn knew of Nellie's bolt before Frank did, and his guilty knowledge sent him looking for company.

He might also be protecting himself. What drives him to Frank's side cuts more deeply than anyone suspects. Yet, having written in *Golden Child* a crime novel, Fitzgerald scatters enough clues throughout *Spring* to rouse an alert reader's suspicions. At age fifty-two, Selwyn is twice the age Nellie was when Frank first met her. The years he worked for Frank's father, besides easing him into the role of older lover so common in Fitzgerald, also harks to *Dombey and Son,* which bulked large in *Freddie's* (e.g., 7, 47, 52). The wife of the eponym of Dickens's 1848 novel runs away with the manager of the House of Dombey. Selwyn is the accounts manager at Reid's, and, even though *Dombey* goes unmentioned in *Spring,* Fitzgerald's prior use of it (it is also referred to in *Bookshop* [43]) suggests that it might have been on her mind during the writing of *Spring.*

Selwyn never flees Moscow with Nellie. But he has bonded closely enough with her, behind Frank's back, to ponder such a flight—at her behest, if he can be believed (181). His having reneged at the last minute does not mitigate his betrayal of his boss, longtime friend, and fellow exile. Like a character in Henry James, he betrays those closest to him. Being stood up by him forces Nellie to decide on the spot whether to go to England alone, take the children with her, or return to Frank. Nor can the wounds Selwyn dealt Nellie and Frank be healed by the regret he sometimes displays (77).

Selwyn is less of a hypocrite, though, than he is a battlefield of warring impulses and drives. At times, the unreason and amorality of Dostoevsky's underground man explains his conduct better than does Tolstoyan nonviolence. Though his poetry stems from a series of conscious choices, his life is ruled by compulsion. But the pious, openhanded Tolstoy had a supercharged libido that persisted into his old age, a trait that humanized rather than tainted his character, his art, and his teachings. Like him, Selwyn is more than just a victim of his sensitivity and high self-expectations—even though he follows his master by plaguing his intimates.

Fitzgerald bolsters her portrayal of him by juxtaposing him against Frank's trading partner, Arkady Kuriatin, the successful merchant whose cherished tablecloth, glassware, and china were all wrecked by the bear cub he brought home as a gift to his son. The outburst he erupts into upon seeing this chaos certifies him as a broadly drawn Russian type. But if broadly drawn, he is also roundly perceived. His peasant gusto, which includes a cruel streak, a vengeance, and a tenderheartedness that declares itself in both acts of generosity and a boozy love of storytelling, again conveys Fitzgerald's view of character as a polygon of warring drives. Kuriatin's widely dissimilar traits infuse the novel with a distinctive Russianness. His drinking and shouting, his tears and laughter, expose his Russian soul in a patently Russian way. Like the rich businessman Lopakhin in

Chekhov's *The Cherry Orchard*, he has retained his peasant origins. But the peasant make-do cunning that has pulled him through adversity has another, no less typical, side. Fitzgerald might have had Chekhov's pushy lowborn Natasha, from *The Three Sisters*, in mind when she has Frank note inwardly in chapter 12, "Like all . . . peasants, Kuriatin was obsessed with the chance to cut down trees" (88).

To say that Kuriatin also enjoys cutting down a business colleague or client is to trivialize. He is never more his shouting, teary self than in chapter 13, when he hosts a lunch for Frank at his club. Furnished with heavy chairs, Rusalochka's stuffs its "bloated, steaming, and streaming customers" with rich pastries and liqueurs while deafening them with music booming from a "great golden organ" (99, 98). Into this stronghold of excess walks an uninvited Selwyn. The luncheon scene at Rusalochka's brings out, however obliquely, his true self, just as it does Kuriatin's. First, his very appearance among the samovars, heavy food scents, and waiters in frog coats reflects his tendency to show up in places where he is unexpected. Next, unfazed by the barbaric pomp surrounding him, he uses a few impromptu words to move an abashed, repentant Kuriatin to confess that he had been trying to cheat Frank on the business deal that brought them together for lunch.

But Selwyn has not reformed Kuriatin. He has, rather, brought out of the rascal a goodness he already possessed—and would sometimes demonstrate. Though unmentioned, Dostoevsky's belief in the power of mystery influenced Fitzgerald's portrait of prerevolutionary Russia as much as Tolstoy's massive harmonies. Like Dostoevsky, Fitzgerald overturns received notions of both probability and behavioral norms and thus deepens our sense of human possibility (as do the book's interiority,

Devil figure, and doubles). The novel's major events defy reason, and effects swerve from their presumed causes. This illogic holds at every level. Frank recalls the Russian Premier Piotr Stolypin being murdered by his bodyguard (49). Mrs. Graham, the English chaplain's wife, knows everything that touches Moscow's British community despite never presumably leaving the church grounds. Lisa's would-be lover, Volodya, meanwhile, performs an armed break-in into Reid's during a convulsive time in Russian history. But rather than acting the daredevil revolutionary, he looks sleepy and "bemused" (124). He is also incompetent. Frank disarms him after he fires his pistol at Frank from point-blank range and, like Chekhov's Uncle Vanya, misses.

Absurdity and black humor stay to the fore of Fitzgerald's rendition of a torn, suffering Moscow. Moral fatigue trumps renewal. Not only will Russians fall in both the Great War and the 1917 coup; the pressures and risks of transacting everyday life in a nation nominally at peace are already huge. Yet this turbulence seems trite and random, the police coming across as tired, inept, and ill-informed. Nor do the English emerge from the dangerous maneuvering morally unscathed. In Lisa, the coming coup has invaded both Frank's home and bed. Also, Nellie would never have asked Selwyn, who is probably also a Red agent, to share her life unless she was already sleeping with him. Like the English visitors to Berlin in Christopher Isherwood's *The Last of Mr. Norris* (1935) and *Goodbye to Berlin* (1939), the members of the Reid circle kick up more trouble among their neighbors than they understand. And, as in Sophocles's *Oedipus Rex,* the trouble starts at home. The innocent Charlie Cooper wants to break up Frank's family. Frank and Nellie both violate their wedding vows. Selwyn betrays both of them, using sex as an expedient with the flair of one of John le

Carré's honey-trap artists. Obeying spymasters who want Frank more closely watched, he builds an elaborate plot around sex that would replace Nellie with Lisa on Lipka Street. It is material in this regard that Selwyn's book of poems, *Birch Tree Thoughts,* though Russian in subject matter, is written, not in the Russian Selwyn speaks fluently, but in English, the language most closely linked to the great game of spying.

The book remains deeply involved in the social history of its day, a sign of this involvement being its attentiveness to trains. A train ride begins Ford Madox Ford's *Some Do Not* (the first volume of his *Parade's End* tetralogy; 1924); likewise, the central scene of Rebecca West's period novel, *The Birds Fall Down* (1966), a political debate between two Russians, takes place on a moving train. These motifs have the same reference point. The 1918 signing of the Armistice in a railway coach made the train a symbol of the transition between the nineteenth and twentieth centuries. This transition stirred Russia deeply. A sealed train carried Lenin from Germany to the Finland Station. Finally, the ever-looming Tolstoy, who expressed his dislike of trains by linking them to disaster in his fiction, died in a train station.

Hewing to this pattern, the first sentence of *Spring* consists of information about a train trip: "In 1913 the journey from Moscow to Charing Cross, changing at Warsaw, cost fourteen pounds, six shillings and threepence and took two and a half days" (5).[16] Because Nellie has taken this long trip, Frank must go to Moscow's Alexander Station in chapter 2 to collect the children she sends home. Nellie's brother Charlie both arrives at and departs from the Alexander Station, which is also where Selwyn first meets Nellie, whom he will later leave stranded at still another train station, in Mozhaisk.

The railway motif, so deeply embedded in Russian turn-of-the-century history, chimes with the theme of *Spring,* as is seen in the book's allusions to *The Cherry Orchard.* If Chekhov's 1904 play begins with the homecoming of a lovelorn Russian widow after a long train ride from Paris, *Spring* (which, like *Cherry Orchard,* includes a domestic servant named Dunyasha) opens with a rail trip from Moscow to London by a runaway English wife equally troubled by sex. The great distance traveled by Nellie is important. Like Balzac, Dickens, and Zola, Fitzgerald wants to show how society's far-flung elements join. Thus notes are sounded that will recur in different contexts. Her complex network of family, friends, and business associates tightens as it expands to include political and paramilitary events. What look like random elements will either fuse or reflect each other. Marx's belief that the proletariat would usher in the golden age was enacted by a clutch of Russian thugs whose attempt to change an unchanging people caused the horrors of collectivization, slave labor, and mass deportation. Similarly, Nellie's circuit between Moscow and London wastes both her time and effort. And, though the effects of this wear and tear has yet to be reckoned, her homecoming leaves her more of a nervous Nellie than she was before setting out.

Another who goes by train from Moscow to London is Muriel Kinsman. Despite appearing but briefly, this unfortunate, who represents a possible direction for both Nellie and Lisa, adds to the book's interdependence theme. Harvey Pitcher's discussion of the esteem enjoyed by English governesses in czarist Russia would have omitted her had she really lived.[17] Muriel has just lost her governess's job, "unjustly," she claims, with a Russian family. (A governess *does* get exploited by her New Zealand paymasters in "At Hiruharama" [1992].) The absence of Mrs. Kuriatin during the bear cub disaster showed Frank the need to hire a woman to watch his kids. But because, responding to his new freedom, he wants a pretty, young governess, he leaves the chaplaincy without hiring Muriel—only to find himself being followed. A chase ensues through lanes and byways so little known that Frank can hardly pick his way through them.

As might be expected in a Penelope Fitzgerald novel, the pursuer in the chase described in chapter 9 of *Spring* is a woman. And she stalks Frank with fervor, finally running him to ground on a path near the river. But the chase has drained so much of her strength that, even though she has been introduced to him, she only tells her quarry that she wants to talk to Frank Reid. When it becomes clear that he will not help her, she says, just before leaving him, that Frank Reid "must be a younger man" (73) than the one she has been addressing. The motif recurs. In chapter 24, Volodya Grigoriev will also tell him that he is old (165). Why should a lovesick university student and a jobless middle-aged governess fire the same parting shot at Frank? As different as they are, both feel thwarted by him, and, like other damaged people, they strike out at the person who has damaged them. Both seek the spot where they can inflict the most pain, too; no longer shielded by a stable marriage, Frank is fair game for the sexual gibe. In line with the book's erotic subtext, Volodya and Muriel both resent Frank sexually. Volodya fears that he has sexual designs on Lisa. Slow-moving, bosomy Lisa, the novel's most radiant figure of female sexuality, vexes Muriel, too, even though the women will never meet, Muriel having surmised that, though Frank's kinsman, she lacks the sexual charms he seeks in a governess. Besides reinstating Frank as a sexual presence, Nellie's bolt from Moscow has shortened the distance between the nursery on Lipka Street and the bedroom.

Sex always looming, Muriel's awareness of the opportunity created by Nellie rouses in her a craving for security. Her desperation makes Frank feel guilty. Nor does the money he puts toward her train fare to London (generous characters take up collections for needy members of their circle in *Offshore* and *Human Voices* as well) ease his guilt. Numbed and dazed by recent setbacks, she resembles him. And lest he forget it, he might bear in mind that she and Nellie, both of whose recent setbacks included valerian drops, spent time, perhaps together, in the same English Tolstoy settlement that Selwyn told them about before they left Moscow from the Alexander Station (21, 65, 75). Fitzgerald's instinct for the off-center detail keeps the Alexander Station in view (Alexander was Russia's czar during the action of *War and Peace*). Perhaps also crossing Nellie's path is the woman who shared Frank's bed with her. After being jilted by Selwyn, Nellie takes the Berlin train to London. But Lisa tells the Reid kids after dropping them off at the Alexander Station that she is needed in Berlin (185), which, incidentally, is where Lenin might have been living in 1913.[18]

These coincidences take on the force of doom, repetition usually portending freedom's loss in a literary work. Frank's hearing a priest's denial of accident in chapter 16, "We never meet by chance" (121), gives his jarring encounters with Muriel and Lisa the look of retribution, even though he would not have met either woman had Nellie stayed with him. The book unfolds in a mood of frustration and turmoil, as the anxiety conveyed by its opening foretells. Not only does Frank find himself wifeless; he is also unable to find his children in the place where they are supposedly waiting. The England that Nellie has fled to offers her little relief from the strain of Moscow. A letter from Charlie cites a black frost, clashes between capital and labor, and a miners' strike that will leave the country without coal during a hard chill (46). Neither do Nellie's brief stints as a teacher and a settlement worker replace the hope she lost when her fainthearted lover failed the tryst he had arranged with her (if he ever intended to keep it).

Other such attempts to brighten one's lot also fail. *Spring* is a moral tale without much morality or joy in sight, its people looking in vain for a sense of who and what they are. Nothing is as it seems; nobody can be trusted; no institution, be it the family, the workplace, or the legal system, is solid. Most flawed of all is the political faction looking to take over the government. Soviet communism will impose machine production upon a feudal-agrarian land. The poor peasant that this land always honored will be either cast off or murdered. The Reds are already squeezing Frank. Foreshadowing the notorious land grabs of the 1930s, though, his worst setbacks are not inflicted upon him by a Russian (Stalin came from Georgia). Their source is a fellow Englishman. The heartache Selwyn wreaks upon those closest to him prefigures the bloodshed caused later in the century when Lenin, Stalin, and Chairman Mao would savage their own people. Fitzgerald's dovetailing of politics and aesthetics runs counter to a Marxist literary criticism that makes light of this bloodshed. With his Marxist contempt for the bourgeois institution of marriage, Selwyn enacts the English novel's traditional commitment, seen in works as different as Henry Fielding's *Tom Jones* and Ford's *Good Soldier,* to defining appearance from reality.

Selwyn is not what he seems to be. "He didn't oppose his will to the powerful, slow and moving muddle around him. . . .

The current of history carried him gently with it" (37), Frank says of him in chapter 5. But *does* he yield to this heaving tide? Here in Fitzgerald's novelistic version of three-card monte; what we see is never what we get. Selwyn's knack for turning up at crucial moments (viz., right after Frank discovers Nellie's bolt from Moscow, the lunch at Rusalochka's, and the moment at Lipka Street when Frank is about to sleep with Lisa) shows him acting out the Leninist imperative to impose oneself on life in order to change it. Selwyn's passion for handicrafts and folk remedies, his pursuit of simple goodness, and his belief in the dignity of poverty all square with communist writ. The industrial capitalism he serves as Reid's accounts manager, despite its great power, will give way, said Marx, to the worker state. It does not smudge this Englishman's communist faith any more than does his love of Russian landscape or his devotion to Tolstoy. Soviet communism was a German import. More vitally, the rebel always contains in himself that which he wants to crush.

Perhaps the characters need more scourging to qualify for atonement. The novel's beginning and end both feature the same sets of events. A woman Frank loves puts his children on a Moscow-bound train prior to taking the Berlin train herself. Then, after a phone call from the stationmaster at the Alexander Station, Frank collects the children and takes them home. This repetition, like the book's others, bespeaks a cyclical pattern that, while mimicking the seasonal flow that dominates Russian life, also disallows progress; repetitions and parallels in Dante, Nietzsche, and Freud connote the limits of human possibilities. But progress in the liberal western sense is not at stake. In Russia, that land "where nature represented not freedom, but law" (177), spring's advent, the great countrywide drama depicted near the novel's end, has a harsh recoil. Yes, it promises rebirth; the days lengthen, the sun shines longer and brighter, and the softening of the earth brings about a fresh green hue together with a welcome fragrance. Double doors and sealed windows open for the first time in months to waft this perfume indoors. With ritual accord, Muscovites leave their air-freshened homes to watch the breaking up of the ice on the river. The "protesting voice" (110) of the water that frees the ice where it lay trapped for months is part of the great drama. There are others. Along with the melting ice and snow that follow the newly freed water downstream slide heaps of trash released from the riverbanks. This ugliness inspires no more thoughts of cleansing and renewal than does the mud that impedes walking, gets tracked into houses, and traps the wheels of carts, leaving long-faced carters pondering ways to trudge to their next destinations without splotching their clothes and spoiling their shoes.

Narrative structure reflects Fitzgerald's awareness of the demands posed by such hardships. Charlie's arrival in Moscow coincides with the first thaw, and Nellie returns home on the first day of spring. In the chapter before her return, Selwyn invites Frank to go with him to the Philharmonic. Because, in Selwyn's words, "Music always makes its effects" (179), Frank's attending the concert would soften his angry response to the confession of guilt Selwyn plans to deliver regarding his adultery with Nellie. The music he invites Frank to hear with him, intriguingly, comes from Igor Stravinsky. It could be *The Rite of Spring,* which debuted in Paris the same year. In any case, Fitzgerald appropriated it for *Spring* because it suits the book's theme so well. Subtitled *Scenes of Pagan Russia,* it alludes to the massive harmonious affirmations cherished by all Muscovites, like the saints' days when work stops, the ringing bells of Moscow's "four times forty churches" (35), and, specifically, the convulsions attending winter's surrender to spring. The collective memories stirred by these occurrences recall D. H. Lawrence's belief that primitive art stems from the unconscious (part one of *The Rite* is called "The Adoration of the Earth"). In Tolstoy, too, the primitive is close to nature and thus morally superior, tapping into a wellspring of human response sophisticates like Flaubert and James cannot connect with.

But if Stravinsky's *Rite* probes ancestral retentions, it can also shock. What it describes in many different registers is the "protesting voice" (110) Frank heard as a boy when he beheld winter's dislodgment by spring. The voice, consisting of discords, dissonances, and arrhythmic percussive clashes, conveys winter's efforts to prolong its stay. This fight to survive is convulsing nature. What, then, is Selwyn thinking of when he invites Frank to hear a program of Stravinsky's music? The jagged melodic line and harsh orchestration of *The Rite* could hardly be expected to sweeten Frank's response to the news that his old friend has been cuckolding him. This counterpoint of intent and mood sounds several times in the book, evoking the poise and precision of the baroque fugue, which flowered in an age when the prevailing faith of deism bespoke an assurance and a confidence Fitzgerald's Muscovites only know from books. The fugue-like rhythms that evoke this sad truth in *Spring* display a rare artistry. Though rich in atmosphere and period detail, the book's backdrop material complements the story so effortlessly that it comes across as imagined rather than researched. While Fitzgerald is developing the countertensions shaping both the earth's renewal and the unraveling of the Russian government, she is also describing the stresses that galvanize these actions.

Mood shift also builds from counterpoint in *Spring*. Nellie's homecoming reaches us as a bald, flat statement of fact. The paragraph preceding it, though, describes the rituals accompanying the heaving, wrenching triumph of spring's restoration. This tonal shift is thematic. It follows a much more ambitious and extended one in chapter 25, which reaches a level of naked expressiveness that is nearly shocking. In keeping with the book's political cynicism, the offspring of Frank's rut with Lisa is her trip with his kids to the family dacha. Much of chapter 25 describes the rundown dacha and its soggy, neglected surroundings. It devotes two brilliantly lyrical pages (171–73) to the annual cycle of the birch, Russia's signature tree, to the scents the birch exudes, and to the growth fostered by its fallen bark on the matted earth floor below. This renewal vindicates Selwyn's having put the birch at the thematic core of his book of poems, *Birch Tree Thoughts*. But it also occurs in the same chapter in which Lisa parts company with the Reids forever. Whereas spring's restoration takes several weeks, love vanishes as suddenly and mysteriously as it had burst forth.

Should we fret? Lisa's asking Frank at first meeting about the family dacha (86) implies that she has been planning her getaway from the start. Little happens in *Spring* without a reason, even if the reason is veiled from us. Selwyn's seemingly inappropriate reference to the vexing renewal of his libido (77) appears in the chapter before he brings Lisa to Lipka Street. This tiny touch foreshadows Lisa's mission at the Reids. (A lie, it also explains that Selwyn misses the sex he had been getting from Nellie.) It is fitting that this mission, or assignment, ends amid a riot of organic growth whose staple of mold and mildew is reclaiming the tumbledown dacha. Perhaps only until very recently, Russia always lacked a political middle ground, a middle class, and middlebrow literature. But the Russian landscape is *all* middle, blurring transitions between beginnings, middles, and ends. It even merges different orders of being. In the forest darkness, the friends who have come to collect Lisa resemble the trees they are standing next to. Just as the previous chapter moved to a climax of physicality, this one unfolds in a realm of inscrutability. Having swathed Lisa's friends and the ubiquitous birches in the same thick darkness, the chapter ends, "She [Frank and Nellie's daughter Dolly] could smell the potent sap of the birch trees. It was as strong inside the house as out" (175). If Dolly, the most precocious Reid child, is moved by this pungency, we should be, too. "The birches are the true forest" (171), we have just been told. Using them both to reveal herself and to do her bidding, Mother Russia has erased the difference between indoors and outdoors as well as between loss and gain. We have walked out of history and stepped into eternity. Though the idea of the inextricability of renewal and decay is trite, Fitzgerald's treatment of it makes it fresh, vital, and profound. The dacha, its shaky, rotting timbers sinking into the mud that the thaw has just formed, symbolizes the defeat of human arrogance, including its recent product, Marxism, by the timeless law of the rustling, heaving eternal forest.

Weighty as it is, Dolly's insight differs only in degree from the one Fitzgerald moved toward but did not describe in the previous chapter—Frank's sexual encounter with Lisa. The erasure of boundaries by the birch-filled forest, recalling the powerful unity created by the Russian Orthodox Church service, during which all the communicants stand facing the altar, reminds us that sex is the great democratizer, toppling barriers created by age, race, and social class. This crescendo also restores the musical motif of fugue, reminding us again of *Spring's* contrapuntal form. Musical references stand as reminders, too. Nellie and Frank's meeting while rehearsing *Scenes from the Song of Hiawatha,* a section of which is called "Hiawatha's Wedding Feast," alludes to the noisy, overly rich meal Frank takes at Rusalochka's in chapter 13. The chorale's composer, Taylor Coleridge, both lived in Croydon, near Norbury, where the chorale was to be performed, and named his son Hiawatha (26–27). The musical references in the book, as is usual in Fitzgerald, connote death and destruction. The Russian Premier Stolypin (1862–1911) was murdered in an opera house (49); Offenbach's *La Belle Hélène* (1864), which is played at rock-concert volume at Rusalochka's (98), tallies the devastation caused by sexual attraction; with its clangs and shrieks, Stravinsky's *Rite of Spring* depicts turmoil.

The associations called forth by Hiawatha, though more subtle, sound another dark note. Hiawatha was the Mohawk chief who built the Iroquois League out of five feuding tribes, creating peace from discord. On the other hand, stridency and chaos dominate *The Rite,* while the political strife that would peak in the Great War and the 1917 Revolution already threatens Fitzgerald's characters. Then Longfellow, besides writing *Hiawatha,* translated in three volumes *The Divine Comedy* (1865–67), a work used for the epigraph of *Offshore* and, later, for the inscription chiseled above the gates of la Ricordanza, the Ridolfi estate in *Innocence* (65). That Frank and Nellie first have sex together in her bedroom on Norbury's Longfellow Road (with its ready-made phallic pun) suggests that Longfellow's relevance to *Spring* transcends the contrast between the unity and harmony of the Iroquois League and the loss and fragmentation plaguing Russia during the novel's present-tense action. (The book's last chapter shows Frank preparing to fold his business and take his family to England.) As we know, this loss and fragmentation flares out. Looming in the background, the figure of Dante evokes the religious faith whose suppression during the communist era robbed Soviets of access to the healing power of the great spiritual truths of the past.

Other contrasts and comparisons between the poem and the novel foretell grief for Fitzgerald's people, as well. The subject matter of *Hiawatha* is as resoundingly American as that of *Spring* is Russian. But whereas *Hiawatha*'s author was the first American to be honored with a bust in the Poets' Corner of Westminster Abbey, Selwyn Crane's *Birch Tree Thoughts*, based on the snippet of it we see (78), can only discredit its author. Frank joins the gestalt. While Longfellow resisted his lawyer-father's wish for him to study law, Frank, who calls himself a coward (11), takes over his father's works, as expected. Then sadness marred the marriages of both the poet and the printer. Mirroring Nellie's miscarriage are the infant deaths of two of Longfellow's six children. Last of all, the poet's first wife died of a miscarriage and his second, who was ten years his junior, burned to death.[19] Suggestively, the burning of the bear cub in chapter 8 of *Spring*, which was taken from a real-life incident, can be traced to the death of *its* mother, who was "shot for sport" (55) by a businessman.[20]

As the bear cub episode proves, Fitzgerald, by kneading the homey into the bizarre, catches the mundane vividness and the lyrical darkness of domestic life in 1913 Moscow. Intense and surreal in its atmospherics, the episode also discloses a carnivalesque sensibility that fits within a Russian satirical-fantastic tradition swathing Gogol and Bulgakov. Yet Fitzgerald plays it straight with her materials. Her daring, digressive art respects the conventions of fiction—its demand for integrity of character, coherence of plot, and a measurable distance between imagination and reality. Like all good novels, *Spring* deals with love and passion, the need for values, and history's tendency to resist them. Infusing all is Fitzgerald's love of Russia. Though familiar with the hardships of daily life, she also sees the comedy, compassion, and ripe human understanding. Her portrayal of Moscow, in particular, is rendered with such confidence and grace that she makes us forget what the place felt like to us before we read her book.

Without question, it discloses more character and personality than the 1975 Moscow depicted in *The Golden Child*, a well-documented product of a tourist with an eye for detail. In contrast to this guidebook version, *Spring* explores Moscow patiently. It is less condescending, more historically aware, and, refreshingly, more liberating, always avoiding the impression that its author's reserve of local color is running thin. Along with Moscow's smells, Fitzgerald recovers its textures, tastes, and sounds. This expansiveness stems largely from hard, slogging research. The notebooks Fitzgerald compiled prior to drafting *Spring* include details, many of which she did not use, on subjects as different as Moscow's weather, greenhouse management, printing, and (with diagrams) heating systems.[21] This fastidiousness translates to lively details (e g., the sounds of electrified trams and church bells that start each workday and the yearly ritual of wrapping public statues in straw to shield them from winter's cold). Such details enrich the book without slowing it. Though jam-packed, *Spring* does not feel congested or fussy. Its curving, rocking rhythms carry steadily through the complex plot.

Sounding notes that will recur in modified form, these rhythms fuse neatly. Speaking in clear, familiar tones, Fitzgerald ignores the rigidities of space and time, yoking 1913 Moscow to an eternal present, the way good music does. Hensher alludes to these harmonics in his reference to the book's "perfect balance between the quotidian and the sublime."[22] The language of *Spring,* without being flashy, is distinctive. Its mythic quality ensures that each word carries its weight, giving us, despite its smooth cadences, the eerie feeling of things left out; something happens, and it is so: "By the time spring came again they [the fallen bark, branches, and twigs of the birches] would have sunk into a sepulchre of earth and moss, and beetles innumerable" (173). The lovely music of this sentence, enhanced by both the religious note struck by the word "sepulchre" and the unexpected comma, makes the complex Tennysonian image vibrate, while the steadiness of the rhythms stabilizes it. Brookner calls *Spring* Fitzgerald's "best novel to date," and Fitzgerald says it is her personal favorite in the canon.[23] There is no argument here. Flat out, the book proves that she is irreplaceable.

The numerous sidelights that emerge after close rereading confirm the book's excellence. Some of them need to be noted. For instance, the Alexander Street Station that Frank goes to in chapter 2 used to be called the Brest Station (14); two chapters from the end, Selwyn reports having seen Frank's hands on Lisa's breasts (183). The incongruity of his appearing at the Reids' at this moment carries into the remote corners of the plot. His patronymic, Osipych, echoes that of Arkady Kuriatin's wife, Matryona Osipovna, who, Frank claims in chapter 7, "was always at home" (52). Yet, though possibly in the house at the time (62), Matryona does nothing to stop the chaos caused by the bear cub in chapter 8. Selwyn's later unbidden appearance at Rusalochka's, while Frank is having lunch with Matryona's husband, reminds us that the Reid kids were guests in the Kuriatin home the day the bear cub was brought there. A Matryona also sleeps near the Reids' dacha (173) the night Lisa runs off to Berlin. Matryona Kuriatin's father has the same first name as Selwyn's (viz., Osip [i.e., Joseph]). Is she his sister? If she and Arkady, who invites Selwyn to join his luncheon party at Rusalochka's, are taking orders from him, they are serving someone who seems to know everything, including the reason why Muriel Kinsman lost her governess's job miles and miles away from Moscow in "the depths of the country" (98, 75, 64).

There are other signs that the book we are reading differs from the one that is developing. Longfellow, whose *Song of Hiawatha* both brings Nellie and Frank together and serves as a reproach to the coming Soviet state, was elected to the Russian Academy of Sciences.[24] The linkages mount. His friend at Bowdoin College, Nathaniel Hawthorne, built "Young Goodman Brown" and *The Scarlet Letter* around a forest mysticism that unpacks the same force as that of *Spring*. Finally, Stravinsky's *Rite of Spring* and Offenbach's *Belle Hélène* (1864) both call attention to the boldness of *Spring*'s narrative design. Sometimes called *The Rape of Helen,* Offenbach's opera-bouffe uses light satire to depict the shattering effects of adultery; Helen's affaire with Paris started the Trojan War. *Rite*'s depiction of spring's arrival as an arrhythmic sequence of torn, menacing sounds has always vexed listeners awaiting a flow of bright, warm melodies. Selwyn Crane's puzzling centricity in *The Beginning of Spring,* traces of which flicker over the action, reminds us that Fitzgerald's book, besides using some of the subject matter found in *The Rite* and *Hélène,* also presents it as part of a larger event she has only allowed us to glimpse.

This tracery of motifs, allusions, and skewed thematic materials shows Fitzgerald's economy at its best. If the pattern of recurrences and returns formed by the tracery (and underscored in the book's last sentence) makes *Spring* look as if its tail is in its mouth, this Uroboros-like image of eternity mimes the seasonal flow that both rules the Russian folk psyche and upholds the traditional concept of Russia as all-swathing and feminine. Fitzgerald's haunting, sensuous description of the birch wood in chapter 25 as at once static and throbbing, empty and heavily potent in its manlessness ("the air was full of floating mealy seed" [172]), anchors the book emotionally and philosophically. It would be hard to find a better vantage point from which to interpret and judge the action of *The Beginning of Spring* than that.

CHAPTER 11

Driving toward Modernity

The Gate of Angels shows Fitzgerald on familiar turf—a shaky, nebulous border between a vanishing world and one groping toward life. Set in 1912, it straddles the lost Victorian world of earnestness and piety, of jowly women and men proud of their whiskers, and the clash of the First World War. For fifty years, Great Britain and Europe in general had basked in an economic system that sustained middle-class life at a high level of physical comfort and financial security. Victorian prosperity, though maligned as prudish and philistine, had created an effect of timelessness, the sense of a safe, self-reproducing world.

The transfer of faith from religion to science in the early years of the last century quenched this confidence. This secularization of the Victorian mind, one of the vital events in all of British history, pervades the action of Fitzgerald's 1990 novel. The fading edifice of the Church of England typifies a land once sustained by great institutions, many of which had been jarred by cynicism and corruption. The damage shows everywhere. A freethinking journalist in chapter 12 is shocked that the woman walking beside him should want to enter a church (45). The master of a rural railway depot says "with controlled fury," "You can't accuse me of being a church-goer" (36). Then the last words spoken about a church rector, who has retired to his study, are "He's frightened" (41). The banners his wife and daughters are making for a suffragists' rally have made him feel passé and irrelevant, and he fears losing more ground.

Fitzgerald calls the novel that records this ferment "a period book," adding, "It was written *about* the time . . . when the whole controversy about mind and body was at its height and [when physicist Ernest] Rutherford had just started his atomic researches."[1] These researchers opposed a long-honored mechanistic tradition. The reigning British school of philosophy disowned themes like the individual's place in the universe or race memory in favor of an empiricism dating back to John Locke. Empiricism seeks practical solutions, not grand designs. With its attentiveness to experiment and observation, it hinges on the primacy of experience. Experience precedes knowledge and belief; all concepts and laws must pass the test of direct experience. This hard-nosed attitude would ramify. Empiricism launched logical positivism, which took hold in the 1920s and ruled the British-American school for the next twenty or thirty years (Gilbert Ryle's rebuttal, *The Concept of Mind*, appeared in 1949). At its core throbbed the verifiability criterion of meaning. The truth of any philosophical proposition must refer to some sense-construct. Though soothing, metaphysics lacks truth value because it bypasses the realm of sense data.[2]

This question grips Fitzgerald's Professor Henry Flowerdew of St. Angelicus's Department of Mechanical Philosophy at Cambridge University: "There's a continuity of scientific thought. . . . The continuity is now being thrown out the window" (23), he grumps. Atomic physics, the hot new cutting-edge field of scientific inquiry, rests on unobservables. But, Flowerdew continues, science cannot comprehend what it cannot measure, and, because no existing scientific instrument can observe atoms, their existence remains moot. Before winning public favor, atomic physics is being attacked as reckless and rearguard, Flowerdew charging that it presumes as much faith

248 / Understanding Penelope Fitzgerald

as religious belief. The atom, he claims, has the same status of God, whom he calls "nothing more than a comforting weakness" (104).

This view limits our ability to respond to the world. Certain choices bypass measurements and scientific proofs. Following a hunch, for instance, will settle many an internal conflict. Though we may never disclaim reason, we do not always know what reason dictates. Sometimes, the heart makes important finds that come later to the brain. Yes, soundness of argument *should* prevail, but often intuition or gut knowledge will warn us that an argument is weaker than it looks. This dynamic enters the novel with the thrice-mentioned proposition, "thought is blood" (10, 14, 47). One experimental physicist declares, "No two people see the external world in the same way. To every separate person a thing is what he thinks it is—in other words, not a thing, but a think" (49).

No quirk or crotchet, this denial of the freestanding integrity of the sensual world would lead later in the century to both chaos theory and Werner Heisenberg's uncertainty principle (25, 143), which claims that it is impossible to observe something without changing it. Fitzgerald does not allude to these later developments because she wants to do philosophy. Rather, she is describing the intellectual firestorm blazing around Cambridge in 1912. Acknowledging this stir, Nan King names some of the world-class Cambridge scholars who were making breakthroughs during the novel's time setting.[3] Many of their finds occurred at the Cavendish, the cold, crowded, underprovisioned lab where James Watson and Francis Crick would later come up with the double helix structure that identified DNA. Good, even great, science can take place in makeshift settings using "apparatus knocked up out of cardboard and string" (21). Like the

BBC of *Human Voices,* the Cavendish shows flawed people using faulty equipment to serve a noble end: "Out of this squalor had come indisputable greatness" (153), Fitzgerald reminds us, saluting the power of the human spirit to trounce adversity. She also agrees with a junior fellow's pronouncement in chapter 3, "These are wonderful years at Cambridge" (22).

So why did she want to call her Cambridge-based novel *Mistakes Made By Scientists?*[4]

Fitzgerald's review of *C. S. Lewis: A Biography,* which saw print the same year as *Gate of Angels,* quotes biographer A. N. Wilson's statement, "Everything on earth is not rational, and attempts to live by reason alone have all failed."[5] Her scientists are either out of step with life or cut off from it. Though pioneers in research, the book's hero and his colleagues park their bicycles in a shed that resembles a peasant's shack (10), but with one key difference. Were the shed built by a peasant, three of its sides, not only one, would fend off attacks from wind and rain. The absence of earthy peasant common sense in the academy persists. In a double oddity, the shed stands near the entrance of St. Angelicus, or Angels. Besides being Cambridge's oldest college, Angels has always banned women from its grounds; since its inception in 1415, no woman, be she student or caretaker, don or visitor, has crossed the book's eponymous gate into the college. Moreover, everybody connected to the college must be a bachelor.

Fitzgerald handworks these edicts with vision and skill, her instinct for the surprising off-center detail making for some dark fun—in the literal sense. The fun starts quickly. First seen as "a patch of darkness" (11), the Master of the College is blind, like the commencement speaker at the low-grade college attended briefly by the narrator of Ralph Ellison's *Invisible Man* (1952). The first words he speaks in the book, addressed to a supposed intruder, convey his passion to control: "This grass [in the Court of Angels] is reserved for the Fellows of the College. Should you be walking on the grass" (11)? This question is put to twenty-five-year-old Fred Fairly, who has already traded the Christianity of his rector-father for a career in science. This career started happily. A possessor if a first-class degree in physics, Fred has been serving as a Junior Fellow at Angels for the past five years. This highly sought-after post now stands at risk. In fact, if Fred had his way, he would scuttle Angels in a heartbeat.

A heartbeat was all it took to change his life. In the book's central event, which took place three weeks before the present-tense action of *Gate* (and which Fitzgerald took from real life), Fred and nineteen-year-old Daisy Saunders are knocked off their bicycles by a runaway cart.[6] The Cambridge couple that found them unconscious in the road picked them up and took them home. Because of the wedding ring Daisy always wore to discourage rough passes from men on the London trams she rode daily to and from work, the Wrayburns assumed that she and Fred were married and put them in the same nursery bed—bathed and naked. As in Terrence McNally's *Frankie and Johnny in the Clair de Lune* (1987), this plotting device works brilliantly. Fred and Daisy, the book's romantic leads, meet in bed, the place where love stories usually end or, at least, point.

But Fitzgerald is not just joking. By inverting the structure of the conventional love story, she is also serving notice that *Gate* differs from those works, like classical tragedies, that sound the pulse of the inevitable. The notice is served early. The title of her first chapter, "Fred's Three Notes," refers to the three notes Fred started writing to Daisy but never finished because, since falling in love with her at first sight, he neither knows where she is nor how to find her. His having both found her and lost her by chance refers to a major premise of *Gate*—that life, erratic and jumbled, resists logic. The logical formulas that the scientists at Angels try to impose on it are mostly irrelevant.

Commenting on this disjunction, Florence McNabb finds *Gate* imbued with "an atmosphere of uneasiness."[7] She is right. Fred met and fell in love with Daisy weeks before the novel's continuous action. In fact, Fitzgerald keeps Daisy out of view till chapter 8 of her twenty-two-chapter book. Even after her appearance, *Gate* weaves in and out, thwarting our expectation of a steadier, smoother narrative pace. But the book's jerky, piecemeal way of conveying information builds moral power, making us consider all sides of the story without forgetting the also-rans and the losers who deserve our attention.

It also puts itself on level ground with what it describes. These sometimes farfetched events may violate probability. Both human nature and human affairs, as Fitzgerald portrays them, are too tricky, evasive, and prone to either accident or ghostly intervention to answer to novelistic convention or rational consistency. It is thus suitable that an insane asylum stands within miles of the university where new discoveries are changing the face of science. The staples of *Gate* are dislocation and discontinuity, giving every action both the potential weight and ambiguity of a nightmare. Fred's introduction to Daisy in a bed, for instance, has a fairytale logic at once impossible and irrefutable. The bizarre force of the book's opening sentence, besides foreshadowing this oddity, defies those fundamental categories that pilot our lives. The world we are introduced to seems to be coming apart as we witness it. Framed as a question to convey an added note of anxiety, the sentence blurs the difference between the stability of solid land and the capriciousness of the sea, always a portent in Fitzgerald: "How could the wind be so strong, so far inland, that cyclists coming into the town in the late afternoon looked more like sailors in peril" (9)?

The next image, one of Fitzgerald's most famous, shows some cows in Cambridge, "a university city devoted to logic and reason," who have been buffeted, spilled, and flipped upside down by the gusts, their hooves aloft, "exhibiting vast pale bellies intended by nature always to be hidden" (9). That the cows keep chewing amid this wildness symbolizes one of the book's chief ideas—the steadiness, reliability, and nurture of women in a crisis. More resilient and resourceful than men, women handle problems better than men. The topsy-turvy cows that will soon right themselves, continuing to work their jaws as if nothing important has happened to them, also give the storm a maternal context, a motif enforced by the high winds, which the ancients believed had the ability to impregnate women. The unpredictability of these winds channels into the indeterminacy motif so vital to the novel. The opening sentences of Ian Hacking's *The Taming of Chance,* still another 1990 book, claim that the laws of chance subvert the determinism intrinsic to causality. "The most decisive conceptual event of twentieth-century physics" Hacking calls "the discovery that the world is not deterministic. Causality . . . was toppled: the past does not determine what happens next. . . . A place was cleared for chance."[8] He adds that Novalis—intriguingly the main figure of Fitzgerald's next book—yoked chance to the miraculous: "The individual is individualized by one single chance event alone, that is, his birth."[9] Fitzgerald, too, puts certain key moments beyond the bounds of measurements and scientific proofs. In *The Blue Flower,* she cites the Moravian belief in chance as "one of the manifestations of God's will" (98). The mind orders, interprets, and evaluates the data our senses provide, often by chance. Perception, she believes, can bypass observables. Inner experience accounts for honor, valor, and decency—compelling virtues in 1912, when religion had declined, ethics were foundering, and social philosophies lacked guidance. An appreciation of the centricity of chance could refresh these stale, decomposing systems.

The awakening of Fred's inner self occurs by chance, as did his landing in the same bed with Daisy. Then, in a different vein, a sudden change of plans at his debating club requires him, "a rank unbeliever" (10), to speak in favor of the existence of the soul. Stretching his mind, Fred argues a position that clashes with his (but not his Roman Catholic author's) beliefs. But reversing his stance on the question of unobservables helps him, jostling him out of his mental habits and forcing him to seek new connections and approaches. One of these that hones his sensibility—while also chipping away at the rigidities of empirical thought—is analogy. In chapter 6, he uses analogy to smooth the mind-body dualism. Though the body needs the mind, he argues, its ability both to sense and avoid danger proves that it also has a mind of its own. Analogously, the mind may have a body of its own, too. The stabs of pain Lord Nelson felt in his missing arm rebuts the idea that everything that happens has a physical cause. And perhaps only a few steps away lies the proof that the mind can survive the body's death (46–47). No, Fred does not attempt these steps. He need not. Bucking orthodoxy—even the orthodoxy of dissent or protest—furthers inner growth. Fred later gives an analogy-based lecture that includes a phrase rarely voiced at Angels, however vital it is to William James's brand of pragmatism, "a rational system for measuring happiness" (154).

Analogy scores again in the court trial described in chapter 18. First discounted as "not much more than a formality" that was "not expected to take long" (139, 141), the trial spins out of control quickly. The driver whose cart suddenly turned into a crowded road and rammed the bicycles of Daisy and Fred is missing along with a possible third cyclist. As in Forster's *A Passage to India,* the patriarchal institution of the law soon goes on trial. At issue is the contempt the law has for women. Regardless of its worth, Daisy's testimony is not be taken seriously. The judge dismisses it by attributing the gaps he finds in it to "menstrual trouble" (144). A previous witness, Venetia Wrayburn, when called by the bench "a housewife" (142), points out that she did all the work for the university degree she never earned due to Cambridge's policy of denying diplomas to women. Many such difficulties, the deep structure of *Gate* suggests, stem from the image of the femme fatale, a product of the same fin-de-siècle male insecurity that haunts the books of Henry James and Ford Madox Ford. The public mood created by works like H. Rider Haggard's *She* (1887) and Oscar Wilde's *Salomé* (1896) helped launch the paradigm of the vampire seductress, a construct that explains the furor kicking up around the innocent Daisy and her prototype, Henry James's Daisy Miller.

The trail ends with a flare-up of male fear and resentment. Thomas Kelly, a middle-aged reporter for the newspaper that printed the story that cost Daisy her probationer's job at Blackfriars Hospital, followed her to London's Liverpool Street Station, where she had gone to catch a train to Cambridge to seek work. Preying on the fears of loneliness and vulnerability waiting to bushwhack her in a strange town, he offers to stay with her. His proposition, though built on the vile premise that all she needs to raise her spirits is a good fuck, she accepts. The stain spreads. The chapter that includes Kelly's proposition, called "Daisy Leaves London," ends with her poignant insight that she and Kelly look cheap because they have made themselves cheap: "He put his arm around her waist, fingering her. What a pair we make, she thought. He doesn't deserve any better, no more do I" (100).

But she does not deliver what Kelly insists he has paid for. He fumes in court that he was "gypped" (140), instigating one of those love triangles, as in *Freddie's* and *Spring*, that wreak such mayhem in Fitzgerald. Most of the mayhem recoils upon Kelly himself. Furious at him for impugning the honor of the woman he loves, Fred ambushes Kelly after he leaves the courthouse and punches him. This drastic show of male force plays out as low comedy. The haymaker that Fred aims at Kelly's jaw lands "just below the ear" (149). But it has enough iron in it either to knock Kelly out—or to let him pretend that he *was* knocked out.

While he lies at Fred's feet in a gentle rain, Skippey, the proponent of the idea that thought is blood (10, 14), turns up unaccountably. The unaccountable and the incongruous continue to rule. While the two scientists, Skippey and Fred, carry Kelly through Cambridge's wet streets, they discuss topics like parasitology and homology. Yet, always prepared to upgrade an effect, Fitzgerald embellishes this bizarre composite image. Yes, the image probes the dualities of spirit and flesh the novel has been addressing. A brilliant piece of physical comedy on its own, it also captures the confusion troubling Fred since punching Kelly. But Fred's later assessment of Kelly, made near chapter's end, creates new comic outlets. Despite the moral seriousness driving them, most of our efforts smack of absurdity: Fred notes of Kelly, "His colour was better now than it had been in court.

Perhaps, like a baby, he simply liked being carried about" (151). Yet the import of these efforts holds firm. Harking to an effect used in *Spring,* the collision that brought Daisy and Fred together occurred on February 26, 1912, near winter's end, and the trial, held in early April, the same day that Fred attacked Kelly, reaches its apogee with Kelly's body sinking into some grass that "had been mowed for the first time that spring" (142, 141, 151). A resurgence of life is about to occur, if it has not done so already.

Remote from the imperatives of both the verifiability criterion and a legal system that would dump a sore-faced man into a pile of wet grass loom the products of the imagination. The best take on the enigma of February 26 comes in a story written by Dr. Matthews, Provost of Cambridge's St. James College. As King reminds us, the story's "undercurrent of twisted sexuality and madness . . . forces us to see the world of the novel in an eerie new light."[10] Analogy, not analysis, justifies this leap; Matthews uses the events of an 1869 archeological dig to shed light on the accident that took place on Guestingley Road more than forty years later and changed forever the lives of Fred and Daisy.

Fitzgerald places the tale in the chapter right before the one that describes the trial because it includes material that, though legally inadmissible, bears upon the courtroom scene. The tale's violent, startling imagery augments the dismemberment motif (from *Innocence*) Matthews introduced in chapter 6 with his reference to a stipulation in a woman's will that her little finger be cut off before her funeral to ensure her not being buried alive (50). That the woman was his sister adds a note of stridency redolent of Fred and Daisy's violent first encounter. The tale puts the corpse of the unidentified missing driver of the cart that smashed into the bikes under the surface of the road where the collision occurred. The female earth, supine but vigorous, pulled the driver under in a way that invokes the corpse jammed up the womb-like chimney in Edgar Allan Poe's "Murders in the Rue Morgue." Both the Matthews story and the Poe story, with its headless corpse, link sex to danger and death. The arm that Matthews's archeologist pushes into a culvert to remove a man he believes trapped there comes out with its flesh "dragged or sucked off to the last shreds" (136).

Rooted in Fitzgerald's unconscious, like the placid cows in the book's first paragraph, such images defy literal interpretation but satisfy both emotionally and poetically. That they refer to Daisy, Fred's beloved—the woman who appears most often on the page and the vehicle of Fitzgerald's feminism—gives them an added charge. "Tall and slender, but solid" (63), Daisy first shows her face in 1908. The fifteen-year-old is living with her mother in south London, now and then changing their lodgings in a series of late-night moves to avoid paying rent. Her father long gone, her mother works in a brewery capping bottles till an undiagnosed illness puts her out of a job. This loss leads by stages to her loss of life. As was vividly shown in the war-blasted London of *Human Voices,* Fitzgerald will both note the major developments breaking around her people and show their impact. Mrs. Saunders and "her tall, good-looking daughter" (66) decide to attend the 1909 opening of Selfridge's, with its unmatched 100 departments and 1,200 sales clerks. Probably not yet middle-aged with a sixteen-year-old daughter, Mrs. Saunders has no clear reason to die from the excursion. Perhaps the effort of pretending that she was not impressed by the gala did her in. Perhaps stealing a coil of artificial hair, which, ironically, she did not want or need, lowered a self-esteem already bruised by her departed husband and crushed her will.

We are never told. Fitzgerald's women are creatures of mystery whose defining acts, like Muriel Kinsman's loss of her governess's job in *Spring,* stay vague. In any case, Mrs. Saunders's death and the loss of income from family property bequeathed to her drive Daisy from the digs she shared with her mother and into the workforce. The job she chooses reflects her coping power. She goes to Blackfriars Hospital, where she hires on as a probationer. Fitzgerald's research into the medical lore and hospital routines of 1912 London enrich the chapters devoted to Daisy's year and a half at Blackfriars, and her descriptions of the long hours, the harsh working conditions, and the strict rules probationers must obey convey a heartfelt pathos. But these chapters also deserve praise for their thoroughness in documenting the era's therapeutic practices. These cut a broad swathe. Fitzgerald records the procedure of treating patients ("the abdominal cases on their backs . . . the fractured skulls on their sides" [79]) and describes the now primitive drugs and instruments the healers of the day used to fight disease and injury. But she always focuses on the human. The paragraph ending chapter 10 consists of many arcane references to physical disorders and their treatment a century ago. The long paragraph, though, ends with three short simple sentences that emphasize the humanity of those being treated—their desperate hold on life, their individuality, and their eagerness to affirm their intrinsic worth: "The patients swallowed gladly. Their names were on the bottles. The doctor had given them something" (82).

Daisy's brutal regimen helps her grow. Undeterred by hours of drudgery, she withstands the rudeness of her chiefs, takes up the slack for the weaker probationers, and, as her advice to some friends of a fainting victim points out, learns to both diagnose and treat an ailment quickly: "Don't move him yet. Give

Driving toward Modernity / 259

nothing by the mouth. Cover him up warm and call the doctor" (167). Perhaps most remarkably, her plight of being overworked and undervalued does not chill her heart. More than an able technician, she loves her patients. Asked if she has a smash, or crush, on a particular one, she growls, "I've got a smash on the whole ward. . . . It's one of my half-days on Wednesday. If any of them have the brass to die when I'm out, I'll make them sorry they were ever born" (88).

Tragically, this gifted, dedicated healer forfeits her career in nursing. Chapter 11 of *Gate* opens thus: "On January 16th, 1912, James Elder threw himself . . . into the Thames" (83). A coded message, Elder's name signals impending trouble to readers familiar with the dangers stemming from bonds formed between young women and older men in Fitzgerald's work. Daisy's fear that Elder's hunger strike will kill him unshackles one of these dangers. A woman in a male-dominated profession, Daisy is a natural victim. She tells a journalist the would-be suicide's story, the printed version of which brings a friend of Elder's to the hospital and saves his life. Daisy, meanwhile, has become the "MINISTERING ANGEL" (96) she is called by the newspaper that ran her story about Elder. But this glory fizzles. Having gone public with hospital business, Daisy broke a rule, and she gets fired despite saving a life in the lone way left to her.

But the ministering angel is also called "the Eternal Woman" (84). These words come from James Elder while he is delirious, which rivets our attention in a book where accident and spontaneity promote more good than the conscious and the planned. Professor Flowerdew struggles with problems rising from the attempt to square what he knows about the constancy of matter with the notion of the conservation of mass (103). Let him. The small daily battles to promote survival fought by an orphaned Daisy pose a stiffer test. There is more to heroism than splitting an atom. A lowly job might demand quick answers every day. The proactive Daisy cannot wait for them to come to her. Sitting around and waiting for answers in her line of work costs lives; opportunity deferred soon becomes opportunity lost. And just as someone's intellect does not proclaim his or her goodness or higher purpose in life, there is no bridge between personal happiness and social welfare. Institutions and customs, traditions and laws, should serve, not thwart, personal growth. Earthy, openhearted, and mischievous, Fitzgerald shows that enshrining them saps life's vigor. Life is all we are given, and we have to make the best of it.

If it takes someone special to act on these ideas, then Daisy does qualify as an eternal woman. Kate Kellaway makes a strong case for her importance by contrasting her with Fred: "Daisy . . . has none of Fred's education but understands a great deal better how to proceed in the world," Kellaway says.[11] Her contrast shows most vitally in chapter 15, where Fred and Daisy take a long walk. The only time in the book when they are alone for an extended time, the chapter set Fitzgerald a great artistic challenge. Within its eight pages, she had to both portray the dynamics of the budding relationship and provide some insights into what kind of future, if any, the relationship holds in store for Fred and Daisy. Friendly signs are absent. Suddenly, the idyll the couple planned looms as a struggle. "Without landmarks, the broad fields deceived" (116), says Fitzgerald of the landscape they must traverse en route to the inn where they intend to rest. But not only does the terrain create vexing tricks with distances; it also forms ruts that impede walking. Yet Fred stays focused on Daisy. Led by his instincts, he tells her to keep her hat off, so he can continue to enjoy looking at her hair

Driving toward Modernity / 261

(116), as much an emblem of female sexual radiance here as it was in *Spring*.

She had said that she only intended to keep her hat off temporarily. Was this an enticement? Expecting "to be impressed by [the] quantities of birds and flowers" (113) she would see on the walk, she prepared mentally for her date with Fred. Her preparations reflect wit. Relying on her nurse's understanding of the power of touch, she takes the opportunity to close with Fred, even at the cost of her comfort. Thus she renounces the dry, hard ground on a cart track to walk with Fred in a muddy rut, where she will not look taller than he and where she can hold his arm to balance herself without looking brazen. The moral genius she displays during the walk includes, as well, knowledge of both when to hold back and when to put out signs of encouragement. Asked if a certain flower is a throatwort, as she has claimed, she answers, "I don't know. . . . I only said it to keep things going" (115). She soon profits from her honesty. Fred's next words, "I'm lost if I can't depend on you" (150), show that this believer in the supremacy of sensory experience has started to learn about the power of mood.

Subtly, Daisy has been controlling her exchange with Fred, buying time until she knows what to do about him. Having just lost her job, she sees that her future, as an uneducated single woman, is uncertain. Her having lost every job she has ever had deepens this uncertainty. But she must tread carefully with Fred. While loath to rush into love as quickly as he, she would like to keep her options open. She will have to be alert to his mood swings. Like any zealous lover anxious to please, he will put himself at a disadvantage, inviting her to spurn both him and his offerings. She says of the "unwelcoming bar" where they have a drink, "I've never been anywhere nicer," and she ignores his sulky retort, "But it's not what you asked for" (117). She also resists using the power his abject devotion has given her over him—this, despite his having unwittingly appropriated her role. Just as Nenna James and Maurice of *Offshore* were both borrowers, Daisy is a giver (118). But she is flexible enough to step out of character. To Fred's request that she think about his marriage proposal, she answers, with perfect emphasis, in the chapter's last line, "I don't say I won't, Fred" (118).

Perhaps some inner demon drives Fred to take Daisy to a production of Christopher Marlowe's *Dr. Faustus,* whose title figure deserts his sweetheart. Even though Fred has sworn to love Daisy forever, the insecurity she has roused in him prods him to warn her that he might defect. How realistic is this warning? Besides the ban forbidding anyone connected with Angels to marry, there is the barrier of social class. Fred's father, as has been seen, is a church rector, whereas the working-class Daisy has always lived in a London slum. Now Fitzgerald's treatment of this second obstacle, if obstacle it be, reflects her awareness of the English novel as a vehicle of social history. The class system, she knows, ran strong in England in 1912. The complexity of its categories, its long-held assumptions, and its absurdity also gave writers in the Jane Austen tradition apparently boundless material. Often, adopting a deceptively light tone, the novel of manners would scrutinize a bourgeois world for flaws that might pass unnoticed under less watchful eyes. The scrutinizers were usually women. Women were supposed to be particularly sensitive to class distinctions, entertaining guests at home while always seeking out intruders—particularly those with designs on their daughters.

In *Gate* the intruder is a woman. But, no gatecrasher, she lacks social ambitions. In fact, it is *her* space that is invaded.

Fitzgerald brings back the motif of the ambassador from *Spring* to sharpen her social criticism. The next time she shows Fred and Daisy together after their country walk, they are punting down the Cam River with Fred's mother and sisters, who have come to meet Daisy. (The Fairly brood, like those of both Frank and Nellie Reid and Desmond and Penelope Fitzgerald, consists of a son and two daughters.) Though not hostile, the ambassadors hold back from Daisy. Mrs. Fairly's first words to her, which could have been said by Oscar Wilde's Lady Bracknell of *The Importance of Being Earnest* (1895), are not framed to help her relax: "We were delighted to have a chance of meeting you, Miss Saunders. . . . We have heard so little about you" (123). Then she snubs Daisy's request that she be called by her first name, withholding the comfort and warmth that would help Daisy feel accepted.

Accepted she is not. If Mrs. Fairly cannot imagine her in the parish, her daughter Julia finds her wanting as a suffragist. These barbs cause regret. Before she reached seventeen, her rejections of sexual overtures had cost Daisy two jobs. But the offsetting kindness she might expect from other women, her fellow underdogs, rarely comes forth. Though crusading suffragists and agitators for prison reform, the Fairly women snipe at her behind her back. The matron at Blackfriars shows courage and grit when she turns away a policeman who had come to the hospital to question James Elder. But, no feminist, she bullyrags Daisy and the other probationers and, before sacking Daisy for taking Elder's story to the press, scolds her brutally. It is as if Fitzgerald's women walked out of a Jean Rhys novel, like *Voyage in the Dark* (1934), the heroine of which gets harder knocks from her own kind than she does from men. With feminist fervor, Venetia Wrayburn, who will house Daisy when she comes to Cambridge to work, trumpets, "Why should . . . any woman . . . have to account for her comings and goings. . . ? All that we have the right to ask is, do the higher elements in her nature predominate" (16–17). But this health food enthusiast and chief of her local Women's Social and Political Union (107–8) will also prod Daisy to leave town, and particularly the Wrayburn home, right after the courtroom fiasco.

Class snobbery pervades all in 1912, despite the era's progressiveness in science and politics. The men working at the *Blackfriars, Vauxhall and Temple Gazette* stay seated and keep smoking when Daisy enters their office in chapter 12 because they can tell at a glance that she is no lady. Daisy herself is snobbish, rejecting an invitation from an unwed Spanish mother in her thirties whose application for a probationer's job at Blackfriars was turned down. Even after she regrets her haughtiness, she cannot stop herself, after hearing that "Mrs. Martinez" is still fertile, from carping, "You ought to know better by this time" (74). *Gate* has taken Fitzgerald far from the small comforts, subtler pleasures, and gentle prodding satire of the traditional novel of manners. The ontological dread Daisy shares with Mrs. Martinez makes the domestic woes recounted by most of Jane Austen's followers look pointless and irrelevant.

But do the tensions that pulsate through *Gate* resolve as a tale of redemption? At times, it looks as if the wedding ring Daisy wears to discourage predatory males has as its real purpose a warning to men of all kinds to stay away from *her*. This warning makes sense from the standpoint of literary history. Though innocent, James's Daisy Miller brought out the worst in practically everyone she met in Europe. Scott Fitzgerald's Daisy Buchanan hid behind her money and the false security of a bad marriage instead of risking happiness with Jay Gatsby.

Like these two women, Daisy Saunders riles nearly everyone she meets. And Fitzgerald includes references to both Maeterlinck's *Pelléas and Mélisande* and Verdi's *La Traviata,* works in which love brings rue, to remind us of Daisy's tendency to vex people. In fact, the heroine of *Traviata,* Violetta, who dies of consumption, is named, like Daisy, after a flower.

But perhaps, as William Gaddis does with Georges Bizet's *Carmen* (1875) in *JR* (1975), Fitzgerald is citing an opera to challenge, rather than point out its relevance to, her novel. She both challenges the convention of closure and subverts reader expectation elsewhere in *Gate*. As has been seen, she omits the book's central incident (the knocking-down of Fred's and Daisy's bikes by a wayward cart). Nor does she bring Daisy and Fred together on the page until she has made it clear that Fred wants to marry Daisy. This time shift hides the links between major plot points. But her critique of logical positivism also includes the strategy of forcing her readers to find their way into the action. The cause-and-effect empiricism that *Gate* spurns includes those storytelling devices earlier novelists had relied upon to condition reader response.

The discontinuity and disjuncture intended to quicken awareness also appears in flat-sounding chapter titles like "A Few Words about St. Angelicus" and "Daisy Leaves London." Redolent of the children's fiction and popular magazine fiction of the day, these titles hide as much as they reveal. The chapter called "How Fred Got His Job in the First Place," with its references to both atomic physics and chaos theory (23, 25), also contrasts the simple and the abstruse. Such polarities apply to Daisy. When Mr. Wrayburn uses *Traviata* to inform Daisy that her marrying Fred will end his career at Angels, she brings his analogy—which is false, anyway, since she is no hooker—

into the bright light of confrontation, where she addresses it straight on.

This plain dealer and straight talker is above all a healer. She will ease pain and suffering whenever she can. In this regard, she calls forth the figure of the interceding female from Christian myth. Any assessment of her should heed Richard Eder's words, from the *Los Angeles Times Book Review*: "Fitzgerald is lucid about science, but her heart seems to be with the mystics."[12] Mysticism certainly infuses the book's finale, where, in Philip Hensher's words, "the opening of a door changes everything."[13] It implies that God works through women, but not through institutional feminism; the same suffragists who would gladly go to jail for their beliefs cold-shoulder Daisy. She must carry out her ministry alone. This she does. After walking down Jesus Lane on her way out of Cambridge, she spots a door "as narrow as a good-sized crack, standing wide open" (166). The door, which leads into Angels, has only been opened twice in the college's history, in 1423 and in 1869 (the time setting of Dr. Matthews's weird tale [130]). Daisy becomes the first woman to set foot in the college after "a human cry of distress" (167) summons her there. She ministers to an ailing person who would have died without her help. But she has also violated a tradition hallowed by five centuries of strict obedience. The "everything" she changes includes much more than she or any of the gowned men who rush into the court to witness the violation can fathom. Like her forbidden visit to the *Gazette*, this violation implies that much of life's crucial work flouts rules and regs, a truth less daunting to Fitzgerald's women than to her men.

Most of the gowned men who rush into Angels' courtyard would argue that all philosophical propositions must refer to sense contents. This argument flips the book's finale upside down, like the cows in the book's first paragraph. An unseen hand seems to have opened the Gate of Angels and then led Daisy to it. But the five minutes she spends reviving the Master of the College also puts her in the path of Fred, giving them a chance to reunite. They have been apart long enough to know that they would be happier together. What is unclear is whether they will *find* happiness. The novel's reported action ends with their roadside meeting, in roughly the same kind of off-key crescendo that marked the finale of *Spring*. Perhaps the parallel between Daisy's last major act in the novel—resuscitating a blind man—and the fact that love is blind will help the lovers, whose meeting, incidentally, occurs in the dark, where objects cannot be seen clearly, if at all. In any case, the parallel shows Fitzgerald's offbeat wit skewering the belief that the senses are our only access to knowledge.

The book includes other acts explainable by divine intervention, like the accident that brought Fred and Daisy together for the first time. The collision that landed them in the same bed resembles similar moments in Graham Greene and Patrick White; in these writers as well as Fitzgerald, God's loving hand convulses those it touches. The three writers also decry the power of reason as an inlet into what is vital and enduring. The biggest decision of Fred's life—that he must marry Daisy— comes to him in a daze. That Dr. Matthews lacks a first name, that Skippey is either a first name or a surname (if not a nickname), and that the Master of Angels has no name at all show the life of reason, particularly if ratified by an academic appointment, to be half a life at best. God, whom these men have dismissed as a soothing fiction, may have diverted Daisy from the sordid hotel room Kelly had booked for them. Reason keeps coming up short in the book's closing chapters. Daisy does not quit her laundry job at the mental home where she works, as she threatens to do after Fred tracks her there. Because the director's work schedule denied her access to him, she can return to her job the next day and thus stay in Cambridge, near Fred.

Like *Spring* before it, *Gate* describes an age when grandeur dignified personal decisions, which were made in both the shadow of global war and in living memory of the time when virtues like honesty and valor counted. Two references to Rudyard Kipling's 1890 poem, "Mandalay" (85, 116), evoke the call to duty that sent so many Britons to outposts like Rangoon, where Venetia Wrayburn's brother served. *Gate* explores Victorian themes like good, evil, and the worth of both institutional and personal responsibility. Daisy's visit to the *Gazette* revives James Elder's will to live, a feat that stumped her chiefs at Blackfriars Hospital. But, besides costing her her job, her enterprise also robs both Blackfriars and the nursing profession itself of a star performer. This same enterprise clashes, too, with today's easy knowingness and self-protective irony. In contrast to the lad literature coming from writers like Martin Amis, Nick Hornby, and Irvine Welsh, *Gate* traffics in behavior that evokes high-stakes gambling, even transcendent adventure.

But the book shuns the florid strokes found in much adventure writing. Too accomplished to go heavy on the signals, Fitzgerald impresses us by what she withholds. There is no busy psychology in *Gate*, no untoward action. The book's leading ideas are implied, and this is its strength. Rather than belaboring a point, *Gate* may foreground it against patterns from Fitzgerald's earlier work. In addition to restoring the motif of the ambassador, from *Spring,* it introduces in chemist George

Holcombe, the smitten sidekick who concocts a plan, allegedly helpful to the hero, that will shift the hero's ladylove to him. *Spring* also supplies the train station as a plot device. The action of *Gate* heats up after Daisy and Kelly travel from the Liverpool Street Station (which also figured in *Bookshop*) to Cambridge.

Other oblique touches help the book. Noting the irony generated by its historical setting, King calls Cambridge's philosophy faculty "an extraordinary concentration of brain power soon to be dispersed by the winds of a brutal war."[14] An important irony put forth by the book's physical setting caught Frank Kermode's eye. Speaking of the finale, Kermode refers to "the gate that should not be opened—which it is, at the very time when, just a few blocks away, scientific men are opening the atom."[15] To these deft strokes may be added the mismatch created by the show of "tree-tops on the earth ... [and] legs in the air" in a "university city devoted to logic and reason" (9). Fitzgerald's eye for incongruity holds steady. Daisy, the book's sanest character, works in a madhouse. "He said he'd take me on for the ironing. We have a lot of incontinents here" (157), her explanation of how she got her low-grade service job, not only conveys important information; it also alludes subtly to Fred, whom she is addressing at the time.

This small stroke typifies *Gate*. Fitzgerald is getting more thematic mileage out of fewer materials. If *Gate* differs from her earlier novels in texture and tone (Angels's musty, grubby residence halls could have come out of a Charles Palliser novel), it is because she has followed Kipling's advice to flee success; any artist who hopes to develop must hazard new subjects and techniques. Always an economical writer, the Fitzgerald of *Gate* discloses a new subtlety and severity. Like all good books, *Gate* leaves us with questions at the end. But this indefiniteness is a plus. The best writers step lightly, keep moving, and leave their dazzled readers to sort it out for themselves.

The ability of indirection and obliqueness to cover so much thematic ground in *The Gate of Angels* bespeaks great storytelling. Disquieting and compelling in a way that few writers are, Fitzgerald creates a world of images, ideas, and people capable of changing the way we view life. *Gate*'s controlled irony and deadpan wit impart a quiet intensity that makes other novels look soggy and loose. A book this nimble comes along rarely, even from the best writers. Along with *Spring*, it comprises Fitzgerald's brilliant, barbed farewell to the new old century she was born into and that ended just a few distressing years ago.

CHAPTER 12

Kind of Blue

Episodic in structure, like Fitzgerald's first five novels through *Freddie's, The Blue Flower* envisages the life of Friedrich, or Fritz, von Hardenberg (1772–1801), the Romantic poet from Germany later known as Novalis. Fitzgerald explains in her author's note that her information for the novel came from a German-language collection of Novalis's work, both published and unpublished, that appeared between 1960 and 1988. This five-volume source stirred both her moral imagination and her artistry. It also jogged her memory. Like *Edward Burne-Jones* (1975), *The Knox Brothers* (1977), and *Charlotte Mew and Her Friends* (1984), *Blue Flower* contains biographical data. But it is no biography. Nor was it intended as one, even though Fitzgerald was writing the life of English novelist L. P. Hartley (1895–1972) when she died. The Fitzgerald of *Blue Flower,* as always, uses precise, evocative language to go past surfaces and into motives. But the last novel she wrote is more of a shapely, nuanced text than a collection of insights and ideas. Its epigraph, from Fritz von Hardenberg, "Novels arise out of the shortcomings of history," claims that every true tale needs a jolt of fiction, usually in the form of imaginative energy or narrative design; no historian can imagine a single turn of human inconstancy. But the imagination has more work to do. In the service of art, the fiction writer must also shape the dullness and deformity she traffics in. An understated authorial presence missing from Fitzgerald's three biographies imbues *Blue Flower*. She knows more than she is telling in her 1995 novel. This subtlety and indirection intrigue us. Richly expressive of her developing economy of means, her sentences hint at the feelings behind them, and she is conversant with a broad range of feelings.

Dread and hope coexist in the novel. Her Fritz is portrayed as the flawed juvenile of the traditional bildungsroman who tries to clear a path through the plod and catastrophe of everyday. He faces more catastrophe than plod. A reality that wielded more force in the 1790s than in the 1912 time setting of *Gate of Angels* was death. This horror comes forth quickly. In the second chapter, a visitor to the Hardenbergs talks of the childhood deaths of his two brothers (by scarlet fever) and a sister (by consumption, or tuberculosis). Such losses were not rare. Childhood mortality pounded many homes, Fritz's mother outliving all but one of her eleven kids. It is no shock that death should dominate a book whose hero died at age twenty-eight. But death's dominance also taught survival skills. Fritz's mother married the boy's father after smallpox took the father's first wife. Others adjust to death as circumstances dictate. Employees marry their bosses' widows, and apprentices, their mentors' daughters or nieces; a professor's junior colleague or favorite student may wed *his* orphaned daughter, too.

The gap between artistic propriety and the toil of everyday life makes up the core tension of Fitzgerald's novel. Guy Mannes-Abbott feels this tension resounding immediately. Fritz is returning home in the first chapter, called "Washday," with a friend: "Fitzgerald introduces the poet to us surrounded by the family's damp underwear."[1] Dampness loads the air. It also produces a surprise. The motifs of cleansing and redemption, supported by Fitzgerald's decision to open her novel on the annual washday of the Hardenberg family, carry less force than the awkwardness felt by Fritz's hapless houseguest, Jacob Dietmahler, as he nears the "great dingy snowfalls" (1) of sheets and small clothes being dumped into baskets. Richard Holmes said of the twenty-two-year-old Dietmahler's arrival in Weissenfels, "He plunges headlong into laundry (rather than poetry)."[2] Though these words blunt Fritz's idealism, they also refer to the proud, aristocratic Hardenbergs' display of their dirty linen in public. The display works as a signal. During our time with them, the family will be constantly trying to sort itself out as its problems grow—often to its embarrassment, regret, and fear of scandal.

The Hardenbergs of Weissenfels, a Saxon town of two thousand people near Leipzig, do belong to the nobility. But they live modestly, having been squeezed financially by King Friedrich of Prussia's involvement in the Seven Years' War. Their home, though big, is shabby and rundown. To save money, they lace their breakfast coffee with burnt carrot powder, and most of their furniture is faded and frayed. In sorrier shape are their estates in Oberwiederstadt and Schlöben. Fritz's father, the Baron, or Freiherr, "a small, stout" (5) Moravian, lacks the cash to refurbish them. As a peer, he is forbidden to hold a range of well-paying jobs open to members of the middle class. At the time he comes before us, he has been supporting himself and his growing family—he fathers two children during the course of the novel—as a Director of Salt Mines. Conservative, as befits both his noble birth and Moravian faith, he dislikes new ideas, particularly the revolutionary ones sprouting in France. Snobbery tempts him, too. His manners, though not coarse, are conspicuously less refined than those of some of his wealthier social inferiors, a truth that vexes him as the book develops.

He is not the only one in the home who is vexed. The family's genteel poverty has burdened Fritz, the second of his parents' eleven kids and their eldest son. Their expectations of him have wavered. A "dreamy, seemingly backward little boy" (9), Fritz began showing signs of genius after fighting off a serious illness at age nine (much like William Gaddis's Wyatt in *The Recognitions* [1955]). But this genius included a maverick streak. When he was ten, his insistence on the unity of body and soul got him expelled from the Moravian school his parents had sent him to. His rebelliousness stayed with him. Though told by his father to study theology and the law, he took courses in history and philosophy. But then, like Giancarlo Ridolfi of *Innocence* and Frank Reid of *Spring,* he left home for career training. He did so gladly. This tall, thin, pale youth with outsized feet welcomed his father's suggestion that he become an Inspector of Salt Mines. In keeping with the purity of his ideals, he saw the mining industry not as drudgery but as a mystical dialogue with the King of Metals. He wants to mine salt. To improve his chances, he studies office management and administration with one Colestin Just, a family friend serving as both a magistrate and tax inspector for the mining town of Tennestedt.

His apprenticeship under Kreisamtsmann (i.e., county official) Just focuses the novel. Fritz accompanies Just on a business trip to Grüningen, which is also the home of the former Kapitän Johann Rudolf Rockenthien, a warm, cheerful man who greets Just as "my oldest friend, my best friend" (66). Aptly, Just had called Rockenthien "someone who keeps his doors open" (65). The doors leading to the family's "quite recently built" (65) manor house are, in fact, standing open as Just and Fritz approach them. Another friendly sign is the light shining from the manor's windows. As she did with the Gate of Angels that supplied the title of her last book, Fitzgerald deploys basic female sexual symbolism to universalize her drama. She even restores the culvert of Dr. Matthews's ghost story, though perhaps in a way rankling to some feminists. Rockenthien's "peaceful-looking" (66) wife first appears lying prone on a sofa. Nor will this mother of six rise when introduced to Just and Fritz. Like Joyce's Molly Bloom, who is always seen abed in *Ulysses,* Wilhelmina comes before us lying flat, like the fruitful earth, not helpless but in a state that will help her fulfill her womanly purpose of creating new life.

But it is her daughter from an earlier marriage who charms Fritz. She compels him at more than one level. Her people, he has seen, though not as well born as his own, are jollier, have better manners, and seem to enjoy life more. But he later delays asking his father the Freiherr's permission to announce his engagement to Sophie von Kühn, an action his mother supports because, should the Freiherr object to the union, she would have to stand by him.

Her fears about conflicting loyalties pass quickly. Though the Freiherr questions both the background and the living arrangements of the arriviste Rockenthiens (159), he consents to the engagement. Yet the wedding gift he chooses for Sophie suggests opposition to the upcoming marriage. In chapter 48, he insisted that he would never part with Schlöben, one of the family's long-held estates. But the following chapter ends with his announcing his plan to give Schlöben to Sophie. He sounds sincere. Besides lacking money of her own, Sophie has been sick, two operations having failed to make her strong and healthy. The stability provided by a fixed residence could comfort and refresh her. But what if the residence were Schlöben? How could living in a tumbledown wreck like Schlöben mean anything to Sophie but toil and grief?

Perhaps the Freiherr is conveying indirectly his disapproval of Sophie's marriage to his son. Perhaps the mischief comes from Fitzgerald. Having loved Schlöben for many years, the Freiherr may well believe that he is giving Sophie a gift beyond diamonds. King Charles of the Austro-Hungarian Empire gave Vienna's magnificent Schönbrunn Palace to his daughter Maria Theresa as a wedding gift. After accepting the palace, she moved into it and spent most of her married life enjoying its luxuriance and splendor. Sophie von Kühn, another German-speaking bride-to-be, dies before her wedding. But, even had she lived to marry Fritz, she would not have survived in a bedraggled ruin like Schlöben. The mischief has taken a dark turn. If the Freiherr wanted to stow Sophie in frowzy Schlöben to speed her death, so that Fritz could remarry and give him grandchildren, he need not have bothered. Sophie would die at fifteen, and Fritz became engaged about a year and a half later (but without marrying his fiancée).

The news of this second engagement in Fitzgerald's afterword redirects our attention to Sophie. This is intended. Sophie's death in Jena, Germany's foremost university town, widens the gap that Fitzgerald had opened between Daisy Saunders and Cambridge in *Gate*. Robert Adamson said that when Johann Gottlieb Fichte arrived in Jena in May 1794 as the University's Professor of Philosophy, "the University was at the height of its renown." Adamson adds that August Wilhelm Schlegel had filled the Chair of History since 1789 (Fitzgerald claims that he taught literature and aesthetics [31]). The playwright Friedrich Schiller also taught history to students who included in their ranks Fritz Hardenberg, Friedrich Hölderlin, and Ludwig Tieck.[3]

In keeping with the widespread Romantic belief (seen in Wordsworth's idiot boy and milkmaids) that the marginal and the dispossessed hold better insights into the character of an age than the regal and the rich, Fitzgerald also calls our attention to Johann Wilhelm Ritter. Despite his lack of formal education, this threadbare physicist believed famously that the impulses traveling between the mind and the body transmitted electrical charges (45). But he does not play the role of brilliant outsider-rescuer, as would suit the radical politics of the day. All the brainpower clustered in Jena cannot help Sophie. In fact, her three operations, all of which included the then latest advances in surgical procedures, may have sped her death. Though handsomely paid for his private lectures on female disorders (208), the distinguished professor who cut her open would have helped her more by leaving her alone.

Fitzgerald and Fritz Hardenberg mesh well. Like Edward Burne-Jones, her first book subject, Fritz saw art as a medium for the dialogue of souls. Obsessive images crowd both men's work, many of which were left unfinished. Fritz's unfinished work includes the novel, "Die Lehrlinge zu Saïs" ("The Novices of Saïs"), *Hymns to the Night* (1800), a book of poems inspired by Sophie's death, and the bildungsroman, or novel of education, "Heinrich von Ofterdingen," which includes the myth of the blue flower.[4] Jennifer Howard explains how the action of "Heinrich" draws less from objective reality than from the depth and vivacity of its author's feelings.[5] Fritz would call the driving impulse behind the quest for the flower universal. Speaking of his book-in-progress, he says, "Perhaps it will not be a novel. There is more truth, perhaps, in folk tales" (110). Like Kafka and the Stravinsky of *The Rite of Spring,* he prefers to probe the collective spirit of a people rather than use a set of made-up characters to move a plot.

Harking to the Romantics' emphasis upon the individual over the group, a young man hears from a stranger, "I have no craving to be rich, but I long to the see the flower." The stranger adds, "It is as if until now I had been dreaming, or as if sleep had carried me into another world" (62, 111). Note the echoes from the English Romantics. From the last stanza of Keats's "Ode to a Nightingale" comes the questioning of the sleep-wake dualism. Possibly awake for the first time, the stranger wonders if he had slept away his whole life up to now, while the power of his tale-telling evokes the mariner in Coleridge's "Rime of the Ancient Mariner." But his dream has not only defied reason; it is also his gift to the young man, the rest of its audience having disclaimed it (63, 111). The dream belongs to the imaginative young man alone. The supremacy of the imagination is thus proclaimed together with, perhaps, alas, the egocentric thinking, emotional excess, and loss of received standards that critics like T. S. Eliot and Kenneth Burke loathed in Romantic verse.

Like Faust's journey, Fritz's begins as an affair of the mind —a craving for unlimited, boundless knowledge. But instead of indulging Faust's passion for the dark and the strange, Fritz seeks unity; to him, as to Walt Whitman, our thoughts and deeds express the universe. This kind of grand unification had also been preoccupying Fitzgerald. Not only does a character in *Spring* say, "Life makes its own corrections", the teenaged Junior Temporary Assistant, Willie Sharpe, too, speaks in *Human Voices* of "general aims for all humanity" (58) that rest on the moral and political equality of all. Fred Fairly of *Gate,* besides repeating the twice-spoken proposition, "Thought is blood" (10, 14, 47), keeps finding evidence of the mystery of unity. He notes that the same classroom techniques he used teaching Sunday school help his students at Cambridge. His words to them, "All thinking is done in precisely the same way" (154), break down distinctions in a way friendlier to the synthesizing imagination of a poet or a religious mystic than to a physicist's analytic bent. Even Fitzgerald's introduction to L. H. Myers's *The Root and the Flower,* which came out in 2001, a year after her death, quotes a passage in which the trilogy's hero says of himself, "Deep in his heart he cherished the belief that some day the near and the far would meet."[6]

The speaker's belief in the oneness of creation chimes with the teachings of the German transcendentalists who influenced Coleridge and, through him, Thomas Carlyle (author of an essay on Novalis). A leading transcendentalist of the day whose passion for synthesis touched many was Fichte, who denied the separation of mind and matter. Fichte also tried to turn philosophical precepts into rules of action; fully developed thought, he claimed, declares itself as activity.[7] For Fritz, too, all abstractions have to meet the test of experience. His search to unify the inner and the outer, as well as philosophy and poetry, has led him to a belief in "universal language, [which existed at] a time when plants, stars, and stones talked on equal terms with animals and men" (61). Recovering this old unity, he says, will raze barriers between the seen and the unseen as well as between past and present.[8] It is this dissolution of daily reality into myth that makes his job as a miner so exciting to him. No limp-wristed decadent, this youth who walked thirty-two miles in one day dives into life full bore.

The youth's concept of life as a seamless, interacting whole brings shocks when applied directly to existence. Not only did his "mystical spiritualism" get him expelled from school at age nine.[9] The little brother he saves from drowning in chapter 4 rewards him by making him eat his words about his belief in death's sameness to life: "You said that death was not significant, but only a change in condition" (12), Bernard insists; no cause for alarm, the death he was spared from was a logical corollary of Fritz's claim that all is one. Six-year-old Bernhard has hard-focused a belief that his brother only reads and prattles about. His words stymie Fritz in one of the book's frequent disruptions of narrative flow. A disquieting sense of menace pervades the everyday in *Flower*, another example being the return of the dismemberment motif from *Innocence* and *Gate*. That the dismembered body part is once again a finger, some fingers, or a hand reshapes the hand in Michelangelo's ceiling on the Sistine Chapel into a claw, invoking the rapacity our animal origins have bred into us. That the dismembered person, like Chiara Ridolfi's Aunt Mad, is an innocent victim or a loser posits life as a battlefield or Darwinian jungle in which only the lucky few keep all their body parts.

No, Fritz does not lose a finger, a hand, or the flesh from one of his arms. But a woman who has fallen in love with him notes inwardly in chapter 17, "She would rather cut off one of her hands than disappoint him" (63). Back in chapter 9, Fitzgerald used the dismemberment motif to test Fritz's belief that all things commune with each other. In a moment of anarchic clarity, Fritz has the chance to enact his philosophy of self-transcendence, but not in a way he had foreseen. He does not grab a horse's slithery tongue as Florence Green did in *Bookshop*. Rather, he must hold in his mouth two fingers lost by a fellow student in a duel until he and a medic arrive at an anatomy theater, where the fingers can be reattached. The bloated mixture of dirt, blood, and saliva that is making him gag en route to the theater gives him his comeuppance, as he admits (34). As well he might; the job of joining the practical to the ideal faces many worries, some of which can shake our sides with either laughter or rage.

These worries also prefigure the accelerating death drift that overtakes the Hardenbergs. In Fitzgerald's earlier work, blocked desire led to heartache and isolation. *Flower* shows it inducing death. Fitzgerald's afterword reminds us, "At the end of the 1790s the young Hardenbergs . . . began to go down, almost without protest, with pulmonary tuberculosis" (226). Their collapse completes a pattern. Two of the Hardenberg children loved a girl who would die of tuberculosis. The brilliant piano work of another, Anton, sends Bernhard to the same riverside where he will later drown, as he may have intended.[10] The boy's yearning for the infinite, like that of his brother Fritz, has curdled into a death wish. More clearly than in any other Fitzgerald novel, Thomas Mann's great 1948 parable of music and evil, *Doctor Faustus,* forms a ghostly paradigm to *Flower,* even though there is no pact with the devil. Music, the most potent and magical of the arts and the most difficult to analyze, can send the golden-voiced Bernhard into binges of self-destruction. Others sense his self-destructive bent. At the end of chapter 49, when he visits Sophie's sick house, he is told, "You shouldn't have come here" (204). Though he is called "Angel" (8, 204) by his family, the shakiness of his grip on life has made him a bringer of bad luck, an evil spirit like the gargoyles seen outside—but never in—Gothic churches.[11]

Fritz's faith in the supremacy of the imagination has posited an organicism that, like the one found in music, is stubbornly nonutilitarian and self-reflexive. Eons from the optimism of Whitman and Robert Browning, *Flower* denies our capacity both to trump forces that look overwhelming and live to the hilt. Part of Fitzgerald's fascination with Fritz's doomed love bond with Sophie, called by W. A. O'Brien "the most profound experience of his life," comes from an age difference that marks most of the other troubled sexual ties she writes about.[12] (Advisedly, she withheld the birth dates of both her mother and stepmother in the Genealogy section of *The Knox Brothers* [x–xi] as well as any reference to her husband's date of birth anywhere in her writing.) When they meet in 1794, Fritz is twenty-two and Sophie is twelve. This age difference colors O'Brien's reading of the relationship, one that evokes that of another German-language writer, Franz Kafka (1883–1924), with *his* fiancée. Called by Alan Bennett a man "who wanted to be somebody and nobody at the same time," Kafka dallied with the prostitutes of Prague while keeping his fiancée at bay.[13] Though he wrote many letters to Felice Bauer of Berlin, he avoided spending time with her. Their rare meetings usually fell flat because he sabotaged them. As a writer, he had the rhetorical skills to control the engagement by conducting it through the mails.

Though not plagued by Kafka's anxieties, Fritz may have used the same approach-avoidance strategy with Sophie. The strategy may have also been unconscious. Unlike Kafka, Fritz did want something hot and vital from his beloved. The sexually aggressive phrase he uses with her in conversation, "those succulent looks of yours" (147), conveys this lust. But the same lust that thrilled him also chafed. Speaking of a "regressive infantilism" that may have carried a charge of pedophilia, O'Brien claims that Fritz was all too glad to postpone sex with Sophie. This delaying game, whether intended or not, filled some important needs. Besides giving Fritz time to sort out his feelings, it also supplied "a delightful obstacle" that helped him conjure up "an endless promise of future bliss."[14]

But why Sophie? An answer to this question invokes the genius with which *Flower* blends subject matter, literary history, and technique. We see little of Sophie; as in Henry James, her bond with Fritz is talked about more than it is acted upon. But Fitzgerald's twofold tactic of avoiding extended descriptions of her and limiting her appearances on the page heightens the book's subjective strain, in deference to the age's preference for the imagination over reason. Perhaps Fritz sees and hears her as little as we do; he falls in love with her before seeing her face. Yet she wins his heart totally, a conquest that must be accepted as a given.

Probing the inner realities that govern the action of *Flower,* Fitzgerald faces the conquest squarely. What little she shows us of Sophie is not impressive. Sophie lacks the witty lucid tongue found in the prepubescent Christine Gipping of *Bookshop,* Tilda James of *Offshore,* and Dolly Reid of *Spring.* O'Brien cites her "poor grammar and spelling," and Gabriel Annan says, "She could barely write a letter. What she liked were presents and fun."[15] A budding scholar she is not. She misspells and mispronounces words, and her teacher stopped teaching her when put off by her lack of progress. Then there is her lack of reticence and modesty. This "very noisy" (90) girl with a double chin laughs unbecomingly. And even if her wine drinking, pipe smoking, and tobacco chewing were not unusual pastimes for preteen German girls in the 1790s, Fitzgerald knows that they would repel most of today's readers. In fact, she included these details to make us wonder anew why the sensitive youth who would soon become Novalis could be so awed by Sophie.

Our skepticism is soon tempered. Like Frances Green of *Bookshop* and Daisy Saunders of *Gate*, Sophie is a fighter. She endures three surgeries without anesthetic, and, though still ailing, musters the courage to show up at the engagement party the Hardenbergs give for her. Once in Weissenfels, she also transcends the weakness and pain conveyed by both her late arrival and the cap she is wearing. When asked for a lock of her hair by Fritz's smitten brother, Erasmus, she laughs. Her sickness having made her bald, she has no hair to give. Her burst of laughter is perhaps her greatest moment. Laughing at the unspeakable is the best way to tame it. It restores a balance that helps us respond rationally and wisely. This restoration must have cost Sophie dearly. But she does not complain. Like that of Daisy Saunders, her heart is right, even though she lacks formal schooling.

She knows instinctively, for instance, how to present herself to young men. Having learned of Fritz's arrival at her home in Grüningen, she makes sure to catch his attention. Not only does she stand by a window, a symbol of communication; she also taps on it when she senses his presence in the room. Fritz's visit has been on her mind. To prepare for it, she let her hair down in the back rather than putting it up, as her mother would have preferred. Her mother is miles from her thoughts. In the next chapter, no sooner does Fritz introduce himself to Sophie than she touches her flowing hair. Her maneuver works. Later, while he is trying to summon up a mental picture of her, he thinks first of her hair.

He is too dazzled to conjure up an image of her face. It is a further tribute to her that the artist he hires to paint her picture fails to do so. He has become infatuated with her, too. He cannot catch her likeness any more than Parenti, the ace couturier in *Innocence*, can make a dress for the beautiful Chiara Ridolfi.

Female beauty hamstrings men. Fritz will twice call Sophie "cold through and through" (113, 136) because what beguiles him in her has also routed both his memory and powers of analysis. His frustration cuts deep. Yet he also courts it. He could not suppress it if he wanted to. Herein lies Sophie's rough magic. She offers him mystery, which poses a greater imaginative challenge than would a girl who appealed to his intelligence.

His first response to her, framed before he has seen her face. "Let time stand still until she turns around" (67), shows that she —or, more properly, her carefully arranged hair—has launched him into an eternity, where everyday standards and distinctions count for nil. Even more than Daisy Saunders, she is Goethe's Eternal Woman; men who turn their minds to her cannot think beyond the love she has roused in them. Goethe's appearance in *The Blue Flower* calls our attention to the point. Though his sensibility is tamer than that of Fritz, or Novalis, his belief that beauty defies categories and precedents to set its own agenda applies directly to the younger man: "Rest assured, it is not her understanding that we love in a young girl. We love her beauty, her innocence, her trust in us, her airs and graces, her God knows what—but we don't love her for her understanding." (189).

Fritz's own understanding has scaled dizzy new heights. The headiness of his response to Sophie tallies with the neoplatonic doctrine of love as reminiscence. Being with Sophie stirs his recollection of the divine, which is why he calls her "my guardian spirit," "my Philosophy, [and] my heart's blood" (154, 157). Sophie's name means wisdom, and Fritz believes that knowing her has blessed him with divine insight. His yearning for her also reflects the soul's desire to reunite with ultimate beauty (i.e., God). If she is ordinary, her ordinariness only matters because Fritz has beatified it.

But what price beatification? How long could she continue as his joy and his wisdom? It is difficult to sustain both harmony and passion in any erotic bond, let alone one like Fritz and Sophie's, where the eroticism is marred by pedophilic cravings. What will happen when the stars fall from his eyes? Sophie's early death removes the need to ask the question. But the question makes sense, anyway, because, when Fritz and Sophie agreed to marry, they both wanted their tie to reach into old age. How realistic was this wish? If she validates his faith in God, his overweening response to her also calls forth the figure of the destructive female, as is seen in Coleridge's "Christabel," Keats's "La Belle Dame sans Merci," and Heine's "Lorelei." The ailing Sophie embodies disease and death, the TB that will soon kill her being rampantly contagious. This hindsight decrees that her first words in the novel, spoken in response to her mother's asking why she is looking out the window, should be, "I'm willing it to snow" (67). Snow's association with death in works like James Joyce's "The Dead" and Robert Frost's "Stopping by Woods on a Snowy Evening" foreground Sophie's answer to her mother. But also at stake in the scene is Freud's belief, dramatized so stunningly in D. M. Thomas's *The White Hotel*, that even in sex's wildest, most leaping moments of joy can be glimpsed the end of both sex and love. Wordlessly, Sophie and Fritz have held a mirror meeting that graced both of them with a prophetic insight. But sustaining this flame-tip of mutual recognition would have crushed them. As a few questions asked by Sophie's older sister in chapter 41 show, Fritz is unaware of the practicalities of marriage. When asked how he expects to support Sophie, he blurts out an array of ridiculous options. "Courage makes us dreamers, courage makes us poets" (157), he also peals, forgetting that it does not pay the rent or put food on the table any more than it can teach Sophie how to cook, sweep floors, or do laundry. The piles of dirty wash shown in the book's first scene cast long shadows.

Perhaps his euphoria has blotted out the toil of keeping house. It is with reason that Fitzgerald refers to him in narration as Fritz and not Hardenberg or Novalis; he is callow and unready. One of his verses includes the line, "Never does the heart sigh in vain" (78). The line is repeated twice (105, 133). Perhaps Fritz had intimations of his early death, a logical enough byproduct of his yen for the infinite. A love that loses out to death before it is consummated is more heartrending than one cooled by the compromises and discontents of marriage. Whereas sex became a bitter doom to Keats and an act of guilt to the incestuous, bisexual Byron, Fritz Hardenberg, or Novalis, always saw perfection in Sophie. Chapter 22 of *Flower* is called "Now Let Me Get to Know Her." But the chapter brings no intellectual recognition. Fritz keeps talking over Sophie's head, and, without being evasive or coy, she keeps thwarting his efforts either to pitch their discussion to a lofty philosophical level or to pump it up with emotion.

She is following no plan. She is young, carefree, and innocent, which excuses her in his eyes, as it would in those of Goethe, from cultivating conversational chic. As O'Brien says, Fritz has been turning her into his "first major work of fiction."[16] The object of his passion is thus only an accessory to the passion itself. Mona Knapp, who reviewed *Flower* in *World Literature Today,* would agree. After noting the drabness of Sophie's talk and her near illiteracy, Knapp says, "Perhaps Sophie's vacuous nature should highlight the fact that romantic yearning itself, not its object, becomes the true source of creativity."[17] Fritz's poetic sensibility has redeemed the ordinary. By assigning Sophie more beauty and depth than almost anyone in his circle does, Fritz, who first saw her standing by a window, creates, thanks to her, a window beyond life's commonness.

But it slams shut quickly. The success of his bond with Sophie declares itself in terms he would find rankling. Like a husband who is the last to know of a big change on his wife's part (Frank Reid comes to mind), Fritz is ignorant of Sophie's plans to have surgery (192). But he has connived at his ignorance. He was not told because he does not want to know. In the chapter following her first operation, he writes in his notebook the phrase, "The wound I must not see" (195). He never finishes the Sophie-inspired *Hymns to the Night* and, the year after Sophie's death, he asks another woman to marry him (225). Nor is he with Sophie during her final overthrow. In fact, he may have avoided her during the last weeks of her life (220, 225). No Byronic hero he. If he risks all for love, scales love's heights, and plunges into despair, he also recovers quickly.

Sophie might have died more happily had she chosen to marry "stumpy little Erasmus," Fritz's younger, less charismatic forester-brother. Erasmus's falling from a horse strikes an eerie chord with her deathbed impression of the sound of horses' hooves (8, 88, 225). This acausal connection matters. Asmus fell from his horse en route to Sophie, whom he rushed to meet after learning of Fritz's love for her. The love that seizes him straightaway rivals Fritz's in both purity and intensity. When Fritz returns to Weissenfels after seeing Sophie for the last time, Asmus is the lone family member waiting for him. He wants news of Sophie, just as he will ask Goethe his opinions on sexual love—because he is worried about Sophie's happiness, not Fritz's (185). He fell in love with Sophie with the same blinding speed as Fritz did.

This speed is dramatized to convey its surge. The last sentence of chapter 23 explains that Asmus has left Weissenfels to meet Sophie (88). By the time chapter 24 begins, he has already spent time with her and fallen in love with her. Then he tells Fritz that Sophie is so far beneath him intellectually that he should forget her. But her talk with Asmus, drab as it might have been, has opened places in his psyche where her alleged stupidity lacks meaning. It is love that prompts him to ask for a lock of her hair in chapter 44. Sophie's illness has remained an issue with him—but not a deterrent. When he wonders in chapter 49 if the Freiherr, the Baron, will block Fritz's marriage to a girl whose sickness may have barred her from childbearing, he is voicing an indirect wish (203). The father's ban would create a chance for Asmus himself. So strong is the youth's love for Sophie that her barrenness would not stop him from wedding her himself—even if he would have to cross his father to do it.

In a Chekhovian blend of irony and pathos, this one-sided, self-scourging love comes closer to the Romantic ideal than that known by Fritz, who is developing into Germany's greatest Romantic poet. Erasmus's is the heart that sighs most longingly. Word of his doomed love reaches us by means of the irony of discrepant awareness. But Fitzgerald gains more than economy and narrative drive by ending chapter 38 of *Flower* with the observation: "Karoline perceived that Erasmus had fallen in love with Sophie von Kühn" (145). Karoline's observation has recoiled on her. The two love triangles that enrich the book are more poignant than any similar grouping in Fitzgerald's earlier work for two reasons: Karoline is the daughter of Colestin Just, the tax officer and magistrate (47) to whom Fritz has been apprenticed. At twenty-seven, she is also becoming a domestic drudge (52, 55), a fate she hopes Fritz can save her from. And he has given her reason to expect a marriage proposal. Right after meeting her, he calls beautiful, and then she becomes the first person to hear his story of the blue flower (49, 62–63). She has also, unfortunately, become his confidante; she must hear twice (69, 70) that he has fallen in love with Sophie.

Karoline may be more vexed by Fritz than Erasmus is. After protesting that Fritz could not have lost his heart to paltry, bad-mannered Sophie, she must acquiesce when he, her secret love, says, "You don't grasp the nature of desire between a man and a woman" (74). Later, she will reject a suitor because he is younger than she (143). But being five years Fritz's senior never worried her. Capable, loving, and well read, the verbally skilled Karoline offers Fritz much more than the unformed Sophie. "How could he?" (104, 106) she asks twice in disbelief upon learning that she has lost out to the pudgy twelve-year-old. But she is appealing to reason, which as Goethe will say, is irrelevant to the heart's impulses. She had intuited this truth herself (55–57). It is only when it leaves her alone in the cold that she denies it.

Karoline, who will later marry a younger cousin she dislikes (226), is one of several women in the book condemned to drabness; better to have a man at home than to droop in isolation, like Faust's Gretchen or Margaret, spinning her wheel and musing about a beloved who is out of reach. Karoline deserves better—which Fritz will not give her. In the last line of chapter 15, after rousing in her expectations he will not fulfill, he tells her that he intends to call her Justen (57) rather than Karoline. Minutes before, he had called her the thesis to his antithesis (56). What she wants is his heart. What she gets is a new name she does not need and the news that she has become a cog in a dialectical scheme. By renaming women, men shape them to fit their own wishes. They are acting like gods. Fritz's mother's real name was Bernardine, but because her husband did not like it, he called her by her middle name, Auguste (17). Sophie is Fritz's philosophy and spirit's guide. Yet during her last, fatal, sickness, he says, "I love Sophie more because she is ill" (217). He can control her more easily; she cannot fight back from a sickbed. He is also risking less. Besides putting her in debt to him morally, the help he extends to her evokes his pity, a response directed to one's inferiors, whereas compassion presumes an equality that threatens him.

Exempt from the dominance-dependence pattern he prefers is Frederike, or Frau Leutnant Mandelsoh, who enters the action slamming to the ground a water bucket (99). The bucket, we soon learn, she intends to use to drown some unwanted kittens. Both this association with death and the splash created by the bucket foreshadow Frieke's role in the plot. Her husband stationed in France, she has come to Grüningen to care for her ailing sister, Sophie. She was a good choice as Sophie's caretaker. When we learn, at the end of chapter 52, that she is the same age (twenty-two) as the innocent, lovesick Erasmus, we are shocked (212). This "exquisite dancer" (178) is in tune with life's rhythms. Perhaps her competence and good sense comforted Sophie and extended her life. Acting prudently, she kept Fritz away from Sophie during a bad spell. Though Fritz calls her "a bully . . . a lance-corporal masquerading as a woman" (217), he is quickly reminded that he refused to look at the entry wound from Sophie's recent surgery, a wound that Frieke, who was on hand for all three of Sophie's surgeries, has to dress regularly.

But Fritz's broadside does crease its target. Separated from her soldier-husband, Frederike has had plenty of time to ponder the drawbacks of sexual love. She is also right to keep Fritz from Sophie during her worst days—even though she does not have to try very hard. The last thing Sophie needs to boost her spirits is one of Fritz's arias of eternal devotion. Fitzgerald commends the Mandelsoh's initiative, all the more for its rarity among eighteenth-century women. She must have enjoyed noting in her afterword that Frieke divorced her husband in 1800, remarried, and lived till age seventy-five, unlike most of her counterparts, who died in their twenties or earlier (226).

The scenes in *Flower* reflect unerring dramatic judgment. Fitzgerald writes with friendly, fluid ease, as if she knows her characters personally, and her descriptive passages are both lyrical and precise. It is as if she brought all of her resources—her talent and craft, thought and feeling, courage and vulnerability—to the book. The critical distance she maintains between us and Fritz lends insight into Sophie's illness, a development Fitzgerald carefully manages to spare us the toil of having to fill in the gaps. Sophie's reference to a pain in her left side is the first sign of her fatal disorder. On the next page, the action of which unfolds weeks later, the pain signals "Sophie's first serious illness" (137), a tubercular hip. In chapter 41, she is taken to a rest home to recuperate, always an act of futility in Fitzgerald. Sophie's health does not improve any more than Fitzgerald's mother's or Charlotte Mew's sister Caroline Anne did in similar retreats. Her later appearances find Sophie looking yellowish and smaller than she was; she has started to smell. In chapter 47, she is operated on—unsuccessfully, we soon learn—for a tumor.

Though these developments compel us, most of the book's virtue comes from its evocative powers; mood and tone trump the exigencies of plot structure in *Flower*. Fitzgerald enjoyed this kind of artistic challenge, a kite that tugs hard at the string that keeps it from flying away. The book's epigraph, from Novalis, "Novels arise out of the shortcomings of history," explains why novels attract us. Our taste for continuity and closure rises from the disquiet we feel when faced, as we are most of the time, by turmoil and the refusal of pattern. *Flower* shapes the defining events in the lives of Fritz and his circle. But it also repels quick or confident value judgments.

The book downplays conventional narrative modes like anecdote and character development—along with plot—to describe actions both personal and world-historical. To a lesser degree, Fitzgerald is following the examples of Yeats, Eliot, and Pound by confronting life's messiness with technical innovations. First, she subverts the optimism that usually goes hand-in-glove with the coming-of-age story. Her hero does not break free at the end to a wider, finer world. The heroine dies. But even had she lived, she might have bored Fritz, or worse; what she needed was not a husband, but a nursemaid, a job ill suited to him. Perhaps he even chose her because he knew she would not live ("I love Sophie more because she is ill" [217]). Sustaining a passion as mighty as his would take a miracle. And the passion's decline would embitter him. Had his awareness of her flaws not cooled his heart, in fact, he would have sunk in our esteem.

Fitzgerald's subversive streak has held in place. By explaining in her afterword what happened to all the book's characters, she is subverting subversion. But this defiance of postmodernism's love of inconclusiveness is a healthy sign; good artists elude definitions. Let Fitzgerald be explicit. *Flower* continues to keep us alert. The strident, off-key chapter endings that make us question how carefully we have been reading the text return from *Gate*. Also restored from *Gate* are those bald, teasing chapter titles. In chapter 53, "A Visit to Magister Kegel," Sophie's stepfather asks her old teacher to resume the lessons he had stopped some three years earlier. Kegel does come to the Rockenthiens' home in chapter 55, "Magister Kegel's Lesson," but without being magisterial. The lesson he tries to give, which collapses in a squall of house pets, ends early—as will the life of his pupil. Kegel, meanwhile, is too minor a figure to have his name featured in two chapter titles, particularly near book's end.

But if Fitzgerald's meaning hangs just out of reach, the care she took orchestrating *Flower* stops us from faulting her. First, the book demonstrates admirable control and selection. Rather than describe the surgery Professor Stark performs on Sophie without anesthetic at the end of chapter 47, Fitzgerald notes the two preliminary incisions Stark makes on his patient and then jumps to the point of view of the curious landlady in whose house the surgery is taking place: "Frau Winkler, waiting below on the bottom stair, had been able to hear nothing, but now her patience was rewarded" (194). This jump-cut leads to another. The action leaps from the pain-racked Sophie and her squeamish fiancé, a tactic that produces great tension because of the ordeals that have been undermining the fiancé's belief in the supremacy of both individual experience and the life of feeling.

A dubious subjectivity also occupies the novel's midmost point. Chapter 28 of the fifty-five-chapter book records entries from Sophie's diary extending from January 8 to March 14, 1795. Fitzgerald's having made the chapter one of the book's shortest is thematic, largely because the diary entries comprising it are short and flat, revealing little curiosity, linguistic flourish, insight into people, and, at least once, knowledge of grammar. The March 12 entry typifies the dullness of the mind behind the diary: "Today was like yesterday and nothing much happened" (108). Once again, Sophie flops by objective standards; she lacks charm and brains. But, rather than maligning her, Fitzgerald is issuing a challenge; in order to grasp the mind-set of Fritz and his times, we have to sink our biases about human worth. To dismiss Sophie as a dolt is to disrespect Fritz's feelings—and to dampen one's own reading of the novel.

Yet the hollowness of the middle chapter, like the book's many heated conversations that break or wander off before gaining resolution, denies *Flower* the traction most great fiction provides. It is not realistic enough to be a novel. Like a poem or a dream, it unfurls in a dreamscape bristling with jumbled but resonant symbols. Events are set off by images. Occurring out of view, the expected death comes, but without the expected emotions. Agile but puzzling, *The Blue Flower* is Fitzgerald's strangest book.

We keep feeling that she knows more than she is telling. In Beckett's sense, the teller and the tale are one. In what she might have known would be her last novel, Fitzgerald went back further into her personal past than ever before. Sophie died just after turning fifteen. Fitzgerald was eighteen when her mother died. But this loss, brutal as it was, only flattened her temporarily. Her later graduation from Somerville, the Oxford college where Christina took her degree, stands as an act of homage as well as an academic triumph. Penelope recreated herself in her mother's image. This pattern recurred in *The Bookshop,* when the devastation and the clamor wreaked by a poltergeist fused the spirits of a frightened eleven-year-old Christine Gipping and her sixty-year-old employer Florence Green (Christina's middle name was Frances). The fusion evokes Christian myth. The argument, popular among Christians, that God chastens those

He loves, hinges on the belief that, by hurting us, He is joining us to His Son in suffering.

Fitzgerald's modification of this transference in *Flower* imbues the book's deep structure. But it leaves no telltale signs of self-indulgence. The curiosity and anxiety with which we respond to Sophie, rather, builds suspense. Without dominating the novel's action or smudging the precision of Fitzgerald's technique, Christina Hicks Knox's spirit helps make *The Blue Flower* a complete, compassionate work.

CONCLUSION

History Illuminated

Penelope Fitzgerald's novels look plain and rambling at first glance, but fuller, stranger, and more stirring the more we invest in them. Certain passages need to be reread, as if their pure, intuitive truth cannot be grasped the first time around. She has, first of all, an instinctive gift for the sequencing of events that can produce an unsettling effect that questions the conventions of comedy. She will also enhance these effects by not leaning too hard on them. There is a refusal in her work to overplay effects and emotions. At first puzzling in its disdain for drama, this restraint turns out to be one of her chief virtues. Her mazes have their turns and surprises, which unfold cunningly. Larger associations will emerge at their own pace as big dramatic scenes are kept from interfering with wider patterns. Thus Sophie von Kühn's death in *The Blue Flower* goes unreported till the book's afterword; *The Gate of Angels* ends before Fred Fairly and Daisy Saunders confront each other in one last try at bonding; Nenna and Edward James of *Offshore* part company, probably forever, without saying goodbye. But to call Fitzgerald's theme the recalcitrance of life is to come up short. Her renderings of physical sensations, like her rhythmic, sensuous descriptions of the birch wood in *The Beginning of Spring*, are exhilarating, giving objects a dramatic edge and potency.

Such moments improve our grip upon the actual. The novels depict the collisions of a highly developed inner reality with an acute sense of an outer reality that often frustrates or disappoints. This battle of inner and outer makes Fitzgerald a religious writer, one to whom everything counts because it comes from God. What also stops her sharp eye for small, inconspicuous things from producing catalogs of dull regularity is her power to disclose the existential within the ordinary. She can, for instance, voice with rare, moving clarity how it feels to be trapped in the nether world of the self, remote from God. The genre she used progressively to lead our sympathies to exciting, unexpected places is the historical novel. Though often scorned as a branch of Gothic romance, the historical novel houses the rewards of both fiction and nonfiction. When well done, it both illuminates history and transcends it ("Novels arise out of the shortcomings of history"), revealing constants of the human heart. Some writers today see history *as* fiction. Because we cannot always know what happened, let us invent it, as Thomas Pynchon, Don DeLillo, and William T. Vollmann have been doing with the shards of American history they have unearthed. These men have succeeded because they know, as Novalis did, that history needs a charge of imagination to put ways of living on a par with ways of feeling. Any historical setting can be imagined into existence. What counts, as Henry James enjoyed reminding us, is the quality of the imagining.

Fitzgerald meets James's standards. She bolsters her historian's attention to minute analysis with the seasoned journalist's awareness of the drama in the story she is telling. History furnishes the costumes, living arrangements, and eating habits (like the Christmas ritual of serving pig snouts and ears boiled in peppermint schnapps in *Flower*) of Fitzgerald's people. Her last three novels are splendid, disarming evocations of things past. They prove that good writing refreshes our awareness of what we have already seen, literally or not. But they do not supplant confrontation with nostalgia. Fitzgerald takes us inside her people to describe historical forces as embodied motives.

The best historical fiction combines the virtues of regional and social literature. Most importantly, it delivers emotional truth through the lives of imaginary, but ordinary, people. By ascribing to Erasmus Hardenberg purer, finer feelings for Sophie von Kühn than those felt by his brother, Fritz, Fitzgerald conveys the texture of events long smoothed out by the generalizations found in conventional histories. The period detail found in her work also addresses issues of inequality between men and women. Annie Asra's choice of clothes for her BBC job interview in *Human Voices* and the impulse that tells Sophie how to seize Fritz's attention spell out the process by which women outclass their much older men in the canon—but usually to no avail. With historical accuracy, Fitzgerald looks at the skewed power relationships between men and women, and, like V. S. Naipaul, but in a gentler vein, the steps by which political turmoil swamps ordinary lives. Her practice of interlinking fictional characters with icons like Noël Coward in *At Freddie's* or Antonio Gramsci in *Innocence* also imparts a convincing realism because these linkages are both historically apt and very contemporary in their psychology.

The same claim can be made for the remarks of Goethe in *Flower*. Fitzgerald has created an array of colorful, credible people, some borrowed from real life. She also uses multiple points of view to capture both their isolation and their impulse to bond; like an Anita Brookner character, Jeff Haggard of *Human Voices* and Selwyn Crane of *Spring* both yearn to connect with others while carefully guarding their privacy. Fitzgerald has put herself in the shoes of these people without patronizing them. Benefitting from the compression built out of crisp wording and sharpness of detail, she uses conflictiveness like theirs to hint at deeper mysteries and truths. The ineffable always beckons her. The Thames River, with its unforgiving tides and undertows, is a primitive force that the houseboaters in *Offshore* have to withstand; it is a font of legends and the muse of the painter Sam Willis. It is also a setting for childish pranks and games that may be more disturbing than funny. A function of her artistic intent, even Fitzgerald's mischief carries an undercurrent of gravitas. Because she cares for what is to be said and the best way to say it, her prose has a heightened aesthetic charge that suits her attentiveness to the complex truth of human feeling.

A crackshot writer with a wicked turn of phrase, Fitzgerald also hates pretension. Her vision is unsparing and honest, and her emotions ring true. Voicing her candor and compression is an exceptionally disciplined prose that gives her work a sure sense of mood, place, and character. Elizabeth Hay credits her in the Toronto *Globe and Mail* with "a mind so sharp and funny, an imagination so rich, and a heart and moral reach so huge that you want to get down on your knees and give thanks."[1] In *New Republic,* Gertrude Himmelfarb calls her "one of the great novelists of her generation."[2] These women hit the mark. Ignoring Fitzgerald is a crime against ourselves. Her books touch the heart and lodge in the memory. Rather than aiming to win a jury verdict, they make us think. She holds no truck with behaviorism, the theory that human personality stems, not from inner forces, but from the self's encounter with positive and negative stimuli in the environment. Great teaching occurs at the bedraggled, tumbledown Temple School in *At Freddie's*. Thameside living in *Offshore* has an aura of pathos but also of glory because of its daily struggles against great odds. It also spells out Fitzgerald's faith in the resilience of the human spirit, the courage fueling our quest for freedom and self-determination on hostile grounds.

Her heart is vividly alive. The thoroughness of her research and her keen artistic judgment have created a wide variety of cultural backgrounds for her books, while her eye for the telling moment, as with her description of the unlucky bear cub in *Spring,* can generate writing that looks and feels like more than writing. Serious fiction respects itself and its audience. Fitzgerald thus tempers her audacity. Her sometimes spiraling, percussive prose fuzzes up and blurs as artistic propriety decrees, and her restrained, elegant irony finds ways to build tension between big dramatic scenes. Her peerless style brings it all home. Penelope Fitzgerald cannot write a dull sentence, and not only the English novel but also the English language itself gains from this.

Notes

Chapter 1—The Benefits of Starting Late

1. Harriet Harvey-Wood, "Penelope Fitzgerald," *Guardian,* May 3, 2000, 22.

2. Dinitia Smith, "Penelope Fitzgerald, Novelist, Is Dead at 83," *New York Times,* May 3, 2000, B10.

3. Ibid.

4. Avrum Fenson, "The School of Soft Knox," *Globe and Mail* (Toronto), December 2, 2000, D8.

5. Anita Brookner, "Moscow before the Revolution," *Spectator,* October 1, 1988, 29–30; A. S. Byatt, "A Delicate Form of Genius," *Threepenny Review* (Spring 1998): 13–15; see also Byatt, introduction to *The Means of Escape* (Boston: Houghton Mifflin, 2000; Boston: Mariner Books, 2001), ix–xxx.

6. Philip Hensher, "Perfection in a Small Space," *Spectator,* October 21, 2000, 44; Hermione Lee, "Listening Carefully," *Times Literary Supplement,* October 20, 2000, 20; Richard Eder, "Penelope Fitzgerald, Her Family's Eyes and Heart," *New York Times,* August 31, 2000, 8E; Harvey-Wood, "Penelope Fitzgerald," 22.

7. Penelope Fitzgerald, "How an Artist's Vision Becomes Ours," *New York Times,* sec. 2: 1–2, October 29, 1989.

8. Penelope Fitzgerald, *The Golden Child* (London: Duckworth, 1977; Boston: Mariner Books, 1999), 71. Citations are to the Mariner edition.

9. Byatt, "A Delicate Form of Genius," 13.

10. Penelope Fitzgerald, *The Bookshop* (London: Duckworth, 1978; Boston: Mariner Books, 1997), 69. Citations are to the Mariner edition.

11. Penelope Fitzgerald, *Offshore* (London: Collins, 1979; Boston: Mariner Books, 1998), 53. Citations are to the Mariner edition.

12. Penelope Fitzgerald, *The Gate of Angels* (London: Collins, 1990; Boston: Mariner Books, 1998), 23. Citations are to the Mariner edition.

13. Blake Morrison, "Looking Backward," *New Statesman*, November 10, 1978, 30.

14. John Bayley, "Innocents at Home," *New York Review of Books*, April 9, 1992, 14.

15. Penelope Fitzgerald, *At Freddie's* (London: Collins, 1982; Boston: Mariner Books, 1999), 121. Citations are to the Mariner edition.

16. Penelope Fitzgerald, "What He Did for His In-Laws," *New York Times Book Review*, February 7, 1988, 19.

17. Penelope Fitzgerald, *Edward Burne-Jones: A Biography* (London: Joseph, 1975; London: Hamish Hamilton, 1989), 188.

18. Penelope Fitzgerald, *Human Voices* (London: Collins, 1980; Boston: Mariner Books, 1999), 130. Citations are to the Mariner edition.

19. Joan Acocella, "Assassination on a Small Scale," *New Yorker*, February 7, 2000, 82.

20. Penelope Fitzgerald, *The Blue Flower* (London: Flamingo, 1995; Boston: Mariner Books, 1997), 10. Citations are to the Mariner edition.

21. Houghton Mifflin Books, "A Reader's Guide: *The Gate of Angels* by Penelope Fitzgerald," http://www.houghtonmifflinbooks.com/readers_guides/fitzgerald_gate.shtml.

22. Amazon, "High Spirits: The Great Penelope Fitzgerald on Poltergeists, Plots, and Great Masters," http://www.amazon.com/exec/obidos/tg/feature/-/10326/002 5437/39 5118461 (1998).

23. Ibid., 4.

24. Fitzgerald, *The Means of Escape*, 71.

25. Penelope Fitzgerald, "The Great Encourager," *New York Times Book Review*, March 10, 1991, 7.

26. Penelope Fitzgerald, introduction to *A Month in the Country*, by J. L. Carr (London: Penguin, 2000), xii.

27. Amazon, "High Spirits," 1.

28. Ibid., 3.

29. Penelope Fitzgerald, *The Knox Brothers* (London: Macmillan, 1977; Washington, D.C.: Counterpoint, 2000), 208.

30. Penelope Fitzgerald, "To Remember Is to Forgive," *New York Times Book Review,* February 13, 1994, 7.

31. Penelope Fitzgerald, *Charlotte Mew and Her Friends: with a Selection of Her Poems* (London: Collins, 1984), 41, 40, 48.

32. Smith, "Penelope Fitzgerald, Novelist, Is Dead at 83," B10.

33. Penelope Fitzgerald, *The Beginning of Spring* (London: Collins, 1988; Boston: Mariner Books, 1998), 15. Citations are to the Mariner edition.

34. Amazon, "High Spirits," 3.

35. Mary Kaiser, "English/Notes," *World Literature Today* (Spring 2000): 377.

36. Jerome K. Jerome, *Three Men in a Boat (To Say Nothing of the Dog)* (New York: A. L. Burt, 1889; Authors Directory, 2001), http://authorsdirectory.com/b/3boat110.htm/. Citations are to the Authors Directory online edition.

37. Susannah Clapp, "Finishing Touches," *London Review of Books,* December 20, 1984, 20.

38. Jack Wakefield, "A Choice of First Novels," *Spectator,* November 17, 2001, 49.

39. Margaret Walters, "Women's Fiction," *London Review of Books,* October 13, 1988, 20.

40. Arthur Lubow, "An Author of a Certain Age," *New York Times Magazine,* sec. 6, August 15, 1999, 30.

41. Peter Kemp, "Snakes in the Grass," *Listener,* September 20, 1979, 387.

42. Ruth Gorb, "The Gentle Ghost of Keats in a Neighbour's Bathroom," *Express & News* (London), November 16, 1979, 16.

Chapter 2—Hearts that Yearn

1. Carl Sandburg, ed. and comp., *The American Songbag* (New York: Harcourt, Brace, c. 1927), 463.
2. Fitzgerald, "To Remember Is to Forgive," 7.
3. Smith, "Penelope Fitzgerald, Novelist, Is Dead at 83," B10.
4. Penelope Fitzgerald, "A Character in One of God's Dreams," *New York Times Book Review,* May 11, 1997, 7.
5. Fitzgerald, "What He Did for His In-Laws," 19.
6. Amazon, "High Spirits," 3.
7. Penelope Fitzgerald, "Confessions of a Pretty Monster," *New York Times Book Review,* June 28, 1992, 7.
8. Fitzgerald, "A Character in One of God's Dreams," 7.
9. Fitzgerald, "How an Artist's Vision Becomes Ours," 1.

Chapter 3—Saying It Right

1. Penelope Fitzgerald, "From Waterloo to Watermelon," *New York Review of Books,* November 1, 1992, 3.
2. Jonathan Raban, "The Fact Artist," *New Republic,* August 2, 1999, 39–40.
3. Richard Eder, "Two Bicycles, One Spirit," *Los Angeles Times Book Review,* January 12, 1992, 7.
4. Edward Wheeler, "A Literary Guide," *Commonweal,* September 10, 1999, 32.
5. Harvey-Wood, "Penelope Fitzgerald," 22.
6. Smith, "Penelope Fitzgerald, Novelist, Is Dead at 83," B10.
7. Penelope Lively, "Five of the Best—New Fiction," *Encounter,* January 1981, 56.
8. Byatt, "A Delicate Form of Genius," 13.
9. Ibid.
10. Philip Hensher, "The Sweet Smell of Success," *Spectator,* April 11, 1998, 31.

11. Raban, "The Fact Artist," 39.

12. Amazon, "High Spirits," 3.

13. Houghton Mifflin Books, "A Reader's Guide: *The Blue Flower* by Penelope Fitzgerald," http://www.houghtonmifflinbooks.com/readers_guides/fitzgerald_blueflower.shtml.

14. Nina King, "The Heart Has Its Reasons," *Washington Post Book World,* February 23, 1992, 8.

15. Ibid.

16. Penelope Fitzgerald, introduction to M. R. James, *The Haunted Dolls' House and Other Stories* (London: Penguin, 2000), xi.

Chapter 4—The Great Museum Sideshow

1. John Mellors, "Anon Events," *Listener,* September 29, 1977, 410.

2. Susannah Clapp, "Suburbanity," *New Statesman,* October 7, 1977, 483.

3. Mellors, "Anon Events," 410.

Chapter 5—Oh, to Be in Suffolk

1. Valentine Cunningham, "Suffocating Suffolk," *Times Literary Supplement,* November 17, 1978, 1333.

2. Byatt, "A Delicate Form of Genius," 14.

3. Houghton Mifflin Books, "A Reader's Guide: *The Bookshop* by Penelope Fitzgerald," http://www.houghtonmifflinbooks.com/readers_guides/fitzgerald_bookshop.shhtml.

4. Smith, "Penelope Fitzgerald, Novelist, Is Dead at 83," B10.

Chapter 6—On the Reach

1. *Lennon and McCartney 60 Greatest Hits* (Winona, Minn.: Hal Leonard, n.d.), 49, 52.

2. John Ryle, "New Music," *New Statesman,* September 7, 1979, 349.

3. Victoria Glendenning, "Between Land and Water," *Times Literary Supplement,* November 3, 1979, 10.

4. Judy Cooke, "Bull's Eye," *New Statesman,* October 10, 1980, 22.

5. Penelope Fitzgerald Papers, Harry Ransom Humanities Research Center, University of Texas at Austin, box 8, folder 7.

6. Mollie Hardwick, "A Water-Colour Novel," *Books and Bookmen,* December 1979, 16.

Chapter 7—Keepers of the Discs

1. John Lukac, *Five Days in London: May 1940* (New Haven: Yale University Press, 1999), 84.

2. Ibid., 85–86.

3. Virginia Woolf, *The Diary of Virginia Woolf* (New York: Harcourt Brace Jovanovich, 1984), 5:287.

4. David C. Cannadine, *Aspects of Aristocracy* (New Haven: Yale University Press, 1954), 132.

5. Susan Salter Reynolds, "Human Voices," *Los Angeles Times Book Review,* June 6, 1999, 11.

6. Alfred Corn, "Broadcast News," *New York Times Book Review,* May 9, 1999, 7.

7. Gillian Reynolds, "Auntie at War," *Punch,* October 15, 1980, 28.

8. P. H. Newby, "BBC Seraglio," *Listener,* October 2, 1980, 445.

9. Raban, "The Fact Artist," 42.

10. Lively, "Five of the Best—New Fiction," 56.

Chapter 8—Stagers

1. Roxana Robinson, "In Short: Fiction," *New York Times Book Review,* September 8, 1985, 24.

2. Penelope Lively, "Backwards & Forwards: Recent Fiction," *Encounter,* June 1982, 88.

3. Anthony Thwaite, "Stagers Old and New," *Observer,* March 28, 1982, 31.

4. Penelope Fitzgerald, "Best Nuisance, Earth Mother," *New York Times Magazine,* April 19, 1993, 85.

5. Acocella, "Assassination on a Small Scale," 86.

6. "George Arliss," in *Who's Who in the Theatre*: *1912–1976* (Detroit: Gale, 1978), 1:68–69.

Chapter 9—Stumbling into Geopolitics

1. Giuseppe Mammorella, *Italy after Fascism: A Political History, 1943–1963* (Montreal: Mario Casalini, 1964), 261.

2. Norman Kogan, *A Political History of Postwar Italy* (New York: Praeger, 1966), 105–6.

3. Penelope Fitzgerald Papers, box 2, folder 3.

4. Martin Clark, *Modern Italy 1871–1982* (London: Longman, 1984), 368.

5. Paul Ginsborg, *A History of Contemporary Italy: Society and Politics, 1943–1988* (London: Penguin, 1990), 148.

6. Ibid., 216.

7. Ibid., 138, 184.

8. Fitzgerald, "What He Did for His In-Laws," 19.

9. Byatt, "A Delicate Form of Genius," 13.

10. Emily Leider, "In Short: Fiction," *New York Times Book Review,* May 10, 1987, 20.

11. Acocella, "Assassination on a Small Scale," 86.

12. "Research Notes for *Innocence,*" Penelope Fitzgerald Papers, box 2, folder 1.

13. Mammorella, *Italy after Fascism,* 294.

14. "Rough Draft for *At Freddie's,*" Penelope Fitzgerald Papers, box 5, folder 10.

15. Frank Rosengarten, "An Introduction to Gramsci's Life and Thought," http://www.soc.qc.edu/gramsci/intro/engbio/html, 2.

16. Clark, *Modern Italy,* 368.

17. John Gross, "Books of the Times," *New York Times,* April 28, 1987, C17.

18. Rosengarten, "An Introduction to Gramsci's Life and Thought," 1.

19. Ibid.

20. Fitzgerald, "To Remember Is to Forgive," 7.

21. Penelope Fitzgerald, introduction to Jane Austen, *Emma* (Oxford: Oxford University Press, 1999), ix–x.

22. Richard Eder, "Innocence," *Los Angeles Times Book Review,* May 3, 1987, 4.

Chapter 10—Degrees of Exile

1. Brookner, "Moscow before the Revolution," 29.

2. Jonathan Penner, "Moscow on the Eve," *Washington Post Book World,* June 11, 1989, 1.

3. Leo Tolstoy, *War and Peace,* trans. Louise and Aylmer Maude, ed. George Gibian (New York: Norton, 1996), 475.

4. Paul Stuewe, "Of Some Import: Fiction," *Quill and Quire* (February 1989): 27.

5. Penelope Fitzgerald Papers, box 8, folder 4.

6. Harvey-Wood, "Penelope Fitzgerald," 22.

7. Lesley Chamberlain, "Worried Norbury," *Times Literary Supplement,* Sept 23–29, 1988, 1041.

8. Harvey Pitcher, *The Smiths of Moscow: A Story of Britons Abroad* (Cromer: Swallow House, 1984), 84; Harvey Pitcher, *When Miss Emmie Was in Russia: English Governesses during and after the October Revolution* (London: John Murray, 1977), 228.

9. Penelope Fitzgerald Papers, box 8, folder 4.

10. Pitcher, *The Smiths of Moscow,* 21.

11. Penelope Fitzgerald Papers, box 8, folder 4.

12. Ibid., box 4, folder 2.

13. Ibid., box 4, folder 3.

14. Simon Brett, "From Moscow to Rummidge via Oxford," *Punch*, September 30, 1988, 50.

15. "St. Benjamin," *Catholic Online*, http://saints.catholic.org/saints/saint.php?saint_id=338.

16. Pitcher also says in *Miss Emmie* that the *Russian Year Book* for 1911 said that the rail trip from London to St. Petersburg, "depart[s] Charing Cross 9 A.M., £fare 15. 18s, 3d, duration of journey 51 1/4 hours" (53).

17. Pitcher, *When Miss Emmie Was in Russia*, 35.

18. Ibid., 143.

19. "The Humanitarian and Critical Temper: Henry Wadsworth Longfellow," Sculley Bradley, Richard Croom Beatty, and E. Hudson Long, eds. *The American Tradition in Literature*, 3rd ed. (New York: Norton, 1976), 750–53.

20. Pitcher, *The Smiths of Moscow*, 53, 79.

21. Penelope Fitzgerald Papers, box 6, file 13.

22. Hensher, "The Sweet Smell of Success," 34.

23. Brookner, "Moscow before the Revolution," 30; Amazon, "High Spirits," 3.

24. "Biography of Henry Wadsworth Longfellow," American Poems, http://www.americanpoems.com/poets/Longfellow/.

Chapter 11—Driving toward Modernity

1. Amazon, "High Spirits," 2.

2. See A. J. Ayer, *Language, Truth and Logic* (London: V. Gollancz, 1936; New York: Dover, 1952), xi, 35. Citation is to the Dover edition.

3. King, "The Heart Has Its Reasons," 8.

4. Amazon, "High Spirits," 2.

5. Penelope Fitzgerald, "The Man from Narnia," *New York Times Book Review*, February 18, 1990, 11.

6. Edward Burne-Jones talked of "having heard of two young bicyclists, a man and a woman, perfect strangers, who

crashed ... were picked out of a hedge, and woke up to find themselves in the same bed" (*Edward Burne-Jones,* 230).

7. Florence McNabb, "Briefly Noted," *Belles Lettres* (Fall 1992): 54.

8. Ian Hacking, *The Taming of Chance* (Cambridge: Cambridge University Press, 1990), 1.

9. Ibid., 147.

10. King, "The Heart Has Its Reasons," 8.

11. Kate Kellaway, "A Bicycle Built for Two," *Listener,* August 23, 1990, 23.

12. Eder, "Two Bicycles, One Spirit," 3.

13. Hensher, "Perfection in a Small Space," 44.

14. King, "The Heart Has Its Reasons," 8.

15. Frank Kermode, "Playing the Seraphine," *London Review of Books,* January 21, 2001, 15.

Chapter 12—Kind of Blue

1. Guy Mannes-Abbott, "Angelic Voices," *New Statesman and Society,* October 6, 1995, 38.

2. Richard Holmes, "Paradise in a Dream," *New York Review,* July 7, 1997, 4.

3. Robert Adamson, *Fichte* (London: W. Blackwood and Sons, 1881; Freeport: Books for Libraries Press, 1969), 42–43. Citations are to the Books for Libraries edition.

4. "Novalis: Hymns to the Night," http//:www.logopoem.com/novalis/. For commentary on the *Hymns,* see Wm. Arctander O'Brien, *Novalis: Signs of Revolution* (Durham, N.C.: Duke University Press, 1995), 256–71.

5. Jennifer Howard, "The Book Club," *Washington Post Book World,* January 7, 2001, 13.

6. Penelope Fitzgerald, introduction to L. H. Myers, *The Root and the Flower* (New York: New York Review Books, 2001), x.

7. Adamson, *Fichte*, 41.

8. See O'Brien, *Novalis*, 81–118, esp. 112–14, for Hardenberg's theory of signs and semiotics.

9. Dagmar Herzog, "Love in the Time of Tuberculosis," *Women's Review of Books*, October 7, 1997, 7.

10. Frank Kermode, "Dark Fates," *London Review of Books*, October 5, 1995, 7.

11. O'Brien, *Novalis*, 118.

12. Ibid., 27.

13. Alan Bennett, *Writing Home* (London: Faber, 1994), 147.

14. O'Brien, *Novalis*, 41, 39.

15. Ibid.; Gabriel Annan, "Death and the Maiden," *Times Literary Supplement*, September 15, 1995, 20.

16. O'Brien, *Novalis*, 29.

17. Mona Knapp, "World Literature in Review: English," *World Literature Today* (Spring 1998): 372.

Conclusion—History Illuminated

1. Elizabeth Hay, "Penelope Weaves Her Last Fictional Web," *Globe and Mail* (Toronto), December 2, 2000, D9.

2. Gertrude Himmelfarb, "A God-Haunted Family," *New Republic*, October 16, 2000, 69.

Bibliography

Works by Penelope Fitzgerald (Chronological)

Novels

The Golden Child. London: Duckworth, 1977. Boston: Mariner Books, 1999.

The Bookshop. London: Duckworth, 1978. Boston: Mariner Books, 1997.

Offshore. London: Collins, 1979. Boston: Mariner Books, 1998.

Human Voices. London: Collins, 1980. Boston: Mariner Books, 1999.

At Freddie's. London: Collins, 1982. New York: Godine, 1985. Boston: Mariner Books, 1999.

Innocence. London: Collins, 1986. Boston: Mariner Books, 1998.

The Beginning of Spring. London: Collins, 1988. Boston: Mariner Books, 1998.

The Gate of Angels. London: Collins, 1990. Boston: Mariner Books, 1998.

The Blue Flower. London: Flamingo, 1995. Boston: Mariner Books, 1997.

Short Stories

The Means of Escape. Boston: Houghton Mifflin: 2000. Boston: Mariner Books, 2001.

Biographies

Edward Burne-Jones: A Biography. London: Joseph, 1975. London: Hamish Hamilton, 1989.

The Knox Brothers. London: Macmillan, 1977. Washington, D.C.: Counterpoint, 2000.

Charlotte Mew and Her Friends: with a Selection of Her Poems. Foreword by Brad Leithauser. London: Collins, 1984. Reading, Mass.: Addison-Wesley, 1988.

Essays

"How an Artist's Vision Becomes Ours." Review of a special exhibit of Antonio Canaletto's work at New York's Metropolitan Museum of Art. *New York Times,* October 29, 1989, sec. 2, 1–2.

"Best Nuisance; Earth Mother." *New York Times Magazine,* April 18, 1999, 85. Short essay on Victorian land reformer, Octavia Hill (1838–1912).

Introductions

Austen, Jane. *Emma.* Oxford: Oxford University Press, 1999, v–x.

Carr, J. L. *A Month in the Country.* London: Penguin, 2000, vii–xiii.

James, M. R. *The Haunted Dolls' House and Other Stories.* London: Penguin, 2000, vii–xiii.

Myers, L. H. *The Root and the Flower* New York: New York Review Books, 2001, vii–xiii.

Book Reviews

"What He Did for His In-Laws." Review of *The Memoirs of Marco Parenti: A Life in Medici Florence,* by Mark Phillips. *New York Times Book Review,* February 7, 1988, 19.

"Do You Have the Courage to Cry." Review of *The Pilgrim's Rules of Etiquette,* by Taghi Modarressi. *New York Times Book Review,* August 13, 1989, 7.

"The Man from Narnia." Review of *C. S. Lewis: A Biography,* by A. N. Wilson. *New York Times Book Review,* February 18, 1990, 11.

"The Great Encourager." Review of *Ford Madox Ford,* by Alan Judd. *New York Times Book Review,* March 10, 1991, 7.

"Lasting Impressions." Review of *The Kelmscott Press: A History of William Morris's Typographical Adventure,* by William S. Peterson. *New York Times Book Review,* December 5, 1991, 19.

"Confessions of a Pretty Monster." Review of *Diaries,* by Antonia White. Edited by Susan Chitty. Vol. 1. *New York Times Book Review,* June, 28, 1992, 7.

"The Only Member of His Club." Review of *Evelyn Waugh: The Later Years 1939–66*, by Martin Stannard. *New York Times Book Review*, September 23, 1992, 1, 38.

"From Waterloo to Watermelon." Review of *The Death of Napoleon*, by Simon Leys. *New York Times Book Review*, November 1, 1992, 3.

"Doers and Viewers." Review of *The Invention of Truth*, by Marta Morazzoni. *New York Times Book Review*, May 23, 1993, 3.

"To Remember Is to Forgive." Review of *Excursions in the Real World: Memoirs*, by William Trevor. *New York Times Book Review*, February 11, 1994, 7.

"Where Am I." Review of *The Following Story*, by Cees Nooteboom. *New York Times Book Review*, October 16, 1994, 13.

"It Never Rains Indoors." Review of *London*, by John Russell. *New York Times Book Review*, November 6, 1994, 3.

"Innocence and Experience." Review of *Blake*, by Peter Ackroyd. *New York Times Book Review*, April 14, 1996, 5.

"A Character in One of God's Dreams." Review of *Reality and Dreams*, by Muriel Spark. *New York Times Book Review*, May 11, 1997, 7.

"No Home on Earth." Review of *The Mad Dog: Stories*, by Heinrich Böll. *New York Times Book Review*, September 28, 1997, 12.

"The Preacher's Life." Review of *The Ultimate Intimacy*, by Ivan Klima. *New York Times Book Review*, February 22, 1998, 18.

Interviews

"The Gentle Ghost of Keats in a Neighbour's Bathroom." By Ruth Gorb. *Express & News* (London), November 16, 1979, 16.

Amazon, "High Spirits: The Great Penelope Fitzgerald on Poltergeists, Plots, and Past Masters." http://www.amazon.com/exec/obidos/tg/feature (1998).

Research File

Penelope Fitzgerald Papers. Harry Ransom Humanities Research Center. University of Texas at Austin.

Criticism and Commentary

Acocella, Joan. "Assassination on a Small Scale." *New Yorker,* February 7, 2000, 80–88. Particularly helpful on the transition between the early and late novels.

Adamson, Robert. *Fichte.* London: W. Blackwood and Sons, 1881. Freeport, N.Y.: Books for Libraries Press, 1969.

American Poems. "Biography of Henry Wadsworth Longfellow." http://www.americanpoems.com/poets/Longfellow.

Annan, Gabriel. "Death and the Maiden." *Times Literary Supplement,* September 15, 1995, 20.

Ayer, Alfred Julius. *Language, Truth and Logic.* London: V. Gollancz, 1936. New York: Dover, 1952.

Bayley, John. "Innocents at Home." *New York Review of Books,* April 9, 1992, 13–14.

Bernard, April. "Wild Lyrics." *New Republic,* August 22, 1988, 36–38.

Bradley, Sculley, Richard Croom Beatty, and E. Hudson Long, eds. "The Humanitarian and Critical Temper: Henry Wadsworth Longfellow." In *The American Tradition In Literature,* 3rd ed. New York: Norton, 1976, 750–53.

Brett, Simon. "From Moscow to Rummidge, via Oxford." *Punch,* September 30, 1988, 50–51.

Brookner, Anita. "Moscow before the Revolution." *Spectator,* October 1, 1988, 29–30.

Byatt, A. S. "A Delicate Form of Genius." *Threepenny Review* (Spring 1998): 13–15. Very insightful about Fitzgerald's blends of narrative modes like farce and deadpan comedy.

———. Introduction to *The Means of Escape,* by Penelope Fitzgerald, ix–xxx. Boston: Mariner, 2001. An amplification of the above essay, with useful references to the short stories.

Cannadine, David. *Aspects of Aristocracy.* New Haven: Yale University Press, 1994.
Catholic Online. "St. Benjamin." http://www.saints.catholic.org/saints/saint.php?saint_id=338.
Chamberlain, Lesley. "Worried, Norbury." *Times Literary Supplement,* September 23–29, 1988, 100–101.
Clapp, Susannah. "Finishing Touches." *London Review of Books,* December 20, 1984, 20.
———. "Suburbanity." *New Statesman,* October 7, 1977, 483.
Clark, Martin. *Modern Italy 1871–1982.* London: Longman, 1984.
Cooke, Judy. "Bull's Eye." *New Statesman,* October 10, 1980, 228.
Corn, Alfred. "Broadcast News." *New York Times Book Review,* May 9, 1999, 7.
Cunningham, Valentine. "Suffocating Suffolk." *Times Literary Supplement,* November 17, 1978, 1333.
Diski, Jenny. "Elements of an English Upbringing." *American Scholar* (Autumn, 2000): 140–42.
Eder, Richard. "Innocence." *Los Angeles Times Book Review,* May 3, 1987, 3–4.
———. "Two Bicycles, One Spirit." *Los Angeles Times Book Review,* January 12, 1992, 3, 7.
———. "Penelope Fitzgerald, Her Family's Eyes and Heart." *New York Times,* August 31, 2000, 8E.
Fichte, Johann Gottlieb. *The Science of Rights.* Translated by A. E. Kroeger. Philadelphia: F. Lippincott. London: Routledge and Kegan Paul, 1970.
Ginsborg, Paul. *A History of Contemporary Italy: Society and Politics, 1943–1988.* London: Penguin, 1990.
Glendenning, Victoria. "Between Land and Water." *Times Literary Supplement,* November 23, 1979, 10.
Gross, John. "Books of the Times." *New York Times,* April 28, 1987, C17.
Hacking, Ian. *The Taming of Chance.* Cambridge: Cambridge University Press, 1990.

Hardwicke, Mollie. "A Water-Colour Novel." *Books and Bookmen,* December 1979, 16–17.

Harvey-Wood, Harriet. "Penelope Fitzgerald." *Guardian,* May 3, 2000, 22.

Hay, Elizabeth. "Penelope Weaves Her Last Fictional Web." *Globe and Mail* (Toronto), December 2, 2000, D9.

Hensher, Philip. "The Sweet Smell of Success." *Spectator,* April 11, 1998, 31–32.

———. "Perfection in a Small Space." *Spectator,* October 21, 2000. 44–45.

Herzog, Dagmar. "Love in the Time of Tuberculosis." *Women's Review of Books,* October 1997, 6–7.

Himmelfarb, Gertrude. "A God-Haunted Family." *New Republic,* October 16, 2000. A cogent argument in favor of Fitzgerald's supremacy as a novelist.

Houghton Mifflin Books. "A Reader's Guide: *The Blue Flower,* by Penelope Fitzgerald." http://www.houghtonmifflinbooks.com/readers_guides/Fitzgerald_blueflower.shtml.

———. "A Reader's Guide: *The Bookshop,* by Penelope Fitzgerald." http://www.houghtonnmifflinbooks.com/readers_Guides/fitzgerald_bookshop.shtml.

———. "A Reader's Guide: *The Gate of Angels,* by Penelope Fitzgerald." http://www.houghtonmifflinbooks.com/readers_Guides/fitzgerald.gateofangels.shtml.

Howard, Jennifer. "The Book Club." *Washington Post Book World,* June 7, 2001, 13.

Jerome, Jerome K. *Three Men in a Boat (To Say Nothing of the Dog).* http://www.authorsdirectory.com/b/3boat110.htm.

Kellaway, Kate. "A Bicycle Made for Two." *Listener,* August 23, 1990, 23.

Kemp, Peter. "Snakes on the Grass." *Listener,* September 20, 1979, 386–87.

Kermode, Frank. "Booker Books." *London Review of Books,* November 22, 1979, 12.

———. "Dark Fates." *London Review of Books,* October 5, 1995, 7.

———. "Playing the Seraphine." *London Review of Books,* January 25, 2001, 15.

King, Nina. "The Heart Has Its Reasons." *Washington Post Book World,* February 23, 1992, 1.

Knapp, Mona. "World Literature in Review: English." *World Literature Today* (Spring 1998); 331–32.

Kogan, Norman. *A Political History of Postwar Italy.* New York: Praeger, 1966.

Lee, Hermione. "Listening Carefully." *Times Literary Supplement,* October 20, 2000, 22.

Leider, Emily. "In Short: Fiction." *New York Times Book Review,* May 10, 1987, 20.

Lennon and McCartney: 60 Greatest Hits. Winona, Minn.: Hal Leonard Publishing Company, n.d.

Lesser, Wendy. "Penelope." In *On Modern British Fiction,* edited by Zachary Leader. 107–25. Oxford: Oxford University Press, 2002.

Lively, Penelope. "Five of the Best—New Fiction." *Encounter,* January 1981, 53–59.

———. "Backward & Forward: Recent Fiction." *Encounter,* June 1982, 86–89.

Logopoeia. "Novalis: Hymns to the Night." http://www.logopoeia.com/novalis.

Lubow, Arthur. "An Author of a Certain Age." *New York Times Magazine,* sec. 6, August 15, 1999, 30. Both a pioneering study and a thoughtful, nuanced analysis, the first of its kind by an American.

Lukac, John. *Five Days in London: May 1940.* New Haven: Yale University Press, 1999.

Mammorella, Giuseppe. *Italy after Fascism: A Political History, 1943–1963.* Montreal: Mario Casalini, 1964.

Mannes-Abbott, Guy. "Angelic Voices." *New Statesman and Society,* October 6, 1995, 38.

McNabb, Florence. "Briefly Noted." *Belles Lettres* (Fall 1992): 54.

Mellors, John. "Anon Events." *Listener,* September 29, 1977, 410.

Morrison, Blake. "Looking Backward." *New Statesman,* November 10, 1978, 30.

Newby, P. H. "BBC Seraglio." *Listener,* October 2, 1980, 445.

O'Brien, Wm. Arctander. *Novalis: Signs of Revolution.* Durham, N.C.: Duke University Press, 1995.

Penner, Jonathan. "Moscow on the Eve." *Washington Post Book World,* June 1, 1989, 1.

Pitcher, Harvey. *When Miss Emmie Was in Russia: English Governesses during and after the October Revolution.* London: John Murray, 1977.

———. *The Smiths of Moscow: The Story of Britons Abroad.* Cromer: Swallow House, 1984.

Raban, Jonathan. "The Fact Artist." *New Republic,* August 2, 1999, 39–42.

Reynolds, Gillian. "Auntie at War." *Punch,* October 15, 1980, 28.

Reynolds, Susan Salter. "Human Voices." *Los Angeles Times Book Review,* June 6, 1999, 11.

Robinson, Roxana. "In Short: Fiction." *New York Times Book Review,* September 8, 1985, 24.

Rosengarten, Frank. "An Introduction to Gramsci's Life and Thought." http//:www.socqc.edu/gramsci/intro/engbio/html.

Ryle, John. "New Music." *New Statesman,* September 7, 1979, 349.

Sandburg, Carl, ed. and comp. *The American Songbag.* New York: Harcourt, Brace, c. 1927.

Smith, Dinitia. "Penelope Fitzgerald, Novelist, Is Dead at 83." *New York Times,* May 3, 2000, B10.

Stuewe, Paul. "Of Some Import: Fiction." *Quill and Quire,* February 1989, 27.

Thwaite, Anthony. "Stagers Old and New." *Observer* (London), March 28, 1982, 31.

Tolstoy, Leo. *War and Peace.* Translated by Louise and Aylmer Maude. Edited by George Gibian. New York: Norton, 1996.

Wakefield, Jack. "A Choice of First Novels." *Spectator,* November 17, 2001, 48–49.

Walters, Margaret. "Women's Fiction." *London Review of Books,* October 13, 1988, 20–22.

Wheeler, Edward. "A Listener's Guide." *Commonweal,* September 10, 1999, 32–34.

Woolf, Virginia. *The Diary of Virginia Woolf.* Edited by Anne Olivier Bell. 5 vols. New York: Harcourt Brace Jovanovich, 1984.

Index

Page ranges in bold indicate extended discussion.

Acocella, Joan, 10, 178, 190
Adamson, Robert, 276
Ambler, Eric, 77
Amis, Kingsley, 93
Annan, Gabriel, 283
Arliss, George, 181
Armin, Robert, 176
Austen, Jane, 52, 64, 176, 262; *Emma,* 205

Baddeley, Hermione, 180
Balzac, Honoré de, 213, 231
Bauer, Felice, 282
Bayley, John, 7
Baylis, Lilian, 9, 76
Beatles, The, 53; "Please, Please Me," 111; "She Loves You," 111
Beckett, Samuel, 209; *Waiting for Godot,* 63, 181
Beerbohm, Max, 186
Bellow, Saul, 49, 50
Bennett, Alan, 282
Berenson, Bernard, 186
Bergman, Ingrid, 186
Bizet, Georges: *Carmen,* 265
Blake, William, 17, 51
Bowen, Elizabeth, 202
Brahms, Johannes, 192
Braine, John, 93
Brett, Simon, 223–24
Brookner, Anita, 4, 214, 243, 299
Browning, Robert, 282

Bulgakov, Mikhail, 241
Burke, Kenneth, 278
Burne-Jones, Edward, 3, 8, 19, 20, 57, 277
Byatt, A. S., 4, 5, 52, 53, 59, 100
Byron, Lord, 287–88

Camus, Albert, 16
Canaletto, Antonio, 5, 6, 47
Cannadine, David C., 139
Capone, Al, 154
Carlyle, Thomas, 279
Carr, J. L.: *A Month in the Country,* 14–15
Carr, John Dickson, 88
Cavendish Laboratories, The (Cambridge), 12, 88
Chamberlain, Neville, 138
Chaplin, Charlie, 53
Charles (King of the Austro-Hungarian Empire), 276
Chaucer, Geoffrey: "The Monk's Tale," 88
Chekhov, Anton, 21, 49, 126, 210, 289; *The Cherry Orchard,* 167, 227–28, 231; *The Seagull,* 223; *The Three Sisters,* 221, 224, 228; *Uncle Vanya,* 229
Christie, Agatha, 39, 73, 90; *The Mysterious Affair at Styles,* 88
Churchill, Winston, 46, 138–39, 141

Clapp, Susannah, 31, 85
Coleridge, Samuel Taylor, 279; "Christabel," 286; "The Rime of the Ancient Mariner," 278
Coleridge, Taylor, 240
Connelly, Michael, 90
Conrad, Joseph, 27, 120; *The Secret Agent,* 102
Cooke, Judy, 102
Corn, Alfred, 141
Cornell, Katherine, 183
Coward, Nöel, 177, 181, 299; *Cavalcade,* 59; "Mad Dogs and Englishmen," 59; *Private Lives,* 59
Crick, Sir Francis, 248
Cunningham, Valentine, 98

Dante, 36, 99, 127, 235; *The Divine Comedy,* 240; *Inferno,* 195, *Purgatorio,* 195
Darwin, Charles, 280
Debussy, Claude, 27, 147
de Gaulle, Charles, 155
Delaney, Shelagh: *A Taste of Honey,* 181
De Lillo, Don, 4, 298
De Sica, Vittorio: *The Bicycle Thief,* 187
Dickens, Charles, 10, 53, 135, 213, 231; *Bleak House,* 206; *Dombey and Son,* 161, 226; *Oliver Twist,* 67
Donne, John, 123
Dostoevsky, Fyodor, 227–28; *The Brothers Karamazov,* 196, 216

Doyle, Sir Arthur Conan, 215; "Dancing Men," 88; "His Last Bow," 87; "Speckled Band," 88
Dreiser, Theodore: *Sister Carrie,* 188
Durkheim, Emile, 31

Eder, Richard, 5, 49, 208, 266
Edward VIII (King of England), 150
Eliot, T. S., 123, 278, 293; "The Love Song of J. Alfred Prufrock," 27, 30, 39, 157; *The Waste Land,* 120
Ellison, Ralph: *Invisible Man,* 250

Fellini, Frederico: *The White Sheik,* 187
Fichte, Johann Gottlieb, 46, 276, 279
Fielding, Henry, *Tom Jones,* 234
Fitzgerald, Desmond (Penelope's husband), 2, 3, 263; Penelope's use of in her work, 18–23, 130, 133–34, 169, 182–83, 185
Fitzgerald, Penelope Knox: awards and critical acclaim, 4–5, 135, 300; family background and career outside of writing, 1–3; family relations, 9–11, 17; feminism, 18–19, 41–43, 100–101, 202–3, 254, 263–64, 266; music, 11, 27, 147, 222, 239–40, 281; narrative technique and style, 5–8, 16, 29–30, 45–47,

48–64, 134–36, 158–59, 208–11, 242–43; politics, 8–9, 12–15, 23–25, 31–33, 52, 71–72, 88; ontology, 11–13, 15–18, 27–28, 33–34, 44, 46–47; sex, 17, 35–42, 63–64, 83, 124–26, 128, 171–73, 179–80, 193–95, 223

—Works by

At Freddie's, 8–11, 22, 27, 35, 36–37, 39, 43, 44, 56, 57, 62, 76, 111, **160–83,** 188, 193, 197, 200, 203, 207, 226, 255, 271, 299–300

"At Hiruharama," 231

"Axe, The," 13, 16

Beginning of Spring, The, 4, 6, 7, 10, 12, 21, 24–25, 30, 32–33, 36, 39–41, 43, 54–56, 58, 83, 108, 137, 192, 205, **212–45,** 256, 258, 267–70, 283, 288, 297, 299, 301

"Beehrenz," 13–14

Blue Flower, The, 2, 4, 11, 16, 24, 27, 33, 36, 43, 46, 47, 63–64, 114, 212, 252–53, **271–96,** 297–99

Bookshop, The, 4, 6, 7, 11, 14, 22–23, 29, 30, 43, 46, 53, 58, 60–61, 80, **93–110,** 111, 113, 127, 146, 161, 188, 190–91, 201, 210, 226, 269, 280, 283–84, 295

Charlotte Mew and Her Friends, 19, 21, 35, 67, 162, 190, 208, 271

Edward Burne-Jones: A Biography, 57, 271, 311–12

Gate of Angels, The, 2–4, 6–8, 10, 12, 17, 24, 25, 28–29, 31, 36, 37, 41, 46, 49, 59–60, 64, 80, 161, 174, **246–70,** 272, 276, 279–80, 284–85, 293–94, 297

Golden Child, The, 1, 5, 7, 9, 18, 25, 29, 58, 60, **64–92,** 98, 105, 106, 113, 137, 140, 142, 203, 223, 226, 242

"High Spirits," 11–12

Human Voices, 5, 9, 10, 15, 17, 20, 25–28, 30, 39, 41, 44, 46, 49, 50, 52–53, 56–58, 62, 76, 111, **137–59,** 160, 168, 174–75, 179–80, 183, 188, 194, 201, 207, 220–21, 233, 249, 257, 278–79, 299

Innocence, 9–10, 17, 21, 31, 33, 35–37, 43, 52–54, 59, 61–62, 64, 117, 171, **184–211,** 216–17, 220, 240, 256, 274, 280, 284–85, 299

Knox Brothers, The, 3–4, 19–20, 58, 133, 208, 271

"Means of Escape," **37–40**

Means of Escape, 4, 13

Offshore, 4, 10–11, 17, 21–25, 30, 33–34, 37, 41, 43–44, 51, 53, 58–61, 64,

Fitzgerald, Penelope Knox, works by (*continued*)
67, **111–26**, 137, 139–40, 146, 152, 154, 157–58, 160–61, 168–69, 173–74, 178–79, 188, 205, 233, 240, 262, 283, 297, 299–300
"Our Lives Are Only Leant to Us," 23
"Prescription, The," 117
"To Remember Is to Forgive," 44

Fitzgerald, Scott: *The Great Gatsby*, 264

Flaubert, Gustave, 213, 237; *Madame Bovary*, 29, 192

Ford, Ford Madox, 14, 254; *The Good Soldier*, 67, 234; *Parade's End*, 230; *Some Do Not*, 230

Forster, E. M.: *A Passage to India*, 52, 89, 135, 254

Franco, General Francisco, 138

French, Thomas Valpy (Penelope's maternal grandfather), 133

Freud, Sigmund, 71, 99, 206, 235; *Civilization and Its Discontents*, 196

Frost, Robert: "Stopping by Woods on a Snowy Evening," 286

Gaddis, William: *JR*, 265, *The Recognitions*, 274

Gaskell, Elizabeth: *Cranford*, 158

Genet, Jean, 181; *The Maids*, 188

Ginsborg, Paul, 187

Glendenning, Victoria, 112

Goethe, Johann Wilhelm von, 285, 287–88, 299; *Faust*, 289

Gogol, Nikolai, 241

Gorb, Ruth, 305

Gramsci, Antonio, 31, 64, 185, 187, 197, 200, 202, 299; *The Prison Notebooks*, 199

Granville-Barker, Harley, 182

Greene, Graham, 18, 33, 202, 267; *Brighton Rock*, 6; *The Confidential Agent*, 74; *The End of the Affair*, 149; *A Gun for Sale*, 6, 74

Gross, John, 199

Hacking, Ian: *The Taming of Chance*, 252

Haggard, H. Rider: *She*, 254

Haley, Bill and His Comets: *Rock around the Clock*, 111

Hammett, Dashiell, 90; *The Maltese Falcon*, 88, 91

Hardenberg, Friedrich von. See Novalis

Hardwick, Mollie, 130

Hardy, Thomas, 53, 113; *The Return of the Native*, 99

Hartley, L. P., 108, 271

Harvey-Wood, Harriet, 1, 5

Hawthorne, Nathanael: *The Scarlet Letter*, 244; "Young Goodman Brown," 244

Hay, Elizabeth, 300

Heine, Heinrich, 5–6; "Der Asra," 147; "Die Lorelei," 286

Heisenberg, Werner, 248

Hensher, Philip, 4, 56, 59, 243, 266

Herodas, 86
Herzog, Dagmar, 313
Hill, Octavia, 162
Himmelfarb, Gertrude, 300
Hitchcock, Alfred: *The Lady Vanishes,* 88
Hitler, Adolph, 138, 151, 154
Hoard, Jennifer, 277
Holderlin, Friedrich, 277
Holmes, Richard, 273
Hopkins, Gerard Manley, 54

Ibsen, Henrik, 123; *Hedda Gabler,* 82, 120
"I Met Her in the Garden Where the Praties Grow" (song), 39
Ionesco, Eugène, 16
Isherwood, Christopher: *Goodbye to Berlin,* 229; *The Last of Mr. Norris,* 229

James, Henry, 15, 38, 202, 204, 223, 227, 237, 254, 283, 298; *The Aspern Papers,* 5, *Daisy Miller,* 254, 264; *The Spoils of Poynton,* 69–70
James, M. R.: "Martin's Close," 60
James, P. D.: *A Shroud for a Nightingale,* 88
James, William, 253
Jeffrey, Lord Justice, 60
Jerome, Jerome K.: *Three Men in a Boat,* 30–31
Joyce, James, 73–74, 178, 215; *A Portrait of the Artist as a Young Man,* 67; *Ulysses,* 139, 275

Judd, Alan, 14
Jung, C. G., 20, 128

Kafka, Franz, 18, 278, 282
Kaiser, Mary, 26
Karsh, Yusef, 56
Keats, John, 61, 220, 287; "La Belle Dame sans Merci," 221, 286; "Ode to a Nightingale," 193, 278
Kellaway, Kate, 260
Kelly, Grace, 186
Kemp, Peter, 34
Kemp(e), Will, 176
Kermode, Frank, 269
Khrushchev, Nikita, 56
King, Nina, 60, 248, 256, 269
Kipling, Rudyard, 269; "Mandalay," 268
Knapp, Mona, 287
Knox, Alfred Dillwyn ("Dilly") (Penelope's uncle), 1, 86
Knox, Christina Hicks (Penelope's mother), 2, 19, 20, 102, 103, 208, 295–96
Knox, Edmund Arbuthnott (Penelope's paternal grandfather), 3
Knox, Edmund Valpy ("Evoe") (Penelope's father), 1, 2, 19
Knox, Ronald (Penelope's uncle), 1, 2
Knox, Wilfred (Penelope's uncle), 1
Kogan, Norman, 309

Laing, R. D., 111
Lawrence, D. H., 17, 37, 38, 117, 203, 237

Lawrence, Gertrude, 183
le Carré, John, 229–30
Lee, Hermione, 5
Leider, Emily, 188
Lenin, Vladimir Ilyich Ulyanov, 230, 234–35
Ley, Simon: *The Death of Napoleon,* 49
Liszt, Franz, 147
Lively, Penelope, 50, 157, 160
Locke, John, 247
Longfellow, Henry Wadsworth, 240–41; "The Courtship of Miles Standish," 224, *Song of Hiawatha,* 224, 240–41, 244
Lubow, Arthur, 32, 33
Lukac, John, 137

Macdonald, Ross, 90
Machiavelli, Niccolo, 191–92, 200
Madam Butterfly (Puccini), 188
Maeterlinck, Maurice: *Pelléas and Mélisande,* 17, 265
Mahler, Gustav, 13–14
Mammarello, Giuseppe, 184
Mann, Thomas, 178; music in, 11; *Buddenbrooks,* 147, *Doctor Faustus,* 147, 281, *Death in Venice,* 5
Mannes-Abbott, Guy, 272
Mantegna, Andrea: "Death of the Virgin," 5
Mao Tse-tung, 234
Maria Theresa (Archduchess of Austria and Queen of Hungary and Bohemia), 276

Marlowe, Christopher: *Dr. Faustus,* 262
Marshall Plan, 185
Marx, Karl, 205, 213, 231, 234–35
McLuhan, Marshall, 182
McNabb, Florence, 251
McNally, Terrence: *Frankie and Johnny in the Clair de Lune,* 250
Mellors, John, 87
Mew, Caroline Anne, 208, 292
Mew, Charlotte, 19–21, 35, 107, 179, 208, 292
Mew, Fred, 10
Michelangelo, 51, 280
Milo, 104
Monteverdi, Claudio, 203
Moore, G. E., 6
Morris, William, 3, 8, 71; Kelmscott Press, 3
Morrison, Blake, 7
Mosley, Walter, 90
Murrow, Edward R., 26
Mussolini, Benito, 184
Myers, L. H.: *The Root and the Flower,* 279

Nabokov, Vladimir: *Lolita,* 6, 95, 96, 98, 103, 105, 110
Naipaul, V. S., 299
Napoleon, 8, 109, 154
Nelson, Lord Horatio, 253
Newby, P. H., 146
Nietzsche, Friedrich, 99, 235
Novalis (Friedrich/Fritz von Hardenberg), 212, 252, 271–96, *passim;* "Heinrich

von Ofterdingen," 277; *Hymns to the Night,* 277, 288; "Die Lehrlinge zu Saïs," 277
Nutcracker Suite, The, (Tchaikovsky), 160

O'Brien, W. A., 282–83, 287
Offenbach, Jacques: *La Belle Hélène,* 222, 240, 244
Olivier, Laurence, 180
O'Neill, Eugene: *The Hairy Ape,* 187
Osborne, John: *Look Back in Anger,* 9, 181
O'Toole, Peter, 180

Palliser, Charles, 269
Penner, Jonathan, 214
Peter the Great, 212
Peter Pan (Barrie), 160
Petrie, Sir Flinders, 76
Phillips, Mark: *The Memoirs of Marco Parenti,* 8
Pinter, Harold: *The Caretaker,* 181
Pitcher, Harvey, 218, 231, 311
Poe, Edgar Allan, "The Gold-Bug," 88; "The Murders in the Rue Morgue," 88, 257
Pollaivolo, Antonio del, 5
Pound, Ezra, 293
Presley, Elvis, 111
Proffitt, Stuart, 50
Pym, Barbara, 18
Pynchon, Thomas, 298

Queneau, Raymond, 16

Raban, Jonathan, 49, 56, 59, 150
Rasputin, 212
Reynolds, Gillian, 141
Reynolds, Susan Salters, 140
Rhys, Jean: *Voyage in the Dark,* 263
Richard, Cliff, 111
Ritter, Johann Wilhelm, 277
Robinson, Edward Arlington: "Richard Cory," 187
Romanov Dynasty, 213
Rossellini, Roberto, 186
Roth, Philip, 4
Ruskin, John, 71; *Stones of Venice,* 5
Russell, Bertrand, 6
Rutherford, Ernest, 7, 247
Ryle, Gilbert: *The Concept of Mind,* 247
Ryle, John, 121

Sartre, Jean-Paul, 16
Sayers, Dorothy L., 73
Schiller, Friedrich, 46, 276
Schlegel, August Wilhelm, 276
Schubert, Franz, 27, 147
Shakespeare, William, 95, 162–63, 176, 182; *As You Like It,* 59; *Henry V,* 59; *King John,* 28, 166, 170, 177, 181–83; *King Lear,* 165; *The Merchant of Venice,* 181; *The Tempest,* 140–41
Shaw, Bernard: *Man and Superman,* 189; *Pygmalion,* 160
Simpson, Mrs. Wallis, 150
Skinner, B. F., 12

Sophocles: *Oedipus Rex,* 229
Sorley, Charles, 107, 110
Spark, Muriel: *Reality and Dreams,* 46, 47
Stalin, Joseph, 154, 184, 234
Stanislavski, Konstantin, 177
St. Benjamin, 224
Steinbeck, John: *The Pearl,* 88
Stevens, Wallace, 5; "The Emperor of Ice-Cream," 90–91
Stevenson, Robert Louis: *Treasure Island,* 88
Stolypin, Piotr, 229, 240
Storey, David, 93
St. Patrick, 72
Stravinsky, Igor, 225; *The Rite of Spring,* 6, 236–37, 244, 278
Stuewe, Paul, 215

Tennyson, Alfred Lord, 243
Thomas, D. M.: *The White Hotel,* 206, 286
Thomas, Dylan, 123
Tieck, Ludwig, 277
Tolkien, J. R. R., 2, 111
Tolstoy, Leo, 67, 82, 225–28, 230, 235, 237; *War and Peace,* 109, 192, 204, 214, 233
Treaty of Versailles, 138
Trevor, William: *Excursions in the Real World,* 19, 44, 201
Turner, J. M. W., 117

Verdi, Giuseppe: *La Traviata,* 17, 265

Visconti, Luchino: *Rocco and His Brothers,* 187
Vollmann, William T., 298
Voysey Inheritance, The (Harley Granville-Barker), 181–82

Wain, John: *The Contenders,* 93
Wakefield, Jack, 31
Wallace, Edgar: *The Four Just Men,* 88
Walters, Margaret, 32
Watson, James, 248
Waugh, Evelyn, 186
Weiss, Peter, 181
West, Rebecca: *The Birds Fall Down,* 230; *The Fountain Overflows,* 199
Wheeler, Edward, 49
White, Antonia: *Frost in May,* 47
White, Patrick, 267; *The Tree of Man,* 67
Whitman, Walt, 64, 278, 282
Wilde, Oscar: *The Importance of Being Earnest,* 263; *Salome,* 254
Wilson, A. N.: *C. S. Lewis: A Biography,* 249
Wittgenstein, Ludwig, 6–7
Woolf, Virginia, 137–38; *Mrs. Dalloway,* 199; *To the Lighthouse,* 89, 199

Yeats, W. B., 157, 293

Zola, Emile, 231